FAUSTUS AND THE PROMISES OF THE NEW SCIENCE, c. 1580–1730

Faustus and the Promises of the New Science, c. 1580–1730
From the Chapbooks to Harlequin Faustus

CHRISTA KNELLWOLF KING

University of Konstanz, Germany, and
Australian National University, Australia

ASHGATE

Published by
Ashgate Publishing Limited
Wey Court East
Union Road
Farnham
Surrey GU9 7PT
England

Ashgate Publishing Company
Suite 420
101 Cherry Street
Burlington, VT 05401-4405
USA

www.ashgate.com

British Library Cataloguing in Publication Data
Knellwolf King, Christa
Faustus and the promises of the new science, c.1580–1730: from the chapbooks to Harlequin Faustus
    1. Faust, d. ca. 1540 – In literature
    I. Title
    809.9'3351

Library of Congress Cataloging-in-Publication Data
Knellwolf King, Christa.
  Faustus and the promises of the new science, c.1580–1730: from the chapbooks to
    Harlequin Faustus / by Christa Knellwolf King.
    p. cm.
  Includes bibliographical references and index.
  ISBN 978-0-7546-6133-7 (alk. paper)
    1. Faust, d. ca. 1540—In literature. I. Title.

PN57.F3K54 2008
809'.93351—dc22

           2008017875

ISBN: 978-0-7546-6133-7

Mixed Sources
Product group from well-managed forests and other controlled sources
www.fsc.org Cert no. SA-COC-1565
© 1996 Forest Stewardship Council
FSC

Printed and bound in Great Britain by
MPG Books Ltd, Bodmin, Cornwall.

Contents

List of Figures

Acknowledgements

Throughout my research on the Faustus topic, I have encountered passionate responses and strong opinions whenever I talked about my interpretation of the various transformations of the legend. Even though the temporal scope of my study prevented an assessment of the contemporary significance of the Faustus topos, my experience at conferences and departmental coffee breaks led me to believe that the Faustus figure describes challenges and moral conflicts that are right at the heart of academic existence. I therefore want to thank all those who sympathized with my fascination for Faustus. My interest in the Faustus topic began with a postdoctoral fellowship awarded by the Swiss National Science Foundation (1997–2000) and I gratefully acknowledge the assistance thus provided. The first two years of this fellowship were spent in the Departments of English and Philosophy at Cardiff University and the final year took me to the Australian National University in Canberra. I was initially positioned in the Humanities Research Centre there and continue to be affiliated to the National Europe Centre at the Australian National University. The final touches to my manuscript were added in the course of guest professorships at the Universities of Vienna and Konstanz. In all these places I encountered interest and constructive comments from colleagues and friends. The list of those to whom I owe a debt is too long to be included in full. Among those who deserve special thanks are Beat Affentranger, Elisabeth Bronfen, Allen Reddick, Christopher Norris, Stephen Copley, Julia Thomas, Karen O'Brien, Martin Coyle, Simon Bronitt, John Gage, Margarete Rubik, Silvia Mergenthal, Judith Salway, Jane Goodall, Peter Bishop and Marie Ray. Christina Winter guided me through the dogmatic controversies of the Reformation and Brian Gibbons kindly read substantive parts of the manuscript. I want to thank Neil Ramsey for his painstaking attention to the stylistic details of the text and Kathleen Olive for the compilation of the index. Erika Gaffney at Ashgate demonstrated unerring belief in my topic and was throughout a pleasure to work with. Thanks are also due to Seth Hibbert for his efficiency in dealing with the production process. The largest thanks of all are due to Peter who nurtured my creative energies with uncounted acts of kindness.

Chapter 1

Introduction:
Radical Explorations of Faustus

The Faustus legend has been popular in various generic guises and thematic transformations for almost five hundred years. It began as an oral tale about the provocative actions of a fictional character modelled on medical doctors, pharmacists, alchemists, quacks, experts in natural magic and performers of fairground spectacles. While not all of these historical characters possessed special knowledge, all of them challenged established beliefs in one form or another. It goes without saying that such personages aroused much talk and gossip, and the tales which surrounded these figures found their way into broadsheets and lampoons depicting Faustus as a petty criminal who could also draw on the sympathies of the public.

Within a short time the Faustus typology established itself in the popular imagination and inspired writers throughout the ages to imagine a version of the myth that would capture the most urgent concerns of their particular period. Its enduring presence in western culture proves that it was easily recognized as an invaluable tool for examining the thoughts and actions of characters who were extraordinary because they either excelled in their intellectual faculties and artistic gifts or simply in the power of their imagination. Since all of these special skills harboured at least a certain potential for wielding power over others, specially gifted intellectuals were always taken to pose a threat to social stability. The resulting need to contain the danger gave rise to nebulous notions of transgression, the exploration of which became a major task of the Faustus tale.

Historical Faustus Figures

Deciding the question of whether Faustus really existed and what he might have been like is of only marginal interest for this study. Rather than follow the elusive steps of an individual, it explores the overt and implied meanings of the stories about this legendary hero. For the purposes of this study it is nevertheless relevant to point out that the fictional Faustus draws on several personages who lived around the same time as Martin Luther. Several travelling scholars appear to have adopted the name Faustus. Johann Sabellicus, who lived around 1480–1540 and travelled

Germany under the name of Georg Faust, became particularly famous.[1] This historical character left behind a trail of offences and frequently had to leave town in a hurry. His bragging, together with his taste for staging sensational spectacles, elicited a great deal of public interest and extraordinary feats were ascribed to him. His infamy was notorious.[2] Descriptions of his evil deeds gave impetus to the growth of the Faustus legend, which in turn helped to consolidate the period's increasing sympathy for characters that subverted authority. In the Faust Books, Faustus' first name is a variant of John. As William Rose points out, there was a historical character who called himself Johann Faust.[3] The fictional John Faustus may be modelled on his historical namesake. However, I would suspect that the Faust Books' choice of first name is primarily a means of alluding to key figures in the life of Christ: John the Baptist and Saint John of the Gospels. The decision to call the hero of the chapbooks John would reinforce the resemblances between Faustus and Christ, which I will discuss at length in the next chapter.

A striking precursor to a figure such as Sabellicus is found in a contemporary and memorable opponent to Aurelius Augustinus, the patron of Martin Luther's monastic order:[4] Faustus of Milevis. Living in Numibia, North Africa, around 350–400 AD, Faustus of Milevis was a key protagonist of Manichean theology. He taught a rationalist interpretation of the Bible, embarked on an uninhibited interpretation of its individual books and questioned the authenticity and ethical import of certain passages. Luther, by contrast, was strongly opposed to an unguided approach to the biblical text, despite having translated the Bible into the vernacular.

The writings by Faustus of Milevis do not survive but Augustine quotes him extensively in his refutation of Manicheanism. A special feature in Milevis' theories concerns the reasonableness of human nature. For example, he said: 'I look upon myself as a reasonable temple of God'.[5] As a young man, Augustine

---

1   See, for instance, Ingrid H. Shafer, 'Pacts with the Devil: Faust and Precursors', accessed 8 February 2007, http://www.usao.edu/~facshaferi/FAUST.html.

2   For a detailed account of historical responses to this Georg Faust, see Philip Mason Palmer and Robert Pattison More, *The Sources of the Faust Tradition: from Simon Magus to Lessing* (New York: Octagon Books, 1966).

3   Rose, William, ed., *The History of the Damnable Life and Deserved Death of Doctor Faustus*, s.l.: George Routledge and Sons, 1925. Mason and Palmer, *Sources of the Faust Tradition*, also document the existence of a Johann Faust (pp. 86–7); beyond this, they demonstrate parallels between Faustus and Paracelsus (pp. 94–5).

4   For a discussion of Luther's philosophical and cultural context, see Heiko Oberman, *Luther: Man Between God and the Devil*, trans. Eileen Walliser-Schwarzbart (New Haven: Yale University Press, 1989).

5   See Philip Schaff's edition of the controversy between Augustine and the Manichaean Faustus, *The Early Church Fathers: Nicene and Post-Nicene Fathers, vol. 4: The Anti-Manichaean Writings* (New York: The Christian Literature Publishing, 1890); Christian Classics Ethereal Library, accessed 23 August 2006, http://www.ccel.org/ccel/schaff/npnf104.html), Book 20, p. 253. See also Friedrich Wilhelm Bautz, 'Faustus von

had been attracted to the Manichean philosophy. His face-to-face encounter with Manichaeus and some prominent members of his movement, however, left him bitter and frustrated, so that he angrily attacked this strand of Christianity. Although initially fascinated by the North African ascetics, Augustine was discomfited by the arcane symbolism of Manicheanism. In particular, he responded indignantly to its polytheistic tendency and objected to its pantheistic adoration of sun, moon and other cosmic bodies. Augustine also indicted the Manichaean sect for its self-centredness and lack of humility. He energetically objected to the Manichaean decision to worship the God of the New Testament while decrying the God of the Old Testament as an arbitrary tyrant, because such an attitude either challenged the supposedly divine authority of the Bible or implied the existence of multiple godheads.

It is important to remember that the teachings of Augustine played a prominent role in Luther's life. While caught in a thunderstorm in 1505, Luther vowed to become a monk, and he chose the monastery of the Augustinian Eremites in Erfurt because this order offered the best resources for pursuing his dogmatic studies. When he heard about a scholar, who travelled Germany under the name of Faustus, his in-depth familiarity with Augustinian theology must have led him to interpret the motives of this character in the light of the controversy between Augustine and the North-African Faustus.

Since the chapbooks present their religious outlook through the lens of the cautionary tale, it is impossible to say whether they aimed to revive the Manichean philosophy. Even if the author of a (lost) original Faust Book was inspired by Faustus of Milevis, this does not mean that he (or she?) must have admired everything about the North African ascetic teacher. A sixteenth-century intellectual who wished to give voice to a positive understanding of the physical world, would in all likelihood have been inspired by Milevis' comment that 'your religion resembles ours in attaching the same sacredness to the bread and wine that we do to everything'.[6] Even if the Faust Books do not directly advocate the pantheistic outlook of the Manicheans, the worship of the 'divine luminaries' of sun and moon fits well with the sixteenth-century chapbooks that describe the life of Faustus. Moreover, the Manichean idea that it is possible to refine and perfect the self through rational application of morality provides an exciting backdrop to a revisionary understanding of sin and damnation.

Whoever was responsible for writing Spies' Faust Book (or its lost precursor) may easily have been aware of the fourth-century Faustus. The name Faustus could

---

Mileve', *Biographisch-Bibliographisches Kirchenlexikon* (1990), accessed 12 February 2006, (1990), http://www.bautz.de/bbkl/f/faustus_v_m.shtml. Also see Friedrich Wilhelm Bautz's entry on 'Aurelius Augustinus', *Biographisch-Bibliographisches Kirchenlexikon* (1990), accessed 15 February 2006, http://www.bautz.de/bbkl/a/augustin_au.shtml, which contextualizes a variety of philosophical developments, or 'heresies' like Manicheanism, Donatism, and Pelagianism.

6   *The Anti-Manichaean Writings*, Book 20, p. 253.

serve as a pointer to the Manichean beliefs that humankind was the epitome of creation. But there are also other points of reference for the arguments in favour of the innate dignity of mankind. One of the most powerful assertions of the human ability to attain a divine frame of mind is Pico della Mirandola's *Oration on the Dignity of Man* (1486):

> Then Bacchus the leader of the muses, in his own mysteries, that is, in the visible signs of nature, will show the invisible things of God to us as we philosophize, and will make us drunk with the abundance of the house of God. In this house, if we are faithful like Moses, holiest theology will approach and will inspire us with a twofold frenzy. We, raised to the loftiest watchtower of theology … shall be prophets, his winged lovers, and finally, aroused like burning Seraphim, filled with divinity, we shall now not be ourselves, but He himself who made us.[7]

A similarly daring celebration of human aspirations can be found in the poem that introduces Giordano Bruno's *On the Infinite Universe and Worlds* (1584):

> Henceforth I spread confident wings to space;
> I fear no barrier of crystal or of glass;
> I cleave the heavens and soar to the infinite.
> And while I rise from my own globe to others
> And penetrate ever further through the eternal field,
> That which others saw from afar, I leave far behind me.[8]

Bruno said about himself that he despised those who are incapable of grasping the sublime and metaphysical dimensions of the infinite. His self-confident description of his achievements and his elitist contempt for inferior minds also resembles Faustus' attitude towards himself and his fellow beings.

But of course, the sixteenth-century Faustus was not merely a proponent of a rationalist type of Christianity; his main claim to fame was that he practiced magic. The Christian type of magician, Johannes Trithemius, Abbot of Sponheim, who had himself argued that the unaccountable appearance of marks in the shape of the cross had been the trigger for the plague, decried Faustus as a charlatan. The Abbot's letter to the court astrologer of the Electoral Palatinate indicts this Faustus for his unhallowed teachings:

---

7   Pico della Mirandola, *On the Dignity of Man*, trans. Charles Glenn Wallis (New York: Bobbs-Merrill, 1965), p. 14.

8   Quoted in Barbara Howard Traister, *Heavenly Necromancers: the Magician in English Renaissance Drama* (Columbia: University of Missouri Press, 1984), p. 6. The reference is to *Giordano Bruno: His Life and Thought*, ed. and trans. Dorothea Waley Singer (New York: Abelard-Schulman, 1950), p. 249.

... he deserves to be flogged so that he cannot dare to continue teaching despicable things which contradict the Holy Church. What else are the titles, which he has assumed than signs of a highly foolish and nonsensical spirit, which prove that he is a windbag rather than a philosopher? He accordingly appropriated the following titles which he thought to deserve: Magister Georg Sabellicus, Faustus junior, originary source of necromancers, astrologer, second in the rank of magicians, chiromancer, aeromancer, pyromancer, second in the rank of hydromancers. Just consider the foolish audacity of this man! ... I crossed the path of this man a few years ago ... When he heard about my presence he fled from the hostel; nobody could persuade him to introduce himself to me. The records of his foolish acts, which, as I note, he sent to you, had also been passed on to me ...[9]

Trithemius goes on to say that this Faustus junior had claimed to possess the entirety of human knowledge and that his own supernatural skills were even superior to those of Jesus. The Abbot concludes his tirade by reporting that, to top it all, Faustus was guilty of pederast abominations.[10]

A magician and necromancer calling himself Faustus also crossed Luther's path in 1533. In the context of discussing the dangers of black magic, Luther's *Table Talks* mention the following episode:

As a necromancer by the name of Faustus was mentioned one evening, Doctor Martinus said finally: 'The devil does not use the service of the magicians against me; if he had had the power and the might to harm me, he would have done so long ago. He has certainly many times held me by the head but he has nevertheless had to let me go. ... He has sometimes given me such a hard time that I did not know whether I was alive or dead. He has also driven me into such desperation that I did not know whether there is a God. ... But I have fought him with the word of God. Otherwise there is neither help nor counsel ... if God does not help us. ...'[11]

Consistent with Luther's fixated belief that the devil is the agent behind all extraordinary events,[12] he describes the travelling magician as an instrument of the devil. But the *Table Talks* do not connect this historical Faustus to the Faustus legend and there is no reference to a pact with the devil.[13] Luther's description shows that he connects Faustus so strongly with the devil that they have almost

---

9 'Introduction' to GFB, p. XVIII. For an account of Abbot Trithemius, see p. XVIII, cf. pp. XVI–XX.

10 For a full reproduction of Trithemius' letter, see Palmer and More, *The Sources of the Faust Tradition*, pp. 83–7.

11 Martin Luther, *Tischgespräche* (Table Talks); in: *Werke: Kritische Gesamtausgabe* (Weimar: H. Böhlaus, 1964), note to vol. 1.1059.

12 Cf. Oberman, *Luther*, pp. 154–7.

13 The Table Talks indeed discuss a pact with the devil but the hero of this particular anecdote is an unnamed wild, young fellow. See Luther, *Tischgespräche*, vol. 6.6809.

become identical. It does not surprise us, therefore, that Luther refused to have any dealings with his contemporary Faustus.[14]

When we compare these historical descriptions of an arrogant megalomaniac and charlatan with the characteristics of the hero of the Faustus legend, we notice a significant discrepancy. It is true that some parts of the chapbooks describe Faustus as someone who likes to impress large audiences with spectacles and silly pranks. In the first two parts of the German and English Faust Books, which are the main focus of my discussion, however, he comes across as an introverted, almost reclusive scholar who only interacts with his amanuensis and his supernatural visitors. His role as a teacher dominates the last part of these Faust Books but his raucous behaviour clashes with his solitary exploration of heaven and hell. Although he is living in a buoyant circle of students and fellow scholars his early musings about the nature of the world concentrate on the landscape of his mind. They describe the inner world of a sensitive scholar in a state of isolation unaffected by his sociable environment.

Even though Faustus is portrayed as a man of the world in the last third of the German and English Faust Books, he interacts less with other people than he does with Mephostophiles and other visitors from the spirit world. It almost seems out of character that Faustus addresses his final lamentation to a group of students to whom he speaks with a great deal of familiarity: 'My trusty and well-beloved friends, the cause why I have invited you into this place is this: Forasmuch as you have known me this many years, in what manner of life I have lived ...' (EFB 177). His choice of words implies that he has been in close contact with a circle of students for his whole life. It is telling that his more public role is elided from the early parts of the narrative. The interest of the literary sections, which have undoubtedly been written at a later stage, revolve around an individual who thinks and acts at a distance from his surroundings. But the egotistic emphasis of these early sections describes a modern character who ponders the nature of the universe on his own instead of discussing it with his fellow scholars.

New Ideas about Human Nature

The Faustus legend, then, portrays a scholar who objected to every sort of restraint. He was undaunted in his examination of all aspects of creation – including heaven and hell – seeking to explain them according to his own intellectual powers. As I will argue in this book, the legend embarked on an uncompromising investigation of sacred and secular matters through its portrayal of a character who wanted to experience and enjoy all aspects of his contemporary world. Numerous stories about his adventures with conjurors, demons and devils emerged during the early phases of modernity and have continued to be written right into the present. In spite of

---

14 For further references to Faustus, see Luther: *Tischgespäche*, vol. 2.1425; vol. 3.3601; vol. 4.4450 and 4.4857.

striking differences in the story's narrative pattern and thematic emphases between its origin in the sixteenth century and later adaptations, it continued to provide a framework for expressing the preoccupations of a particular age. The sixteenth-century Faustus stories were also enmeshed with the establishment of empiricism and the associated successes of scientific experimentation. Closely interwoven with the origin and general spread of the early Enlightenment, my discussion of representative versions of the legend reveals the passions, intellectual curiosities, spiritual cravings and moral dilemmas of a period of reorientation and change.

The radical aspects of the age of Enlightenment have provided the focus for recent influential studies of the period.[15] Beyond confirming that early modernity brought forth groundbreaking ideas concerning human existence and destiny, these studies describe it as a period that has been riven by heated conflicts over the definition of human nature. Contests over proper conduct, acceptable living conditions, and freedom of conscience were embedded within a powerful desire to discover the true nature of the self. Michel Foucault famously describes the preoccupation with the self as one of the prominent changes in the psychological outlook of early modernity, yet he cautions that 'the meticulous rules of self-examination' emerging in the seventeenth century called into existence new forms of social control.[16] The painstaking and perpetual self-analysis required by early-modern ideology implanted its social norms in the conscience of the individual, who then became the guardian of the state's moral principles.

The individual who strives for self-knowledge is seen as having internalized the instruments of social control. Yet it cannot be denied that an equally important reason for the introspective gaze was to fathom the hidden potentials of the self. This emphasis on introspection might have evolved as a consequence of realising the dangers of being open about one's convictions. Talking about the blossoming of creative energy in Renaissance Italy in spite of rampant despotism, the nineteenth-century critic Jacob Burckhardt argues:

> Despotism ... fostered in the highest degree not only the individuality of the tyrant or Condottiere himself, but also of the men whom he protected or used as his tools – the secretary, minister, poet, and companion. These people were forced to know all the inward resources of their own nature, passing or permanent; and their enjoyment of life was enhanced and concentrated by the desire to obtain the greatest satisfaction from a possibly very brief period of power and influence.[17]

---

15 See Margaret Jacob, *The Radical Enlightenment: Pantheists, Freemasons, and Republicans* (London: Allen & Unwin, 1981); and Jonathan Irvine Israel, *Radical Enlightenment: Philosophy and the Making of Modernity* 1650–1750 (Oxford: Oxford University Press, 2001).

16 Michel Foucault, *The History of Sexuality, vol. 1: Introduction*, trans. Robert Hurley (New York: Vintage, 1988), p. 19. Also compare his *The Order of Things: An Archeology of the Human Sciences* (New York: Vintage Books, 1970).

17 Jacob Burckhardt, *The Civilization of the Renaissance in Italy* (London: Allen & Unwin, 1944), p. 82.

A social environment poisoned by mistrust, fear and abuse enticed scholars to become creative in order to obtain property and social position, but it also forced them to think about the nature of intellectual integrity. The withdrawal into the self may have started as a defensive mechanism against despotic abuses, but the struggle for intellectual survival nevertheless generated unexpected energies. Someone who is embedded in a stable social environment may remain in a state of unreflected wellbeing, but an oppressive environment challenges its inhabitants to muster their 'inward resources' in order to escape from its debilitating violence. This is why culture and art flourished under the despotic rulership of Renaissance Italy. Although living in a less explosive environment, northern-European intellectuals similarly objected to the forces of control and pushed for new political and personal experiences.

It took a while before the quest for one's inner resources became a major concern. In the Romantic period, Coleridge was an eloquent voice to advocate such an approach to the self. He also pointed out that there was a wide discrepancy between human potential and what was realized of it in an actual state of existence:

> They and only they can acquire the philosophic imagination, the sacred power of self-intuition, who within themselves can interpret and understand the symbol, that the wings of the air-sylph are forming within the skin of the caterpillar; those only, who feel in their own spirits the same instinct, which impels the chrysalis of the horned fly to leave room in its involucrum for antennae yet to come. They know and feel, that the *potential* works *in* them, even as the *actual* works on them! In short, all the organs of sense are framed for a corresponding world of sense; and we have it. All the organs of spirit are framed for a corresponding world of spirit; though the latter organs are not developed in all alike. But they exist in all ... [original emphasis][18]

In spite of differentiating strongly between the sensitive poet and ordinary minds, Coleridge claimed that all should strive to realize their abstract potential so as to overcome the gaping gulf between real and ideal states of existence. He may have been one of the first to express himself in these terms, but the Aristotelian differentiation between form and content had already emphasized the discrepancy between realized and unrealized potentials. What is new is that Coleridge defines the self in terms of potentialities, claiming that the vital energies of human existence should be employed in achieving ideal states of existence even if these are ultimately unattainable.

By contrast with the Romantic emphasis on exploring and utilizing one's capacities, the late medieval world was hostile to innovations that endangered the established order, and Church authorities made every effort to suppress increasingly vigorous challenges to received definitions of human nature and

---

18 S.T. Coleridge, *Biographia Literaria*, eds. James Engell and W. Jackson Bate (Princeton: Princeton University Press, 1983), I.xii, p. 241–2.

social roles. Traditionally, the Christian church encouraged a certain range of well-defined quests in the form of pilgrimages and other circumscribed religious practices and rituals.[19] However, it attached the most serious warnings to anything that aspired to go beyond its traditional boundaries. Unless the study of the self and the world were conducted as a means to gain spiritual humility, it was decried as sinful self-indulgence. Medieval doctrines cast a long shadow over subsequent centuries and the Calvinist idea that the self was endowed with dangerous qualities survived into the not-so-distant past. A.D. Nuttall illustrates how questions about human nature formed in the competing camps that argued either for humanity's inherent goodness or its inherent depravity:

> from magicians, Platonists, and Hermetists came the idea that human potential was limitless: man could ascend into the firmament of knowledge and become divine; from Calvin and the Reformers came the contrary idea that human capacity was zero: man is totally depraved, naturally damned, deprived of all initiative, whether for moral or intellectual good. Those who escape hell are saved not by merit but by the inscrutable Grace of God.[20]

Orthodox Protestant theology, particularly Calvinism, severely condemned the craving for knowledge, quoting the biblical precedent of Adam and Eve's fall from grace as a potent reminder that the inquisitive propensities of the self had to be curbed.

Natural philosophical investigation, on the other hand, endorsed the positive outlook of hermeticism, valorising the original and 'natural' human qualities because they had been made by God. According to medieval cosmology, the term nature was more or less synonymous with God's creation and it only gradually came to be understood as a part of the oppositional duality of nature and culture. As Enlightenment thinkers strove to emancipate human experience from theological control, nature became further and further removed from its implied creator. The stylistically masterful contests of the later sixteenth and seventeenth centuries between soul and body, then, dramatize not merely the tensions between spiritual and worldly satisfaction but also the strongly diverging views on the natural qualities and propensities of the human being. The prominence of these conflicts in contemporary culture also demonstrated that the worldly contestant was a powerful character who pointed eloquently to the violence with which his claims were suppressed.

The task of exploring the self was gradually made a priority during the eighteenth century and became a prerequisite of Romanticism. But how did this emphasis emerge and develop? During the sixteenth century, all aspects of nature

---

19 Cf. Christian K. Zacher, *Curiosity and Pilgrimage: The Literature of Discovery in Fourteenth-Century England* (Baltimore: Johns Hopkins University Press, 1976).

20 A.D. Nuttall, *The Alternative Trinity: Gnostic Heresy in Marlowe, Milton, and Blake* (Oxford: Clarendon Press, 1998), p. 25.

began to be studied and explored. The great masters of map making, Abraham Ortelius and Gerhard Mercator, were able to represent geographical space with unprecedented accuracy,[21] and the systematic exploration of psyche and mind became an equally urgent objective. Excitement over the remarkable descriptions of the landscape and peoples of the new world reinforced the idea that internal spaces harboured similar mysteries and promises as the world at large. Progress in the understanding of human anatomy, moreover, was a further incentive for the exploration of emotional and intellectual capacities.[22]

Early modernity valued analogical thinking and took for granted strong resemblances between microcosm (self) and macrocosm (world). Christian pilgrimages had also emphasized the symbolic similarities between the experience of unfamiliar places and the experience of self. In strict terms, a pilgrimage followed closely prescribed rituals so that the believer could attune to the sacred quality of the destination and attain a state of mind that was appropriate to the pure reception of the divine spirit. The objective of the spiritual journey was to exclude all worldly distractions so that the believer could become one with the sacred object in the process of experiencing its qualities. The underlying requirement of an effacement of self, however, contradicted an increasingly powerful emphasis on spiritual experience.

The imaginative space of the medieval world was subdivided into three realms: heaven, hell and earth. These spaces were associated with particular parts of a medieval church and there were rituals designed to confirm their respective meanings.[23] After the Reformation, however, mystery plays, religious pageants and rituals disappeared as instruments for guiding the believer in the experience of the sacred.[24] While the late medieval world was characterized by a loss of images and rituals, it nevertheless retained the core metaphors of Christianity: heaven and hell. In an intellectual climate cultivating the pure unmediated experience of abstract ideas, contemporary thinkers set out to explore their meanings and relevance in a climate of ever-expanding knowledge about the material world.

People have always tried to expand the knowledge of their period. They have always – to a greater or lesser degree – tried to gaze across boundaries to answer questions considered either unanswerable or dangerous. And of course, people have always travelled. Some set out to satisfy their cravings to see foreign lands

21 See, for instance, Charles Bricker, *Landmarks of Mapmaking: An Illustrated Survey of Maps and Mapmakers* (Oxford: Phaidon, 1976).

22 An important example is William Harvey's physiological discoveries, *The Circulation of the Blood*, trans. Kenneth J. Franklin and Andrew Wear (London: Everyman, 1990).

23 Cf. for instance Emile Mâle, *Religious Art in France, the Late Middle Ages* (Princeton: Princeton University Press, 1986).

24 For a discussion of the representation of the sacred in the mystery plays, see John D. Cox, *The Devil and the Sacred in English Drama*, 1350–1642 (Cambridge: Cambridge University Press, 2000).

while others aimed to conduct business in foreign parts of the world. Some were mortally afraid to leave their domestic realms, fearing – justifiably – that their journeys would be hazardous and that they would never come back; others spent huge sums on chasing after the mysterious treasures of fable and myth. Many travellers of medieval Europe crossed the 'Spanish Frontier' in order to have access to the exquisite works of Arab scholars in fields such as medicine, astronomy and botany.[25]

Early modernity also kindled an attitude towards curiosity that gave new impetus to the perennial desire to see the lands beyond the horizon. A static world view, according to which all necessary knowledge was contained in the Bible and in traditional lore, was being replaced by the idea that the future harboured vast stores of hitherto unexplored knowledge. It became a moral imperative to harvest these stores for the good of humankind. By the time Francis Bacon propagated the advancement of knowledge as the principle of his society and culture, it had become permissible to ask, inquire and speculate. It would not take long before it became the intellectual's duty to take part in the process of expanding existing boundaries.

The icon prefixed to Bacon's *Novum Organum* (1620) portrays two ships sailing through the columns defining the boundaries of traditional knowledge: *non plus ultra*. One ship is on the point of disappearing on the horizon while the other is shown re-entering the traditional realms, carrying a rich store of information and goods (Figure 1). Here geographic exploration features as the most palpable icon of progress, symbolising the period's tireless efforts to achieve technological improvements and advancements in the understanding of nature. Bacon indeed pursued the project of collecting all branches of knowledge under the principles of a *first philosophy*, a 'common parent of all knowledge', as Jerry Weinberger describes it, which demands that the axioms of every branch of investigation should be deduced from observed data.[26] Of course, Bacon's all-embracing method of investigation was an ideal, and by no means described how things were done in practice. His attempts to establish a hierarchy of all branches of inquiry nevertheless encouraged a rational approach to all questions of human concern.[27]

That people wanted to observe and judge for themselves was characteristic of the period. But Bacon drew a rigid line between scientific observation and religion. In the preface to the *Great Instauration*, he says:

25 For a discussion of the cultural boundary between Arab Spain and Christian Europe, see Peter Linehan, 'At the Spanish Frontier', *The Medieval World*, eds. Peter Linehan and Janet L. Nelson (London: Routledge, 2001).

26 Cf. Jerry Weinberger, *Science, Faith, and Politics: Francis Bacon and the Utopian Roots of the Modern Age* (Ithaca: Cornell University Press, 1985), p. 246.

27 Cf. Sachiko Kusukawa, 'Bacon's Classification of Knowledge', *The Cambridge Companion to Bacon*, ed. Markku Peltonen (Cambridge: Cambridge University Press, 1996).

Fig. 1   Francis Bacon, *Instauratio Magna*, or *Novum Organum*, (1620)
                frontispiece from an eighteenth-century edition of *Opera Omnia*,
                vol. 2, London: M. Gosling, 1730.

My first admonition (which was also my prayer) is that, in things divine, men should confine the sense within its proper sphere. For the sense, like the sun, opens the face of the terrestrial globe, but shuts and seals up the face of heaven. On the other hand, in flying from that evil, they should not fall into the opposite fault, as they certainly will, if they think that any part of the investigation of Nature must be excluded, as if by any interdict. For it was not that pure and spotless natural knowledge, by which Adam gave names to all things according to their kind, that was the origin and occasion of the Fall, but that ambitious and headstrong greed for moral knowledge – of telling good from evil – so that man might desert God and make his own laws, that was the ground and manner of his temptation.[28]

Bacon defended the wish to expand the existing perimeters of knowledge. He also implicitly refuted the argument of the second commandment, which condemns as sinful the desire to conceive an image of that which is outside one's immediate field of experience: 'Thou shalt not make unto thee any graven image, or any likeness of any thing that is in heaven above, or that is in the earth beneath, or that is in the water under the earth' (*Exodus*, 20.4). His argument relies on the assumption that Adam must have been created with a special kind of divinely sanctioned knowledge in order to give the right names to God's creatures. He therefore distinguishes between a pure and an impure craving for knowledge. By proposing a 'natural knowledge', located in prelapsarian times, Bacon is defending himself against the accusation of heresy. Within one and the same passage, however, he commits the logical inconsistency of arguing that the scientific method should steer clear of religious issues while referring to the Bible to prove the existence of a natural, God-given knowledge. With a great deal of hermeneutic liberty he implies that the famous fall from grace may have buried the original and pure human knowledge. He then allows himself to speculate that this knowledge is still alive and, with proper endeavour, might be brought back to the surface.

Probably the most famous passage of *Novum Organum* is the discussion of the 'idols of the mind' where Bacon argues for the existence of ways and means of counterbalancing the distortions clinging to an uninformed perception and interpretation of the world.[29] His utopian description of an ideal society, *The New Atlantis*, then, proposes a careful schooling of the senses by means of which sensory deceptions should be minimized. The House of Solomon, the academy of this utopian society, boasts 'perspective-houses', 'sound-houses', etc., devoted to the comprehensive understanding of sensory perception. The triumphs of their inventiveness are 'houses of deceits of the senses; where we represent all manner of feats of juggling, false apparitions, impostures, and illusions; and their fallacies'.[30]

---

28 Francis Bacon, *Novum Organum, with Other Parts of the Great Instauration*, trans. and ed. Peter Urbach and John Gibson (Chicago: Open Court, 1994), p. 15.

29 Bacon, *Novum Organum*, 1, §§46–68.

30 Francis Bacon, *The Advancement of Learning and New Atlantis*, ed. Arthur Johnston (Oxford: Clarendon Press, 1974), pp. 243–5.

The last of these institutions established for the understanding of sensory perception is specifically devoted to an analysis of sensory illusions. In other words, Bacon posits an educated reason that resists the deceptions of the senses.

An intellectual climate geared towards expanding the boundaries of geographic and scientific knowledge also opened up new approaches to the understanding of the self. In spite of the secularising tendencies of the period, the exploration of the true nature of the self was suspect on religious and political grounds, two areas which were still closely interwoven. The wish to uncover the full potentials of human existence encouraged many to gather together with like-minded people who were keen to bring to light their emotional and intellectual capacities. It is obvious that contemporary society felt threatened by coteries of restless young men gathered in more or less secret circles to question the constrictive standards of their period. Their meetings might concentrate on political, intellectual or religious issues, or they might simply be devoted to boisterous masculine rituals and orgiastic excesses. Regardless of whether it was a case of freemasons pursuing mystical secrets or libertine rakes dedicated to the pleasures of the body, such meetings brought to the surface a whole spate of creative energies.[31]

Scientific Revolutions and the Nature of Change

'Revolution' is an evocative term associated with ideas of far-reaching social, political and economic change. As part of the compound of the 'scientific revolution', it promises an account of the ultimate victory of knowledge over ignorance and superstition. By offering itself as an umbrella term for a confluence of changes and reorientations, however, it encourages a reductive view of historical change.[32]

The idea that historical development occurs through moments of dramatic transformation – referred to by the term 'revolution' – is borrowed from the historian of science Thomas Kuhn. In his influential book *The Structure of Scientific Revolutions*, he argued that intellectual progress went through phases of apparent stagnation until a particular confluence of circumstances enabled a breakthrough,

---

31 Cf. Margaret C. Jacob, *Living the Enlightenment: Freemasonry and Politics in Eighteenth-Century Europe* (New York: Oxford University Press, 1991).

32 Thomas Kuhn argued that the history of science progressed through periods characterized by prevailing paradigms, or generally accepted interpretations of natural phenomena, and radical transitional periods in which the consensus was challenged so that false interpretations of the material world could be replaced by substantially better ones. Kuhn's arguments are informed by a firm belief in the progressive capacities of science to oust the superstitions of previous modes of knowing. In *The Structure of Scientific Revolutions* (Chicago: University of Chicago Press, 1962), p. 160, Kuhn therefore maintains that progress is 'a perquisite reserved almost exclusively for the activities we call science'.

or a paradigm shift, that established a fresh understanding of a whole complex of questions. Although he denied the applicability of paradigm shifts to art, political theory, or philosophy, his ideas nevertheless provided an influential model for cultural change. In particular, it became fashionable to identify the scientific endeavours of early modernity as the driving force behind all other changes. The by now heavily contested term of the 'scientific revolution' prioritized the early modern preference for the scientific methodology of empiricism, claiming that it became a matrix for the introduction of far-reaching ideological changes. The unprecedented significance of natural investigation undoubtedly coincided with dramatic shifts in the attitude towards self and world.

A relevant example concerns the wish to uproot erroneous popular beliefs and superstitions. But it is important to remember here that medieval approaches to the study of nature did not differentiate between scientific investigations and magic. Lynn Thorndike undertook the monumental task of demonstrating that the boundary between science and magic was an early modern invention. It came into existence in order to demarcate the methodological rigour of an empirical science against earlier practices. A special aim of such a division was to eradicate the idea that nature possessed an independent will that would allow it to act in response to the wishes of a magician who sought to unravel its secrets. This is not to say that mediaeval magic did not have its own benefits. It was Thorndike's great achievement to document medieval magic as the precursor and breeding ground of early modern science. In the process of doing so, however, he exaggerated the scientific aim of gaining new knowledge over the deeply human need to be at one with the mysterious powers of field and forest. Bert Hansen describes the early modern shift of emphasis on the material aspects of nature as a means of

> bankrupting magic's metaphysics. The change was not effected overnight, but in the long run the new quantitative and mechanistic approach eventually established a metaphysics which left no room for essences, animism, hope, or purpose in nature, thus making magic something 'unreal', or supernatural in the modern sense.[33]

The more human dimension of magic also established powerful links between arcane scientific practices and new political ideas. It is, therefore, also important to observe that the metaphorical meaning of a scientific 'revolution' refers to scientific views or theories as if they were bad political regimes waiting to be overthrown so as to make room for a superior kind of government. Invoking the associations of the French revolution, the concept of the 'scientific revolution' endorses a naïve theory of progress.[34]

---

33 Bert Hansen, 'Science and Magic', *Science in the Middle Ages*, ed. David Lindberg (Chicago: University of Chicago Press, 1978), p. 497.

34 For an analysis of the meanings of the French revolution projected retrospectively by the twentieth century, see Robert Darnton, *The Kiss of Lamourette: Reflections in Cultural History* (New York: Norton, 1990).

Up to the early seventeenth century, 'revolution' referred to a revolving movement in space or time, and, as Raymond Williams demonstrates, it required a semantic shift before it could describe the act of overthrowing political order.[35] The *Oxford English Dictionary* lists as its dominant and earliest meaning the astronomical description of celestial bodies 'moving round in an orbit or circular course'. At its roots, 'revolution' is a mechanical concept. Associated with the image of the wheel of fortune and the concomitant sense of order, it implies an order in which high and low take turns in rotational sequence. That the change of meaning should have occurred at the beginning of the early modern period is telling; it shows that this period could no longer believe in a perennial recurrence of the same and therefore came to understand 'revolution' as an irreversible change in political and intellectual order.[36] The Copernican revolution, which, according to Hayden White, marked the transition from a naïve to a self-conscious perception of temporality, is similarly an effect of semantic as much as of social and intellectual change.[37] Or as Robert Markley formulates it: 'The processes of reinscribing and deconstructing the binary structures of thought and representation of their culture are precisely what generate the complex forms of new information that have been labelled the scientific revolution'.[38]

In his analysis of the most important concepts, or keywords, of western culture, Williams discusses in detail why 'revolution' became a term for political change. He claims that since shifts in conventional beliefs always at some level threaten the stability of an existing order, struggles for change are necessarily political.[39] Of course, changes in awareness and outlook prepare for changes in social and political order. Or as William Eamon remarks:

> to succeed, a revolution must win the hearts and minds of the people. That statement may also be applied to the Scientific Revolution. To succeed, it had to create a cosmology

---

35 Cf. Raymond Williams, *Keywords: a Vocabulary of Culture and Society* (London: Flamingo, 1983), pp. 270–74.

36 For a detailed overview of the changing meanings of 'revolution', compare the Oxford English Dictionary.

37 Hayden White projects Piaget's model of the four stages which the child has to pass through before reaching cognitive and psychological maturity onto different stages of historical consciousness. In particular, he argues that E.P. Thompson's *The Making of the English Working Class* (London: V. Gollancz, 1980) follows precisely this four partite structure of increasing sophistication and/or disillusionment; cf. Hayden V. White, *Tropics of Discourse: Essays in Cultural Criticism* (Baltimore: The Johns Hopkins University Press, 1978), particularly 'Introduction: Tropology, Discourse, and the Modes of Human Consciousness', pp. 1–26. For Jean Piaget, see, *The Child and Reality: Problems of Genetic Psychology*, trans. Arnold Rosin (New York: Grossman, 1973), pp. 15–16.

38 Robert Markley, *Fallen Languages: Crises of Representation in Newtonian England, 1660–1740* (Ithaca: Cornell University Press, 1993), p. 33.

39 Williams, *Keywords*, pp. 270–74.

and an epistemology that were consistent with the secularistic attitudes that emerged, especially among the urban middle class, in early modern culture.[40]

The changes that ousted an old order were happening at all material and psychological levels. There were conflicts between high and low, religious and secular, elitist and popular, feudal and capitalist-bourgeois factions. They had such profound ramifications on contemporary experience that it was no longer possible to define historical development as a permutation of familiar events. As a consequence it became necessary to think of the present – or rather of the forces that gave shape to the present – as the ferment for unprecedented future constellations.

What is referred to by the name 'scientific revolution' equated the term 'revolution' with the endeavour to achieve enlightenment. The tireless quest for knowledge – or for unhindered access to knowledge – is frequently taken to characterize the early modern period, irrespective of when the starting point of modernity is taken to be. Francis Bacon's claim that knowledge is not a firmly defined entity, but that it can be shaped, re-shaped, and expanded – programmatically outlined in *Novum Organum* – is a major point of reference for such an attitude. Bacon counterposes his *'New' Organum* against Aristotle's accounts of the practices of reasoning, the 'old' Organum. Modelled on the astrological concept of the *magnus annus* (the 'cosmic year'), the old theory had taken for granted 'that history begins to repeat itself in every detail when the heavenly bodies have all regained their original positions'.[41] Bacon rigorously rejects this idea and instead calls for an intellectual history defined as a crusade for progress.[42]

Regardless of how the process of discovering new scientific knowledge was conceptualized, early modernity was a period when extensive amounts of new knowledge and skills were formulated and applied. Furthermore, a significant number of new inventions transformed the daily lives of each and everyone. For example, the invention of the printing press ensured that the subversive claims

---

40 William Eamon, *Science and the Secrets of Nature: Books of Secrets in Medieval and Early Modern Culture* (Princeton: Princeton University Press, 1994), p. 10. For an analysis of the meanings of modernity, see Bruno Latour, *We Have Never Been Modern*, trans. Catherine Porter (Cambridge, MA: Harvard University Press, 1993).

41 Lynn Thorndike, *A History of Magic and Experimental Science During the First Thirteen Centuries of Our Era*, 8 vols. (New York: Columbia University Press, 1923), vol. 1, p. 26. This recalls Northrop Frye's mythic historiography which he subdivides into 'romantic historical myths based on a quest or pilgrimage to a City of God or a classless society; ... comic historical myths of progress through evolution or revolution; ... tragic myths of decline and fall', see 'New Directions from Old', *Fables of Identity: Studies in Poetic Mythology* (New York: Harcourt, Brace and World, 1963), pp. 52–66.

42 That history was immensely important for Bacon is reflected in the fact that he keeps returning to the project of a natural history. For a discussion of the significance of temporal change, see John F. Tinkler, 'Bacon and History', *The Cambridge Companion to Bacon*, ed. Markku Peltonen (Cambridge: Cambridge University Press, 1996), pp. 232–59.

of early modern splinter groups and sects could reach large audiences.[43] Utopian ideas and arguments about the right to decide on religious practices were mostly generally available although they were formulated by a small number of individuals working in the underground.[44]

Science is also frequently described as the motor behind secularisation. Whereas a medieval world view had taken for granted that one's every step was determined by higher forces, it now became possible to imagine that accidents were a product of circumstances which were subjected to mathematical computability.[45] So while confrontations with death and illness continued to be an ever-present factor of life, mechanical views of nature, for example, jeopardized religious ideas about the treatment of the sick body. But the general impact of secularisation has been exaggerated. It is important to keep in mind that while matters of civil administration were gradually removed from the direct influences of the Church, it continued to prescribe the behaviour and beliefs of its members well into the nineteenth century.

The Human Dimension of the New Science

But how did the re-orientations in natural philosophy influence the conception of self and world? And what were the psychological consequences of the new understanding of the world? It seems reasonable to assume that empiricism gained ground because it promised to satisfy the deeply human craving to be in control of the forces of life. Early modernity eagerly embraced empiricism as a harbinger of certainty and stability. In symbolical terms, however, the idea that knowledge should be verifiable lies at the very heart of the Judeo-Christian myth of origin.

The paradoxes and contradictions of empiricism found a resonance through the period with the biblical story of Adam and Eve. Nuttall offers an incisive discussion of early modern controversies over the first couple's craving for knowledge. He identifies numerous moments when Gnostic arguments concerning the supreme spiritual value of knowledge come to the surface of Marlowe's *Doctor Faustus*, where 'the homosexual rake, the spy, with his reputation for atheism, might give expression to a ... momentary shaking of the foundations of Christianity'.[46] Later chapters of this book will discuss how the Faustus stories challenge this 'starting

---

43 Benedict Anderson refers to the Vatican's *Index Librorum Prohibitorum* as evidence for 'the sheer volume of printed subversion'; *Imagined Communities: Reflections on the Origin and Spread of Nationalism* (London: Verso, 1991), p. 40.

44 Cf. Frances Yates, *The Rosicrucian Enlightenment* (London: Routledge, 1972).

45 Cf. Lorraine Daston, *Classical Probability in the Enlightenment* (Princeton: Princeton University Press, 1988).

46 Nuttall, *Alternative Trinity*, p. 48.

point of the Christian drama of redemption', as Erich Auerbach describes it.[47] It will also be shown that the stories operate within a range of subversive Gnostic beliefs that suggest analogies between the Faustus character and Christ, both in his Orthodox definition and in his Prometheus role of challenging God.

An interesting paradox is that empiricist certainty had to be bought at the cost of eradicating the emotional subtleties of experience. Reducing to a cognitive abstraction the multifarious and colourful nature of sensory stimuli, the empiricist outlook threatened to impoverish the experience of self even before notions of individuality had acquired the importance they have now. Social outsiders, who might have identified with Faustus and his radical search for truth, did not simply devote their energies towards greasing the wheels of scientific progress. In retrospect, we tend to assume that since empiricism was the good theory that ousted the flawed scholastic approach to the study of nature, anyone who was smart and thought logically would hail it enthusiastically. As Steven Shapin and Simon Schaffer have demonstrated in their study of the reception of Robert Boyle's discoveries, much more was at stake than a simple competition between different accounts of natural phenomena.[48] The early modern wish to understand the self, and to experience it in its colourful and sensual complexity, ran into difficulties with both scholastic and empiricist methodologies. While Christopher Marlowe's Faustus conducts his personal quest in his dialogue with Mephistopheles, he identifies with none of the various competing camps. On the contrary, Marlowe's Faustus questions all contemporary knowledge and, by doing so, seeks to discover his own understanding of heaven, hell and earth.

The interdependence between scientific and cultural developments has moved into the focus of recent critical debate.[49] But how was change registered in early modern consciousness? I approach the complex causalities through a discussion of how contemporary culture fictionalized – or embedded into stories – the changes it was experiencing. The reciprocity between the history of science and culture strikes us most forcefully in stories that circle around the wish to understand the nature of knowledge.

After the death of the figure (or figures) who travelled by the name of Faustus in the first half of the sixteenth century, the story circulated mainly in oral form.[50]

---

47 Erich Auerbach, *Mimesis: The Representation of Reality in Western Literature* (Princeton: Princeton University Press, 1978 [1946]), p. 151. For Auerbach's discussion of the significance of the Adam and Eve story in Renaissance Europe, see pp. 143–73.

48 Steven Shapin and Simon Schaffer, *Leviathan and the Air-Pump: Hobbes, Boyle and the Experimental Life* (Princeton, NJ: Princeton University Press, 1985).

49 Lorraine Daston and Katherine Park, *Wonders and the Order of Nature,* 1150–1750 (New York: Zone Books, 1998).

50 For a discussion of the historical background, see Frank Baron, *Doctor Faustus from History to Legend* (München: W. Fink, 1978). There are several surviving chapbooks, most important among them the German Faustbuch (1587) and a free translation into English entitled, *The Historie of the Damnable Life, and Deserved Death of Doctor John Faustus* (London: Thomas Orwin, 1592). As Frank Baron demonstrates in his study of the historical

Concerning the historical character(s) on which the story is modelled, Harry Levin comments: 'Sketchy records and sporadic anecdotes trace for us the shadowy – not to say shady – existence of an academic loner, hastily moving on through clouds of local scandal from one German town to another.'[51] However, the popular imagination refused to dismiss him as a charlatan, but instead explored the tragicomic potential of his life. The inevitability of his final damnation was questioned from the moment when his life was first recorded in chapbooks. E. M. Butler offers a detailed overview of the popular versions of the Faustus legend, from its emergence as a Lutheran tale to its interpretation by Thomas Mann as an allegory for the artist's struggle in an oppressive, petty-bourgeois environment. Comparing the fate of Faustus with that of Don Juan, Butler points out that 'the conception of Don Juan, the ruthless, irresistible, conquering male, took Europe by storm; whilst the equally ruthless, titanically aspiring Faust remained caviare to the non-German general public'.[52] Outside Germany, Faustus may not initially have reached the same fairground presence as he had in Germany but Marlowe's *Doctor Faustus* nevertheless continued to be performed during the seventeenth century, ensuring that the idea of the 'titanically aspiring' character became a corner-stone of early modern literature. However, Faustus is never an unequivocal hero or villain, but instead explores the ambiguous interspaces between success and failure. The farcical flipside, moreover, underpins all versions of the tale, even those that purport to describe the damnation and deserved death of an infamous necromancer, to paraphrase the title page of the sixteenth-century Faust Books.[53] And of course the story about Faustus boasted a powerful popular tradition in which the intellectual, moral and religious conflicts of the period were explored with bacchanalian freedom.[54]

This book discusses the narrative traditions about the legendary anti-hero Faustus. Most early versions of the life of Faustus present themselves as cautionary tales, yet they simultaneously tackle some of the most urgent questions of the age: they investigate the foundations of religion, politics and natural philosophy at the same time as they explore the capacity of their hero to realize his wishes and desires.

---

background of the myth, there must have been countless pamphlet versions; see, *Faustus on Trial: The Origins of Johann Spies's 'Historia' in an Age of Witch Hunting* (Tübingen: Max Niemmeyer, 1992). The story of his life was circulated in cheap printed form from the moment when the reputedly original historical Faustus died around 1540 up to the end of the sixteenth century.

51 Harry Levin, 'A Faustian Typology', in *Faust through Four Centuries: Retrospect and Analysis,* eds. Peter Boerner and Sidney Johnson (Tübingen: Max Niemeyer, 1989), p. 1.

52 E.M. Butler, *The Fortunes of Faust* (Cambridge: Cambridge University Press, 1979 [1952]), p. xiv.

53 One instance, among others, is William De Mountfort's dramatic rendition, *The Life and Death of Doctor Faustus Made into a Farce* (1697), introd. Anthony Kaufman, The Augustan Reprint Society 157 (Los Angeles: William Andrews Clark Memorial Library, 1973).

54 Frank Möbus, in: *Faust: Annäherung an einen Mythos*, eds. Friederike Schmidt-Möbus and Gerd Unverfehrt (Göttingen: Wallstein, 1995).

The objective of this book, therefore, is to discover what it felt like to live through and experience the cultural and intellectual changes associated with the rise of empiricism and Enlightenment. It asks how people resisted, supported, or simply lived with these changes. It also seeks to show in what ways technological inventions and new political and scientific aspirations left their marks on contemporary consciousness. Not all texts included in this study are explicitly focused on Faustus but they share the thematic emphasis on the intellectual's quest for comprehensive knowledge of self and world. Parodic derisions of human naivety and gullibility play as important a part in this book as the moving manner in which Milton's Adam persists in seeking to understand the secrets of the material world and human consciousness. Unbounded in their intellectual and emotional aspirations, the Faustus stories embrace a large range of genres, themes and narrative modes, ranging from tragedy, epic, satire, farce and harlequinade. Whether their emphasis is serious or farcical, I argue, most versions blend comic and tragic elements in order to explore the rich tapestry of human fears, hopes and aspirations.

The Mythic Dimension of the Faustus Legend

Finally, a word of warning. The Faustus legend was a popular and often told story in large part because it positioned its hero in a mythic context. Many interpretations of the Faustus legend are somehow incomplete because they define Faustus as a pioneer of a rational opposition to the political, moral and scientific practices of an older era. However, it should be born in mind that the act of re-telling or re-making the tale both confirmed and challenged beliefs about God and the devil; death and life. It articulated archetypal ideas that exceeded all attempts to control them.

Some components of the legend have been added and some have been lost over the ages. But one detail that is germane to all versions of the legend is that Faustus agrees to sell his soul in exchange for twenty-four years of power and pleasure. While the figure of twenty-four years comes across as arbitrary, the number of his good years makes a lot of sense in the light of James Frazer's study of rituals associated with the succession of powerful rulers. Faustus fits well with the myriad of examples studied by Frazer across numerous historical periods and geographic boundaries. If viewed in this light, Faustus can be interpreted as a representative of the archaic king who embodies a god for a limited period of time. Read in the context of Frazer's archetypal god-king, Faustus becomes something more than a mere challenger of the competing factions of early-modern Christianity. Rather than being punished for his presumption at the end of his period of power, he becomes the victim of necessity. This is to say, he has to undergo a violent death in order to mask the slow decay, and natural death, of an aging human being so that kingship as an idea can for ever be identified with youthfulness and virility:

> If the course of nature is dependent on the man-god's life, what catastrophes may not be expected from the gradual enfeeblement of his powers and their final extinction in death?

There is only one way of averting these dangers. The man-god must be killed as soon as he shows symptoms that his powers are beginning to fail, and his soul must be transferred to a vigorous successor before it has been seriously impaired by the threatened decay.[55]*

Of course, the Faustus legend did not grow out of a historical experience of securing, through violent means, the succession of ever-young, ever-powerful rulers. But Frazer's study goes beyond literal examples of this violent tradition when he scrutinizes European folk customs. The ritual replacement of kings and other powerful rulers during carnival, who are beaten and ridiculed at the termination of their temporal rule, for example, are taken to be a substitute for the literal killing of the king. Such examples document the survival of the king's sacrifice in certain rituals and symbolic performances.[56]

Although the Faustus legend emerged at a remove from the violent traditions, whose presence Frazer documents in numerous archaic and non-European societies, it appeals to archaic views about the relations between power and knowledge. Because its transgression against the Christian commandments overlaps with more primordial views according to which the god-king's physical death secures his eternal veneration, the Faustus legend was ideally suited to exploring the boundaries of legitimate knowledge. Of course, the individual versions that were written between the late sixteenth and the early eighteenth centuries are preoccupied with different questions and concerns. However, all versions of the story invite their audiences to expand human boundaries and to question conventional views about the limits of permitted knowledge.

*

This book describes the narrative traditions about Faustus from the moment when oral versions and written stories about a daring rogue turned into a serious investigation of curiosity and useful knowledge. The German Faust Book (GFB), published in 1587, and its English Translation of 1592 (EFB) provide the focus of the first chapter. Concentrating on the value and purpose of existence reflected by these works, it argues that their emphatic references to human dignity collide with the cautionary tale's seeming acceptance of Calvinist hostility towards metaphysical curiosity. A comparative reading of these two Faust Books also identifies other moments when the cautionary tale's damning verdict is challenged. The most important element of these Faust Books consists of a set of journeys, added to the narrative framework of previous Faust Books, which dramatize the hero's desire to see and experience the delights and terrors of heaven, hell and earth. The addition of this travelogue, which sees Faustus' travel through the

55 Cf. James Frazer, *The Golden Bough: A Study in Magic and Religion* (Ware: Wordsworth Editions, 1993), p. 265.
56 Cf. the chapter 'Temporary Kings' in Frazer's *Golden Bough*, pp. 283–9.

three locations that defined late medieval cosmology, marks the moment when a burlesque rogue's tale is transformed into a literary portrayal; one in which an individual is torn between desire for unlimited power and the wish to see and understand that which holds the (material and metaphysical) world in place.

Christopher Marlowe's *Doctor Faustus* has attracted a great deal of scholarly attention. However, a large number of critical studies interpret the Faustus character too narrowly as an 'overreacher',[57] who craves the possession of unlimited intellectual knowledge in a fashion similar to Marlowe's Tamburlaine, who aspires to unbounded military power. However, such approaches fail to come to terms with the meanings and uses of magic. This chapter discusses the play's exploration of the borderlines between mundane knowledge and insight into metaphysical matters. It describes the play's understanding of magic as a form of knowledge that straddles proto-scientific, alchemical investigations, on the one hand, and metaphysical speculations, on the other. Both surviving versions of the play were of course published long after Marlowe's death in 1594. But the attempt to capture Marlowe's authorial intentions is less important than describing the argumentative thrust of the two versions. I place my emphasis on the B-text (1616) which, unlike the more secular A-text (1604), presents Faustus as a more serious seeker for metaphysical knowledge and thus enters into a discussion of the limits of that which can be known.

This book aims to describe the trajectory of the Faustus typology from the moment when the late sixteenth-century Faust Books explored the obstacles in the scholar's road towards secular and metaphysical knowledge to the emergence of Harlequin Doctor Faustus in the 1720s. But for the main part of the seventeenth century there were no attempts to re-fashion and adapt the Faustus typology. At first sight this seems to indicate that, paradoxically enough, the Faustus narrative was not considered relevant to the period when attitudes towards curiosity and knowledge underwent the most far-reaching transformations. But this conclusion fails to consider that the story was passed on through numerous performances of Marlowe's play and that dramatizations or adaptations of Marlowe's *Doctor Faustus*, even if they were not faithful to the original, kept alive the basic theme of a scholar-magician who made a pact with the devil. On another level, the key themes of the Faustus typology entered into every intellectual's attempts to understand the circumstances and consequences of their intellectual quests. Of seminal importance to an essentially Christian society were questions concerning the impact of intellectual enquiry on the salvation of the soul. This is why this chapter begins with the period's most eloquent interrogation of a Christian believer's approach to scientific investigations: Thomas Browne, *Religio Medici* (1642).

---

57 This memorable term for Faustus was of course coined in Harry Levin's study *The Overreacher: A Study of Christopher Marlowe*, Cambridge: Cambridge University Press, 1952.

A book on its own could have been written about Thomas Browne's views of the complicated relationship between religion and the study of nature; the same applies to the other representative voices of the seventeenth century discussed in Chapter Four. However, the purpose of this study is not to present an exhaustive account of some of the period's most prominent figures but to elucidate the spectrum of diverging voices around the interrelations between science and religion. This study, therefore, pays attention to the common denominators of three writers who offered very different explanations of the significance of scientific knowledge for the psychological-emotional complexities of human belief. While Browne's work represents a kind of meditation by which he can come to terms with the contradictions and dilemmas of his intellectual efforts, John Milton's *Paradise Lost* (1667) includes descriptions of states of mind altered by the experience of illicit forms of knowledge. I judge it impossible to exclude *Paradise Lost* because it represents the period's most important investigation of the psychological motivations behind the desire for knowledge. The avowed aim of Milton's description of the origin of the world is to justify the ways of God to man. While the poem claims to condemn Adam and Eve's curiosity, it does not consistently indict the first couple for craving after knowledge. Like the Faust Books, I argue, *Paradise Lost* contains some absolutely seminal moments when the desire for knowledge is not simply excused. Rather, these acts of transgression are shown to be of material necessity for achieving a higher state of consciousness.

Bernard le Bovier de Fontenelle's romantic dialogue between an aristocratic lady and a male scientist about the possibility of other worlds, is the last representative text in my palette of seventeenth-century's views about the psychology and social setting of knowledge. Fontenelle's broadly secular *Entretiens sur la pluralité des mondes* (1686) is conceived as a means of disseminating Descartes' scientific theories. Written some forty years after Browne and twenty after Milton, it expresses an unconditionally positive attitude towards the desire for knowledge. By enacting an imaginary journey through the planetary system, it takes its reader through a space from which all vestiges of a metaphysical quintessence have been erased. The sense of enchantment which clings strongly to the Faust Book's three journeys is hence transformed into a feeling of vertigo and disorientation. Such a situation requires the scientist's reassurance that the laws of nature are unshakeable, however difficult it may be to reconcile the intrinsic scientific facts with the observed characteristics of the world. This also positions Fontenelle's scientist at a remove from the traditional magician. As a scientist, he may be able to influence his period's understanding of natural laws, but he has no control over these laws themselves. Even while he can inspire endless fantasies about other worlds, the serious scientist can be seen as an impotent magician who has lost his ability to influence the course of nature.

At the same time as a modern scientist makes his appearance on the social stage, late seventeenth-century dramatists were once again tampering with the established Faustus plot. The final chapter, therefore, returns to a comparison of the resurgent Faustus narratives which re-design the classical narrative elements of the story. Perhaps owing to the lack of heroism attributed to the new category of the natural scientist, late seventeenth- and early eighteenth-century versions of the tale concentrate on its comic potentials. While they at times satirize the new science, the newly emerging Faustus dramas do not directly interrogate the position of the contemporary natural philosopher. Even though comedy comes to the fore, the Faustus narrative remains inherently tragi-comical. This chapter argues that the humorous dimension of the Faustus typology is the result of popular traditions according to which laughter was a familiar method of depriving the devil of his power and influence.[58] In spite of orgiastic belly-laughs that are meant to have an exorcising purpose, the comedy at the expense of the devil is always tainted by tragedy, because it is never possible to tell the remaining extent of his power. The inherent ambiguities of the devil's comedy is a palpable reminder of the uncertainties about human existence, emphasizing the lack of information about the nature of the soul, the meaning of life, and the possible existence and qualities of afterlife. Comedies, farces and harlequinades, such as Thomas Shadwell's *The Virtuoso* (1676), William Mountfort's *Doctor Faustus Made into a Farce* (1697) and the harlequinades about Doctor Faustus that emerged in the 1720s, therefore, use the farcical mode to explore the ambiguities around temptation, worldly success, spiritual yearning and death.

My study of early modern versions of the Faustus story and contemporary treatments of its key themes traces important changes in the perception of scientific investigation between the late sixteenth and the early eighteenth century, the time frame between 1580 and 1730 loosely circumscribing the period that is sometimes described as the age of the scientific revolution. Observing the interconnections between the Faustus story and the trajectory of the new science reveals that certain fantasies about the ability to control nature evolved at the same time as scientific investigations were being established as a serious occupation. However, my study also contrasts the process of legitimating scientific curiosity with a more basic craving for a harmonious union with nature. It argues that Faustus aims to both gain a mastery over nature but that he also hopes to perfect himself as a result of having grasped the essential truths about the cosmos. My interpretations of the different versions of the tale aim to show that at some level most descriptions of the intellectual's pact with the devil assert a positive view of human existence.

---

58 Ben Jonson's *The Devil is an Ass*, ed. Peter Happé (Manchester, Manchester University Press, 1994) goes to the point of describing the devil as a clumsy and incompetent character. That it was withdrawn or suppressed after its first stage production in 1616 and was only published posthumously in 1640 suggests that the complete comic denial of demonic power was not credible and that a 'true devil' was popularly believed to be far more ambiguous.

Chapter 2

The Insatiable Speculator:
The Hero of the Faust Books

In all early modern versions of the Faustus legend, Faustus is a scholar who is possessed of an insatiable thirst for knowledge. Since he was not satisfied with his culture's received wisdom and conceptions of legitimate knowledge, he resorted to the occult sciences, selling his soul to the devil in exchange for the secrets of magic and necromancy. While the authorities of the period decried him as an arch-sinner, he also inspired awe and admiration. The unquestionable topicality of the material to his contemporaries is evidenced by the fact that a simple rogue's tale was told and re-told through the sixteenth century until the Faust Book published by Johann Spies (1587), along with its English translation (1592), emerged as imaginative masterpieces of the period.

On the face of it, the Faustus narrative is a cautionary tale about the dangerous consequences of an intellectual's unorthodox study of self, world and God. The hero of the Faustus legend, as it was written down in proto-novelistic form in the late sixteenth century, probes into all topical questions of the period. Undaunted by the dangers believed to result from spiritual curiosity, he boldly challenges the ideological edifices of church and state.[1] Thirsting for knowledge, he rigorously disregards his period's warnings about the consequences of acquiring arcane forms of knowledge. His contemporaries viewed Faustus' unlimited desire to control the forces of nature as deeply immoral. As Leslie Shepard points out in his edition of Agrippa's work:

> from the thirteenth century onwards, the Church made an important doctrinal distinction between witchcraft and sorcery. Control of the forces of nature for magical purposes was not necessarily prohibited unless coupled with heresy. Although he made many enemies during his lifetime through his plain speaking, Agrippa was never convicted of heresy – indeed, much of his study and writing took place under the auspices of the Church. His great teacher in the magical sciences was the good Abbot John Trithemius of Herbipolis.[2]

---

1   For a discussion of the role of secret knowledge in early modernity, see Francis A. Yates, *Rosicrucian Enlightenment* (London: Routledge, 1972); see also Margaret C. Jacob, *The Radical Enlightenment: Pantheists, Freemasons, and Republicans* (London: Allen & Unwin, 1981).

2   Henry Cornelius Agrippa von Nettesheim, *The Philosophy of Natural Magic*, introd. Leslie Shepard (Seacaucus, NJ: University Books, 1974), p. 1.

The Church quite happily tolerated scientific investigations as long as the process of gathering knowledge did not give rise to visions of power that threatened to overturn existing hierarchies. In its early days, the study of nature was even thought to be a moral lesson about the miraculous skills of the creator. But when those who studied nature began to think about the logical implications of their discoveries, and in particular, started to question some core beliefs of their society, they came to be indicted for heresy and insubordination. Stuart Clark identifies four closely enmeshed developments:

> the modernization of Aristotle and the naturalizing of magic became key ingredients in natural philosophy from Oresme onwards; apocalypticism and prophesy were thriving in the fifteenth century but received an enormous boost from subsequent religious conflicts; providentialism, evangelism, and Decalogue theology were at the heart of the 'long' reformation of the church; the new pretensions of absolutist theory meant that politics became mystified to an extent unknown in the Western medieval states.[3]

Since the Faustus figure of the chapbooks probes the depths of these four demesnes of early modern intellectual life,[4] it was inevitable that their narratives had to conclude with his damnation. This chapter concentrates on uncovering the conflicting emotions and complex experiences emerging from behind the authoritative verdict of Faustus' damnation.

The Emergence of the Faust Books

With Spies' publication of 1587, the Faustus legend focuses on his quest for first-hand experience of the symbolically conceived framework of contemporary existence and probes into the full complexity of ideas about heaven and hell. Faustus' craving for knowledge also takes him on a journey through the three spheres that form his contemporary universe: heaven, hell and earth. The symbolic significance of this extraordinary travelogue is immediately recognized as a crucial element of the legend and writers as diverse as Christopher Marlowe and Thomas Mann expended their imaginative energies on this element of the story. It is indeed possible to argue that the whole of Part II of Goethe's *Faust* dramatizes Faust's travels through the real and imaginary spaces of his period's culture.

But what kind of person was the sixteenth-century Faustus? Spies' version introduces some passages into the narrative pattern that portray Faustus as a sensitive intellectual, while preserving the older features of the story according to which he is a jealous and petty-minded fairground hero who is hostile towards his fellow magicians: 'he could not abide to see another do anything, for he thought

---

3   Stuart Clark, *Thinking with Demons: The Idea of Witchcraft in Early Modern Europe* (Oxford: Oxford University Press, 1997), pp. 684–5.
4   For a definition of black magic see, Stuart Clark, *Thinking with Demons*, pp. xxx.

himself to be the principal conjurer in the world' (EFB 165).[5] The Spies version freely blends older patterns of the story about a rogue trying to trick the devil with the description of a serious seeker of wisdom. Of course, we can simply interpret this contradiction as an artistic flaw. But recognising that the main character is a bad-tempered villain as much as a sensitive individual searching after metaphysical truths forces us to remain aware of the multiple origins of the Faustus story.

The blatantly uneven literary merit of the different parts of the book prevents an easy identification with the hero of the Faust Books. Since only a small percentage of the population could read in the late sixteenth century, the written version of the story would have circulated among a small circle that may also have been aware of the striking ruptures in approach and stylistic finish. Considering that the Faustus story discusses explosive material in an age of censorship, it is conceivable that these ruptures served as indications that the tale contained more than one ideological point of view. The superior quality of the passages that portray a sympathetic figure certainly provides a noticeable contrast to the cautionary tale's bland condemnation of everything creative, imaginative and passionate.

The book as a whole is subdivided into four separate parts, which may have been taken from different sources: the first part describes how Mephostophiles first appeared to Faustus and became a part of his household; the second embraces an account of three extraordinary journeys during which Faustus gained first-hand knowledge of heaven, hell and earth; the third part describes a whole range of farcical adventures of an impecunious travelling adventurer; and the last part covers the lamentations and death of Faustus.

Since the Faustus legend originated in an oral context, we cannot say with any certainty when and how it first came into existence. An equally impossible task is to determine what its original objectives might have been and to which religious faction it belonged. The pranks played on the Pope and the dismissive comments about the practices of his court in Rome suggest that satirical broadsheets on the Catholic Church contributed to the narrative conception of the rogue's tale. Comments like 'the holy fathers will hear no confession without the penitent bring money in his hand' give vent to anti-Catholic polemics (EFB 130). This is not to say that the Faust Books ascribed unquestioningly to Protestant theological arguments. Rendering the legend in a more literary form, both the German and English Faust Books described behaviour that counted as sinful for any of the multiple strands of Protestantism and Catholicism.

The Faustus story was circulated in a variety of forms. At least three versions of the German chapbook have come down to us. The most influential versions undoubtedly are the Spies edition and its English translation. But it is impossible to say how many earlier versions may have existed. The anonymous writer of the Wolfenbüttel Faust Book, for instance, explains that it is a translation of a

---

5   The abbreviation EFB stands for English Faust Book and GFB for German Faust Book.

Latin manuscript.[6] It is nevertheless doubtful whether all versions derived from such a Latin source. There has been extensive speculation about the date and place of the first origins of the Faust Book, but it will probably remain impossible to document the precise course of the transformation from the rough-and-ready oral tales, lampoons and doggerel verses to the prototype of the Faust Book. What we can conclude with certainty is that the novelistic form of the story originated in an intellectual context – probably in a circle of students – who objected to their period's warnings about unrestrained intellectual activities. The close association with student circles is supported by a historical reference to a group of students who were publicly flogged for writing a glorifying account of Faustus' life just months before Johann Spies published his German version.[7] While its author remains anonymous, it seems likely that it was an individual who, on the basis of numerous oral tales that had long been cross-fertilizing each other, transformed the popular material into an early type of novel.[8]

The Faust Books have their roots in a variety of factors: Lutheran tracts against insubordination,[9] handbills circulated on account of the execution of medical practitioners and calendar makers, to mention only a few. Adrian Johns even demonstrates a close relationship between the emergence of the Faustus figure and the development of the printing press and its uncanny powers of disseminating subversive ideas.[10] Written accounts of the supposedly true adventures of Doctor Faustus began to circulate from the time when a group of travelling scientists or adventurers left behind a trail of scandal. Rather than tracing the origin of these tales, my study will begin at the moment when petty roguery turned into an intellectual scandal and when some anonymous hand used the material to study the inner experiences of a contemporary intellectual. The stated objective behind recounting the abominations of an atrocious sinner, then, served as a façade for an analysis of the intellectual's attempt to break out of the constrictions of his age. But the sober warnings against intellectual quests nevertheless remain important features of the books.

Georg Rudolph Widmann's slightly later Faust Book of 1599 appears to have been published with a view to profiting from a lucrative trade.[11] Although it

---

6   *Das Faustbuch nach der Wolfenbüttler Handschrift*, ed. H. G. Haile (Berlin: Erich Schmidt, 1963), p. 27. See also John Henry Jones's introduction to EFB, pp. 6–7.

7   Jones's preface to EFB, p. 9.

8   Haile shows that several manuscript versions of this novelistic treatment existed, arguing that the original version must have been written in the 1570s. For a detailed discussion of the textual tradition of the individual manuscripts, see *Das Faustbuch*, ed. Haile, p. 9. Also see introduction and annexes to his edition.

9   Cf. Frank Möbus, Friederike Schmidt- Möbus and Gerd Unverfehrt, eds., *Faust, Annäherung an einen Mythos* (Göttingen: Wallstein Verlag, 1995).

10 Cf. Adrian Johns, *The Nature of the Book: Print and Knowledge in the Making* (Chicago: University of Chicago Press, 1998), pp. 324–79.

11 Georg Rudolf Widmann, ed., *Fausts Leben*, ed. Adelbert von Keller (Hildesheim: Georg Olms, 1976 [1880]).

contains the core elements of Faustus' pact with the devil, it lacks the imaginative embellishments of the Spies edition. A further notable difference is that heaven and hell are only explored as part of the dialogue between Faustus and his familiar spirit. The absence of the travelogue, together with the more dour tone of the narrative, suggest that Widmann actually published a version of the Faust Book that predates the addition of Faustus' remarkable journey by which Spies transformed a popular tale into a work of literature. In any case, the absence of imaginative and psychological depth emphasizes the superficial quality of this Faust Book's moralising. The text of Widmann's Faust Book is interwoven with a prefatory discussion of temptation and intellectual arrogance, and the turgid message from a nineteenth-century pedant further smothers the story's challenging dimensions.[12]

The influential English translation of 1592, then, remains faithful to Spies' original but it also takes important liberties. An anonymous translator had a keen awareness of style and introduced many evocative descriptions, as well as replacing reported speech with direct speech. His emendations, however, are aimed at increased fluency and his embellishments add a sense of drama. His most telling liberties relate to the characterisation of Mephostophiles, who has turned into a more likable but also more difficult companion of Faustus.

What's in the Name 'Faustus'?

The shortened form Faust is German for 'fist', a detail which lends the Renaissance figure the defiant physicality of a rebellious radical. The full name Faustus, however, is Latin and means the happy or prosperous man. Could there have been a more inappropriate name? Numerous historical explanations of the Faustus legend have tried to account for this strange name by pointing to the precedent of some historical characters. But what has happiness got to do with the Faustus typology? The simple answer is: everything.

Even though the bulk of the Faustus literature deals with the human quest for happiness, the topic is treated with a certain embarrassment, as if the belief in happiness was a mark of naivety. Absolute happiness may not be within human reach, but this does not mean that the quest for a certain degree of fulfilment must be futile. Different periods have outlined different paths towards this goal. Happiness in the sixteenth century was focused on life beyond death while in the present secular age,

---

12 Cf. Conrad Wolff's prefatory treatise 'Kurtzer, nothwendiger und wolgegründeter Bericht von dem Zauberischen Beschweren und Segensprechen') ('short, necessary and well-founded account of magical incantations and pronouncements of blessings'), in: Widmann, ed., *Fausts Leben*. This nineteenth-century reprint is bolstered with an excessive amount of explanations aimed at preventing susceptible youngsters from imitating Faustus. The fact that such a wordy contextualisation was perceived to be necessary documents the powerful appeal of the legend, particularly after Goethe and other Romantics had embedded the story in a contemporary setting.

it is most closely aligned with the consumption of material goods. In both cases, though, the quest for happiness is an essential component of life, even though the term 'happiness' jars with the religious austerity of Luther, Melanchthon, Calvin and their adherents. Calvinism, in particular, insisted that a craving for salvation was the only legitimate quest for happiness, and otherwise inculcated a deeply negative attitude towards the joys of the here and now. However, the dour emphasis on sin and guilt was not able to eradicate the deeply human craving for happiness. It survived in the form of popular fiction, which continued to be dominated by tales about lucky adventurers obtaining their wishes against the odds.

Darrin McMahon draws attention to the etymological connections between happiness and the early modern conviction that the factors creating this state of well-being happen adventitiously. What is more, he argues that this idea is reconcilable both with antique philosophy and Christian theology.[13] Although Christians believed that nothing happened without the explicit will of God, they nevertheless had to accept that occasionally it was possible for the right circumstances to come together so as to create a moment of worldly happiness. If chance could influence the course of events, why should it not also be possible to take matters into one's own hands?

However, the idea of taking charge of one's own emotional and physical well-being grated against the core beliefs of Protestantism. The Catholic chapbook *Fortunatus*, first published in 1509, provides an interesting point of reference to the Faustus legend. Its eponymous hero stumbles from one misfortune to another until he finally loses his way in the middle of a desolate wood. When he is close to starvation he receives help from a virgin. Though she clearly recalls the virgin Mary,[14] the book refuses to commit itself on this matter, showing that her unearthly character emerged as a result of a strange marriage between the Catholic saints and a more ancient belief in the existence of mysterious, supernatural helpers. In any case, this mysterious helper allows Fortunatus to choose from among a list of abstract benefits: wisdom, wealth, strength, health, beauty and long life. After his disastrous mistake of choosing wealth, the story describes the consequences of his youthful imprudence, but it never suggests that he might have committed a sin.

By contrast with the foolish Fortunatus, Faustus' craving for knowledge almost illustrates the choice Fortunatus should have made, but there are of course very important differences between knowledge and wisdom. A major difference between *Fortunatus* and the Faust Books is that the latter are embedded in a context that questions the idea that those who go in search of their fortune will ultimately find it. A further difference between the heroes Fortunatus and Faustus is that the latter actively conjures up a supernatural helper, while the virgin who helps Fortunatus arrives unbidden. Faustus is not fighting his way through hardships and difficulties

---

13 Darrin McMahon, chapter for *The Enlightenment World*, eds. Martin Fitzpatrick, Peter Jones, Christa Knellwolf and Iain McCalman (London: Routledge, 2004).

14 *Fortunatus*, ed. Gerhard Schneider and Erwin Arndt (s.l.: Müller & Kiepenheuer, 1964), pp. 59–64.

in the hope that some supernatural character will ultimately save him. When Faustus calls for assistance, moreover, there is no ambiguity at all regarding the identity of his helper: it is the devil. Faustus confidently pronounces his conjurations and therefore it can only be the devil – and not the virgin – who arrives to help him.

Since Luther and his followers placed a great deal of emphasis on passive submission to God, the religious experience of early modernity was overshadowed by fear. David Riggs therefore argues: '[w]ithin the world of post-Reformation Christianity, belief in God was inextricably linked to the fear of God; a deity who did not enforce his commandments – a God without sanctions – might as well not exist.'[15] The austere visions of daily life formulated by Calvin and other Reformers after Luther have frequently been noted.[16] By the time the second generation of reformers had taken over the leadership, the believers were enmeshed in a world of fear that left little scope for earthly happiness.

The Ambiguous Theology of the Faust Books

The Faust Books are imbued with Protestant notions about grace and redemption. As William Rose points out, the overt message of the Faust Book is one of deep hostility towards an independent mind, but he also suggests that 'if the Faust Book had indeed been of Catholic origin, there is little doubt that the Madonna and the Saints would have saved him'.[17] But Faustus inhabits a world from which an elaborate hierarchy of interceding saints has been removed. With the disappearance of saints, the sinner was left to plead for his own salvation and there was no help if he pleaded badly. Abandoning trust in the good offices of saints thus meant that humans had to take responsibility for their own souls. But were they able to do so? When Marlowe's play asks whether Faustus' soul is indeed his own (2.1.68), it draws attention to a poignant question about whether the individual believer is in a position to make choices about the best way to take care of his soul.

Regular religious practices and worship perpetuated a belief in abstract notions about the sacred. It is important to keep in mind that the Christian rituals performed in preparation for experiencing the sacred have always pursued the task of embedding the individual within a community of believers.[18] They foster an

---

15 David Riggs, 'Marlowe's Quarrel with God', *Critical Essays on Christopher Marlowe*, ed. Emily Bartels (London: Prentice Hall International, 1997), p. 46.

16 Cf. A.D. Nuttall, *The Alternative Trinity: Gnostic Heresy in Marlowe, Milton, and Blake* (Oxford: Clarendon Press, 1998) or Alan Sinfield, *Faultlines: Cultural Materialism and the Politics of Dissident Readings* (Berkeley: University of California Press, 1980).

17 William Rose, ed., *The History of the Damnable Life and Deserved Death of Doctor John Faustus (1592) Together with the Second Report of Faustus Containing His Appearances and the Deeds of Wagner (1594)* (London: George Routledge, n.d.), p. 29.

18 Cf. Cox, *The Devil and the Sacred in English Drama, 1350–1642* (Cambridge: Cambridge University Press, 2000), p. 50.

attitude of sharing and belonging that dissolves the constraints of individuality. The act of transgression, by contrast, is associated with the assertion of individuality. Because it is supposed to disturb the connectedness between community and God, it is associated with the idea of sin or defilement.

There has been a recent tendency to interpret the eroding significance of religion in early modernity as a stepping-stone on the road towards the rationality that dominated the Enlightenment period. Cultural historians talk about the increasing demystification of religious mysteries, sketching the dismantling of superstition, and atheistic liberation as the success story of modernity.[19] However, such a view fails to acknowledge a host of factors that contributed to the dilapidation of the moral-emotional edifice that had been embodied by the medieval church.

Officially, atheism was a crime that drew draconic punishments on the perpetrator at a time when religion and civil order were still closely intertwined. Owing to the tight entanglements between religious belief and social order, atheism was perceived as a major threat to the norms and standards of medieval society. Giordano Bruno was burned alive for his open commitment to the Copernican theory of the cosmos; when Christopher Marlowe was stabbed he was saved from a trial for atheism, and the last two burnings alive for heresy in England occurred as late as 1611.[20] Even though theological arguments of the period tend to blur the boundaries between heresy and atheism, it is important to keep in mind that the act of gainsaying certain religious orthodoxies is by no means the same as straightforward denial of all metaphysical agency. Oppositional arguments did not necessarily seek to reject religious beliefs as such, but to replace them with what they considered to be better beliefs and practices. Opposition to clerical authority, particularly in regard to civic matters, is one thing. It is quite another to reject religion as a myth that had been established as an instrument of social control.

When 'the Spanish ambassador Gondomar Gondomar estimated the number of English atheists at nine hundred thousand, or a fourth of the adult population', he must have misinterpreted the people's indifference to or ignorance of the core beliefs of Christianity.[21] However, for the zealously competing religious factions, indifference, or refusal to be embroiled in the religious controversies of the period, was almost as objectionable as atheism. Bitter disillusionment over the carnage of the warring parties may have motivated many to reject religion wholesale. But those who lapsed into gloomy indifference were not the problem; serious threats were perceived to come from what William Empson calls 'undergraduate atheism',[22] an uninhibited and irreverent investigation of the rationale and morality behind the core allegories of Christianity and their interpretations. Some

---

19 See for example E.K. Chambers, *The Medieval Stage* (Oxford: Oxford University Press, 1978).

20 William Empson, *Essays on Renaissance Literature*, vol. 1: *Donne and the New Philosophy*, ed. John Haffenden (Cambridge: Cambridge University Press, 1993), p. 82.

21 Riggs, 'Marlowe's Quarrel', p. 44.

22 Empson, *Donne and the New Philosophy*, p. 92.

may indeed have concluded that there was no God, but simply questioning the prevailing religious explanations of life and death was already considered to be a dangerous undertaking.

During the sixteenth century, groups of young men and some women began to assemble in frequently raucous circles to debate the topical concerns of the day. And they did not stop short of the Bible. They observed that the wide interpretive scope of the biblical stories, as, for example, Alan Sinfield comments, 'hardly makes for a persuasive theology. It may lead to the thought that there is no coherent or consistent answer because we are on an ideological faultline where the churches have had to struggle to render their notions adequate.'[23] Intellectuals like Christopher Marlowe were quick to respond to the fact that an inconsistent theological edifice served as the foundation for moral standards and sexual mores. Censorship and other means of social control prevented them from saying openly that the idea of original sin and natural depravity insults the humanity in us. This explains why the cautionary tale that frames the Faust Books conceals some rather subversive claims.

While the Faust Books can be seen to condemn objectionable and unorthodox ideas, they can also be seen to describe a positive alternative to the story of damnation. The abstract reasoning and concrete experiences of Faustus are of course overshadowed by the seemingly tragic course of his life. He is, nevertheless, one of the most powerful characters of German and English literature; a figure who could not fail to elicit at least some sympathy. So as to understand this fictional persona and his significance over a period of some 150 years, I will now take a close look at the cautionary tale and discuss its divergences from other voices of the narrative.

The Structure of the Cautionary Tale

The summaries on the title pages of all versions of the Faust Book draw attention to the tragic conclusion of their hero's life. Johann Spies' influential German version advertises the book as follows:

> History of Doctor Johan Faustus, the widely renowned magician and necromancer [or goetian], how he signed himself over to the devil for an appointed time, what strange adventures he experienced in the meantime, what he did and how he behaved, until he finally received his well-deserved reward. (GFB 1)[24]

---

23 Alan Sinfield, 'Reading Faustus' God', *Critical Essays on Christopher Marlowe*, ed. Emily Bartels (London: Prentice Hall, 1997), pp. 197–8.

24 'Historia von D. Johan Fausten, dem weitbeschreyten Zauberer und Schwarzkünstler, wie er sich gegen dem Teuffel auf eine benannte Zeit verschrieben, was er hierzwischen für seltsame Abentheuwer gesehen, selbst angerichtet und getrieben, bis er endlich seinen wohlverdienten Lohn empfangen.' The modernised spelling is quoted from GFB.

This summary concentrates on the main components of the story, which was already widely known by the late sixteenth century: Faustus makes a pact with the devil and buys the devil's services in exchange for his soul. The formulation that he 'signed himself over to the devil for an appointed time' reminds us of the nature of contracts: it indicates that he signed at a certain moment of his life and agreed that the devil could fetch him at a later date. We are all familiar with the fact that signing a contract involves a time lag between decision and action, which means that contracts 'dispose of' the future. Not surprisingly, the question concerning the precise moment when Faustus belongs to the devil sparked off major controversies. Will Faustus only be damned after the expiry of 24 years, or is merely dealing with the devil and signing the pact sufficient for him to be damned? Here it is relevant to consider that the phrase 'for an appointed time' can both refer to a limited period of time as well as describe a particular moment in the future. Important questions proceed from this ambiguity: What is the nature of the contract with the devil? Is Faustus able to change his mind? Can the contract be revoked or annulled? And, finally, is it valid in the first place?

The title page of the Spies edition quotes the Lutheran version of the following verse: 'Be subject therefore to God, but resist the devil, and he will fly from you,'[25] a gesture by which Spies sought to protect himself against accusations of heresy. No similar precautions were taken with the English Faust Book. Its title page merely announces that the book contains 'The historie of the damnable life, and deserved death of Doctor John Faustus' and it omits the proselytising details of its German original. His life may be 'damnable' – that is to say worthy of damnation – but the phrase does not imply that he was really damned after death. Although it implies the causality that his 'damnable life' brought about 'his deserved death', the simple fact that he dies is not conclusive proof of his damnation.

The title page of the English translation softens the 'damnable' aura of Faustus and simply offers a brief thematic summary of his life:

A Discourse of the most Famous Doctor Faustus of Wittenberg in Germany, Conjuror, and Necromancer: wherein is declared many strange things that he himself hath seen and done in the earth and in the air, with his bringing up, his travels, studies, and last end. (EFB 91)

Here Faustus has received the epithet of 'the most Famous Doctor' and the occupations of conjurer and necromancer are no longer prefixed with gruesome adjectives. The events of his life move into the background while the 'many strange things' encountered on his journeys gain prominence. His adventures in heaven and hell, moreover, have become located in physical spaces: 'in the earth and in the air'. The book itself describes heaven and hell along traditional lines but the introductory summary transforms these mythological localities into physical

25 *Authorized King James Version of the Bible* (1611), *Epistle of St. James the Apostle*, 4.7.

places and thus offers a materialist interpretation of the symbolic cornerstones of Christianity. Importantly, the summary also refrains from any judgement concerning the nature of his 'last end'.

The English version contains no further introductory sections. The Spies edition, by contrast, discusses the fate of its hero both in the dedication to Caspar Kolln and Hieronymus Hoff, two officials in the administration of the duchy of Königstein, and in the preface to the Christian Reader. Spies carefully guards himself and the anonymous author of his book against the suspicion of heresy by referring to a nameless friend in the town of Speyer from whom he claims to have received the manuscript (GFB 4). While insisting that the book's value lies primarily in deterring others from imitation, he also explains:

> Because it is a noteworthy and terrible example, in which one cannot simply see but also sense evidently the devil's envy, deceit and cruelty towards the human race … I have spent so much cost and effort on it with all the more pleasure and hope to do a kind service to all those who allow themselves to be warned. (GFB 4)

The emphasis on palpably experiencing the events of the story goes hand in hand with the attempt to warn his readers against imitation. Spies might well argue that a simple warning is not sufficient but that effective deterrence requires a palpable rendition of the dangers. On the other hand, the immediacy of his narrative also allows his readers to get a better understanding of the meanings and uses of magic. The surprising camaraderie between Spies and his audience, furthermore, appears to be founded on a shared understanding of the challenges and excitements of the Faustus story rather than on a joint resistance to the devil's wiles. His tone of voice suggests that he is not talking to those who are frightened by simple words of warning but addresses likeminded scholars who are able to 'sense evidently' the yearnings and desires associated with the breach of traditional commandments. Their familiarity with these strictures, though, does not mean that they must be deterred by them.

There is a faint line between 'those who allow themselves to be warned' and those who allow themselves to be seduced. But the tone of the dedication suggests that it is far less important to define this line than to adumbrate a coterie of people who know the temptations. The warmth with which Spies addresses the two recipients of his dedication embraces the audience and knits a sense of emotional complicity between reader and writer. It is in this spirit that Spies describes the publication of the book as a 'public testimony of the extraordinary love and friendship which partly dates back to our school days in Ursel and partly began with much visiting and common activities and continues to the present day' (GFB 5). If the two old friends should have belonged to a circle of intellectuals attracted to alchemy and hermetic scholarship, the emphasis on feeling and experiencing gains additional salience, inviting the initiated reader to 'sense evidently' and identify with the passions of a fellow seeker after first-hand knowledge of self and world.

The Faust Books' Attitude towards Magic

Like the Wolfenbüttel manuscript, Spies' version also elaborates on the sinfulness of magic. Rather than merely quoting the biblical passages against sorcery and divination, both versions explain that magic involves a rebellious rejection of God as the most supreme power (a violation of the first and second commandments) and is therefore tantamount to idolatry.[26] The preface spells out that magic is such a sinful pursuit because it challenges the foundations of religious belief. It then enters into an account of various alchemists and magi and, for instance, describes Zoroaster as an Icarus figure 'who was led into the air by the devil and, because he wanted to see all the gods and celestial bodies was burnt by the heavenly fire'.[27] This preface recounts the disastrous punishments for the pursuit of magic in an unemotional, matter-of-fact tone, without the least trace of sympathy for the magician's yearning to see and experience the visible and invisible universe.

In the eyes of contemporary theology, the practice of magic was always in danger of breaching the First Commandment, where the Christian God defines himself as the one and only deity: 'Thou shalt have no other gods before me'.[28] Since magic employs the assistance of spirits, it challenges the supremacy of God, threatening to replace the monotheistic status quo with a struggle between God and spirits – or devils. Some comments are in place here on the understanding of 'spirit'. As with most metaphysical issues, there were at least two factions: some identified all spirits as deeply offensive, satanic emanations and others distinguished between malign and benign spirits.[29] In a world that was obsessed with fear of the devil, in any case, all dealings with spirits were potentially dangerous, particularly if such dealings challenged established beliefs. For this reason, the Christian God was considered unwilling to forgive acts that questioned his sovereignty. If he were to forgive Faustus for his dealings with the devil, he would recognize the power of other supernatural agents and as such question his own supremacy. But as a result, the failure to forgive shows him either to be lacking in kindness or unable to rise above the strictures of his law.

The 'Preface to the Christian Reader', which introduces the Spies version, adds an interesting perspective to this debate. While it announces itself as a preface to the 'Christian' reader and thus claims to address the crowd of God-

---

26 *Das Faustbuch*, ed. Haile, p. 27.

27 *Das Faustbuch*, ed. Haile, p. 29.

28 *Authorized King James Version of the Bible* (1611), *Exodus* 20:3.

29 For an account of the devilish nature of spirits, see W.W. Greg, 'The Damnation of Faustus', *Modern Language Review* 41.2 (1946): 97–107; and for an interpretation of the role of spirits that differentiates between good and bad spirits, see T.W. Craik, 'Faustus' Damnation Reconsidered', *Renaissance Drama*, NS 2 (1969): 189–96. Also compare Keith Thomas, *Religion and the Decline of Magic: Studies in Popular Beliefs in Sixteenth and Seventeenth Century England* (London: Weidenfeld and Nicolson, 1971); and Stuart Clark, *Thinking with Demons*.

fearing Christians, it subverts some important points of Christian dogma. Behind its explicit condemnation of an arch-sinner, it is really forging a bond among a circle of likeminded intellectuals. Giving numerous quotations from the Bible, the Preface appears to condemn the practice of magic, and all associated attempts to overstep the narrow confines of proper Christian behaviour. It is particularly emphatic in its argument that magic is rooted in idolatry. However, the potency of magic is never doubted and several famous examples are quoted in order to illuminate the dangers of these secret and illicit skills. On the other hand, no mention is made of prophecies and miracles wrought with divine assistance. The differentiation between sacred miracles and satanic arts will preoccupy thinkers of the seventeenth century, such as Bernard le Bovier de Fontenelle, Thomas Browne and others.[30] Spies' preface, however, wastes no energy on trying to differentiate between the two; it simply mentions the arguments of the Christian precepts and by doing so appears to indict all practitioners of magic.

The Voice of Rationality

In the preface to the German Faust Book, the gruesome death of Faustus is explained as a direct consequence of his 'shameful vices, gluttony, drunkenness, whoredom and excess until the devil gave him his deserved reward and strangled him in the most abominable manner' (GFB 10). The 'Preface to the Christian Reader' overtly says that this is a truly evil character and describes his eternal punishment as follows: 'However, this is not yet the end of the matter but now follows the eternal punishment and condemnation which amounts to the fact that conjurors of the devil finally follow their idol, the devil, into the abyss of hell and have to be damned eternally' (GFB 10). A number of biblical quotations are given as an evocative reference to the fire and brimstone of hell. For those who believe that the Bible is the literal rendition of the word of God, Faustus is irredeemable. But alternative points of reference appear alongside the conventional tenets of Christianity.

When scrutinized in detail, the Preface to the Christian Reader refutes the Protestant view of human nature. The following comments are disguised as moralising side-remarks:

Is it not a gruesome and frightening bargain if a reasonable human being, created by God according to his image and ennobled so highly in body and soul and richly endowed, should miserably abandon the one true God and creator to whom he owes all reverence and obedience in order to hand himself over body and soul for temporary and eternal damnation to a created spirit who, unlike the dear angels in heaven, who hold on to the justice and purity created with them, is not a good and holy spirit but a damned, lying

---

30 Bernard le Bovier de Fontanelle's *Histoire des oracles*, ed. L. Maigron (Paris: Didier, 1971); for a more detailed discussion of these issues, see chapter 5 of this book.

and murdering spirit who has no continuity in truth and justice but was banished from heaven because of his sins? (GFB 8)[31]

The idea of the 'reasonable human being' is anathema to the Lutheran claims about the natural depravity of mankind. As Heiko Oberman points out, it was an essential element in Luther's thought to take for granted the extreme and insurmountable inferiority of man to God and to insist that the human mind bore no resemblance to the mind of God. Unless reason was harnessed to humility, he argued, it would simply be used in the service of the ever-present satanic tempter.

Luther himself emphatically rejected the idea that human reason could be of any benefit whatsoever for achieving spiritual salvation. Oberman explains:

> First there was the nominalistic subordination of reason to experience, whereby … experienced reality itself becomes the focus for the perception of the world. Furthermore, nominalists sought to distinguish between God's word and human reason. In the realm of revelation, in all matters concerning man's salvation, God's word is the sole foundation – here reason and experience do not prescribe but confirm; here they do not precede but follow.[32]

Because there is no mediation and no guaranteed right understanding of God's word, Luther's theory of salvation is a highly personal affair, and it allows for no certainty. To be human means to be a sinner. But for Luther, any sinner could be saved, provided that he or she was sufficiently repentant. All that was required for salvation was to accept one's sinfulness with humility and to submit to God's grace. Luther's robust fight against the Pope's indulgences was indeed motivated by his conviction that there was nothing anyone could do in order to guarantee their salvation: neither the dedication to a religious life nor the untiring practice of good works might gain one any advantage on the road towards salvation.

The emphasis on the 'one true God and creator' in the quotation above alludes to the idea that only God can create true substances. The German and English Faust Books elaborate on this assumption in the context of the imaginary journey through hell: they emphasize that Faustus is terrified by appearances, referring to

---

31 *'Ist es aber nicht ein greulicher und erschrecklicher Handel, dass ein vernünftiger Mensch, von Gott zu seinem Ebenbild erschaffen und an Leib und Seel so hoch geehrt und reichlich begabt, denselben einigen, wahren Gott und Schöpfer, dem er alle Ehr und Gehorsam sein Leben lang schuldig ist, so schändlich verlassen und sich einem erschaffenen Geist, dazu nicht einem guten und heiligen Geist, als die lieben Engel im Himmel sind, die in ihrer anerschaffenen Gerechtigkeit und Reinheit Bestand haben, sondern an einem bösen, verfluchten Lügen- und Mordgeist, der in der Wahrheit und Gerechtigkeit keinen Bestand hat und seiner Sünde halber aus dem Himmel in den Abgrund der Höllen verstossen worden, mit Leib und Seel zu zeitlicher und ewiger Verdammnis zu eigen ergeben wolle?'*

32 Heiko Oberman, *Luther: Man Between God and the Devil*, trans. Eileen Walliser-Schwarzbart (New Haven: Yale University Press, 1989), p. 120.

the general belief that the devil did not have the power to create material objects. The prefactory passage therefore further emphasises that there is only one creator. The repulsiveness of the devil, then, is emphasized through the contrast between the 'dear angels' and the 'damned, lying and murdering spirit'. The devil is not here described as the counterpart of God but, much like the 'dear angels', he is a 'created spirit'. While God is described as the all-powerful single origin of all creatures and spirits, the passage also suggests that it is easy enough for the angels to be good and dear since justice and purity were created as their natural attributes. Because God also created the devil, we need to conclude that he is responsible for the devil's sinfulness, which means that he damned him for a quality with which he originally created him.

A.D. Nuttall's study of the contemporary relevance of the Gnostic heresy shows that these considerations deeply troubled early modern culture. Formulating a consistently equitable interpretation of the Bible, he argues, was a key objective of the Reformation period. However, the task could only be achieved if God was defined as a jealous and petty-minded character who refuses to forgive offences that endanger his superiority.[33] Nuttall argues that this is why an influential strand of early modern religion tried to replace the admiration for this tyrannical demiurge with a celebration of Jesus as the one who brought the beneficial gift of knowledge to the people. Modelling Jesus along similar lines as Prometheus, of course, introduced a rift into the harmonious understanding of the trinity. The resulting conflicts between God, the father, and God, the son, exposed the inherent injustices of Christian theology while it also placed the devil in a more favourable light. While the Faust Books confront us with some inherent injustices in Yahweh, they also insist that human resemblances to the creator 'ennobles' mankind.

Faustus, the Speculator

The early modern debate about whether it was legitimate to acquire knowledge of the mysteries of nature was closely associated with contemporary views of the devil. Any age's attitude towards the devil is the consequence of a complex layering of legend, folklore and historically specific attempts to imagine him as an embodied figure. This may account for the devil's extraordinary transformational powers, allowing him to appear both in his archaic, horned guise who will torture the flesh of his victims, or as a subtle sophist who assails their conscience. The two extremes of this spectrum describe him either as a physical being, adopting an animalistic guise, or as a metaphysical spirit, providing a foil against which a good Christian could be defined. The devil also demonstrates a large number of human characteristics at the same time as he breaches all notions of what is acceptable for humankind. The secret of his contradictory nature depends on the idea that as an animalistic demon

---

33 Nuttall, *Alternative Trinity*, e.g. p. 16.

he is lower than man and yet, as a psychologically skilled fallen angel, he is higher and endangers all notions of what is considered properly human.

The devil has always been imagined as breaching any attempts to enclose him within a precise definition. Numerous legendary origins define him as a deeply ambiguous and unfathomable figure. In an attempt to explain the cultural roots of the early modern tempter, Bernard McGinn argues that 'satan' is rooted in a word that

> comes from the verb *satan*, meaning 'to oppose', which in its noun form is used in the Hebrew Bible both for human (*2 Sam.* 19:22) and angelic opposers. The most noted occurrence of an angelic opposer is found in *Job* where Satan functions as one of the 'sons of God ... that is, the members of Yahweh's heavenly court'. (*Job* 1:6–12; 2:1–7)[34]

It would go beyond the scope of this study to discuss the diverse traditions behind the biblical occurrences of the devil. I simply want to point out that the clash between a number of different traditional ways of defining the devil left its mark on the writer(s) of the German Faust Book. These writers must have been aware that the Bible forges intimate links between God and devil. So much so, that it is frequently unclear whether the opponent is a vassal acting on behalf of his lord or an adversary using his cunning to overthrow divine power.

The contradictory qualities of the devil cannot have escaped a period that was obsessed with him. Furthermore, awareness of the fault lines in the conception of Satan must have gone hand-in-hand with the attempt to conceal a whole array of theological incongruities. However, not even the severest injunctions against probing the logical foundations of belief could smother the curiosity of independent minds. Critical analyses of cultural projections could not fail to draw attention to the man-made qualities of metaphysical agents. This is why the Mephostophiles imagined by the Faust Books derives his power from a deeply ingrained belief in the existence of metaphysical beings. My interpretation of the Faust Books aims to elucidate the metaphysical framework that gives life and vibrancy to Mephostophiles and adds a sparkle to Faustus' experience of devils, spirits, heaven and hell.

A whole range of different devils appear in the Faust Books but it goes without saying that the most striking among them is Mephostophiles. He may not be a coherent character but this renders him no less attractive to his readers. His first appearance is prefaced by a theological controversy about whether the devil has always been lurking around Faustus, and merely pretends to have responded to his conjurations, or whether the devil was forced to appear by the conjurations. While the emphasis of the story is on whether Faustus is able to repent, a further theological point revolves around the question of whether he broke his tie with

---

34 Bernard McGinn, *Antichrist: Two Thousand Years of the Human Fascination with Evil* (San Francisco: HarperSanFrancisco, 1994), p. xi.

God when he first decided to conjure the devil or whether he only does so when he actually signs his name to a formal pact.[35]

The full complexity of the Faust Book develops around the hermetic reader's concerns with God and metaphysics. Earlier I drew attention to the role of reason in Spies' Preface to the Christian Reader. The initiated circle of readers who agree that a 'reasonable human being' is 'created by God according to his image and ennobled so highly in body and soul' (GFB 8) will in all likelihood have concluded that free will determines the actions of Faustus. Rather than portraying the damaging consequences of his curiosity, this same group is likely to believe that reason directed his decision. In *Paradise Lost*, Milton will claim that 'reason also is choice' and, by doing so, proposes an intimate link between reason and freewill.[36] The cautionary tale of the earlier Faust Books derides knowledge as foolish and vain but the narrative also valorizes reason and progress.

The Faust Books' brief sketch of their hero's background and upbringing mentions that both his natural parents and his foster-father in Wittenberg took special care to cultivate his scholarly faculties. The introductory chapter objects to the idea that they 'might have encouraged his wilfulness in his youth and not have made him study hard' (GFB 14). That he possesses a particular turn of mind and has received his yearning for knowledge by nature is given as the exclusive reason for Faustus' pursuit of the secrets of magic. His friends are excused from any guilt over failing to warn him about the dangers of magic. The text proposes a view of extraneous influence as forms of 'somnia', dreams or futile confabulations. Spies' Faust Book next comments that he had 'a foolish, silly and proud head, which is why he was generally called the Speculator' (GFB 14).

By contrast, the English translation eradicates the idea that Faustus might have had a foolish head and instead says:

> But Doctor Faustus within short time after he had obtained his degree, fell into such fantasies and deep cogitations that he was marked of many, and of the most part of the students was called the Speculator; and sometimes he would throw the Scriptures from him as though he had no care of his former profession: and so began a very ungodly life ... (EFB 92).

This passage explains his ungodly life as the consequence of speculating about mysteries which contemporary theology declared to be forbidden to human investigation.

---

35 Nutall's interpretation of Marlowe's *Doctor Faustus* argues that it builds up dramatic tension around the question of whether Faustus acts on the basis of free will and hence is fully accountable for his actions or whether he can still obtain forgiveness for his sins; see Nuttall, *Alternative Trinity*, pp. 22–41.

36 Cf. John Milton's *Paradise Lost*, in *Complete English Poems, of Education, Areopagitica* (London: Everyman, 1993), Book III, 108. The larger context reads as follows: 'Not free, what proof could they have given sincere / Of true allegiance, constant faith, or love, / Where only what they needs must do appeared, / Not what they would?'; Book III, 103–6.

However, the close causal link between extraordinary intelligence and breach of restraints, explains why his hunger for insight was highly regarded by some while it was taken to be a sign of depravity by others. While the Spies version describes the Speculator as someone who possesses a foolish and proud head, the English translation explains that Faustus acquired his reputation for being a Speculator because he 'fell into fantasies and deep cogitations'. Criticism of his behaviour has been greatly toned down in the English translation, although the formulation that he '*fell* into fantasies' is reminiscent of the *fall* from grace.

The Speculator's imagination goes beyond the simple ability to comprehend. He is also able to create, which explains why he rivals the traditional skills of a jealous God. The formulae of conjuration play an important role in this context, although they are omitted from the narrative. But even if they were quoted in full, they do not offer a guaranteed path towards command over the spirit world. As the burlesque chapbook about the attempt of Faustus' servant Wagner to pursue the same route as his dead master demonstrates, the magical formulae are not sufficient by themselves.[37] Not even the possession of a supernatural spirit is much use to poor Wagner, and he is systematically ridiculed for his ineptitude at handling his familiar spirit, Auerhan (GFB 118). Wagner, and the crowd of alchemical-magical dabblers represented by him, lack sensitivity and imagination. Faustus, however, stands far above the common fairground magician. A reason for this may be found in the etymologically based paraphrase of the term Speculator. As is documented by the *Oxford English Dictionary*, the main meaning of 'speculator' that evolved during early modernity described somebody who could see things through his mind's eyes, somebody who could imagine and call things into existence by force of his imagination.[38]

Not surprisingly, there is a close connection between giving reign to the imagination and pondering over impenetrable complexities. The *OED* traces the first usage of the word 'Speculator', in the sense of 'one who speculates on abstruse or uncertain matters; one who devotes himself to speculation or theoretical reasoning' to the year 1555. The term is, for instance, used by Richard Eden who writes: 'The philosophers, speculatours of naturall thynges, saye that it is engendered of substaunce more watery then fyerie.'[39] The next documented usage is from Thomas Browne who talks about 'The Writers of Mineralls and naturall speculators'.[40] Both quotations from the *OED* point to the borderlines

---

37 Wagner Book, published in same book as GFB: Helmut Wiemken, ed., *Doctor Fausti Weheklag: die Volksbücher von D. Johann Faust und Christoph Wagner* (Bremen: Carl Schünemann, 1961).

38 Cf. the first meaning listed in the *OED* under 'speculate': 'To observe or view mentally; to consider, examine, or reflect upon with close attention; to contemplate; to theorize upon'.

39 Richard Eden, *The Decades of the Newe Worlde or West India* (Arber, 1885 [1555]).

40 Thomas Browne, *Pseud. Ep.* III. xiii. 137.

between early modern science and magic or 'natural magic'.[41] This collective term for a whole range of proto-scientific experimentation as well as weird and wonderful displays by itinerant scholars who pledged to demonstrate the nature of the cosmos to a crowd of gaping spectators is beautifully illustrated by Hieronymous Bosch's painting *The Conjuror*.[42] It renders the mentality of a period when the study of the material world had not yet been divorced from theoretical accounts of its rationale. It was a time when Paracelsus explained the inalienable connections between macrocosm (the universe) and microcosm (the body), form and meaning, body and mind. Then as now, the uninformed crowd preferred spectacles to true insight, demonstrating that a magician's reputation rested on his ability to satisfy an audience which, while enthralled by exciting spectacles of magic, was little interested in learning about the secrets of nature.

The Significance of '*Formae Coniurationum*'

As I have argued before, the Faustus legend is strongly rooted in traditions that would have been branded heretical at the time. While the story challenges the Judaeo-Christian godhead in various ways the most important strand of oppositional thought is associated with hermetic or Gnostic beliefs. But it makes little sense to equate the subversive gist of the Faust Books with the tenets of the various sects and secret societies that were forming at the time. While the narrative structure of the Faust Books expresses powerful elements of oppositional-heretical thought, they do not align themselves with any of them. In other words, the Faust Books are not written in a code that can be made to reveal a secret message. It is entangled too strongly in the mindset of the cautionary tale, on the one hand, and the contradictions of alternative beliefs, on the other.

So what kind of magic does Faustus perform and what skills does he possess? He clearly acts out the magical conjurations described in medieval books of sorcery. Even though the narrative is careful to omit any concrete *formae coniurationum*, it alludes to familiar practices. Accordingly, it says that at a prescribed hour Faustus went into a famous wood and after locating a suitable crossroad 'he made with a wand a circle in the dust, and within that many more circles and characters' (EFB 93). The precise nature of his magical invocation is left vague but his performance of ritual practices is nevertheless described in evocative terms. As noted before, Spies' Preface draws attention to his careful excision of incantatory formulae. While this decision panders to those who want to see the life of Faustus as a cautionary tale, the indirect presence of these formulae renders them more potent than if they had been reproduced. In the absence of a precise description of the '*vocabula*, figures,

---

41 John Batista Porta, *Natural Magick*, ed. Derek J. Price (New York: Basic Books, 1957).

42 Hieronymus Bosch, *The Conjuror*, 1500, painting held in Musée Municipal, Saint-Germain-en-Laye.

characters, conjurations and other ceremonial actions' that 'he put in practice', moreover, the description draws attention to the dramatic nature of the rituals.

However, there is also a sense that the intended readership of the Faust Books would have been familiar with the *formae coniurationum*. That quite some credence was attributed to them is demonstrated by the fact that a booklet containing these omitted formulae appeared in 1609. It was a German publication entitled 'The key to the power over hell or the conjurations and activities of Doctor John Faustus, from the original of the frequently practiced divine art of conjuration'.[43] It was published at a time when the tug of war between zealots and oppositional thinkers had grown less severe, and it appeared among a spate of adaptations, handbills and ballads that vied for popular attention. The reference to an original publication of Faustus' art of conjuration may be fictional but the formulae described in the German booklet are embedded in a system of beliefs that might have been shared by Faustus, if he had been a historical figure.

The title of the booklet describes magic as a divine practice because it confers god-like power on its practitioner. However, the preface contains no subversive comments and is written in the voice of a stolid believer. It describes its reader as 'yearning for art and knowledge' and explains the contents of the booklet as follows:

> Here you will find the right key that will open up hell and, with the help of God, to force, compel and bind the powerful spirits therewith to your obedience ...[44]

The practitioner of magic is further admonished to perform a devout prayer and

> to cleanse himself externally and internally; internally so as to ensure that he is reconciled with God and that he has abstained from all fleshly intermingling for at least three days before he sets to work; externally that he should wash his whole body and wear clean clothes. Hereafter he should make use of the holy cross of Christ, carved either in wood or drawn onto parchment ... (pp. 5–6)

Far from representing an attempt to oust Christianity, the school of magic described in this booklet presents itself as a legitimate offshoot. Importantly, this booklet describes the devil as a helpmate whose abilities can be harnessed for all kinds of good purposes, provided God offers his assistance. From the great adversary of Luther's cosmology, the devil has dwindled into a serviceable spirit of the Christian God. Of course, the published conjurations of Faustus did not necessarily emerge from the coterie responsible for Spies' literary version of the

---

43 *Der Schlüssel von dem Zwange der Höllen oder die Beschwörung und Prozesse des Doctor Johannis Faustae, von der öfters practicirten göttlichen Zauber-Kunst ex originalibus* (Hamburg: L.M. Glogan Sohn, 1609).

44 *Der Schlüssel*, p. 1.

chapbooks. Nevertheless, it shows that there were attempts to continue an older tradition according to which magic and Christianity could exist side by side.

The Appearance of Mephostophiles

After a brief description of his birth, background and upbringing, the Faust Books explains that 'all Faustus' mind was set to study the arts of necromancy and conjuration, the which exercise he followed day and night: and taking to him the wings of an eagle, thought to fly over the whole world and to know the secrets of heaven and earth' (EFB 93). The imagery of this description portrays him as a modern Icarus fired by the desire for unlimited knowledge. Not only does Faustus want to obtain the complete body of knowledge but he also wants to perceive empirically what the world feels like. By doing so he subscribes to the Aristotelean tradition according to which knowledge can only be gained through physical perception, which is to say that he can only receive answers to his burning questions if he sees and experiences all aspects of the universe himself.

The devil is similarly portrayed as a palpable presence. The dogmatic question about whether Faustus conjured the devil or whether he had been lurking in his vicinity from the very first is embedded in the terms of low comedy. The Spies version comments graphically that 'the devil will certainly have been laughing up his sleeve and have shown his behind to Faustus'.[45] The story next associates the appearance of the devil with a vehement outburst of the elements. In spite of its melodramatic potential, the description of Faustus' conjuration of Mephostophiles utilizes elements of archaic beliefs to render the devil physically real: 'then presently the devil began so great a rumour in the wood as if heaven and earth would have come together with wind, the trees bowing their tops to the ground' (EFB 93). The elements rage at the same time as the devil roars, blares and bellows. Alternatively we may imagine that the wild tunes of nature complement the terrifying noises of the devil; so much so that the devil's animalistic noises can be interpreted as a personification of a thunderstorm. Faustus is standing in the midst of thunderclaps and lightning when an ominous fireball races towards him:

> Presently not three fathom above his head fell a flame in manner of a lightning and changed itself into a globe: yet Faustus feared it not, but did persuade himself that the devil should give him his request before he would leave. (EFB 94)[46]

---

45 GFB, p. 16: 'Da wird gewisslich der Teuffel in die Faust gelacht haben, und den Faustum den Hintern haben sehen lassen.'

46 Cf. GFB, p. 17: '*Bald darauf fiel drei oder vier Klafter hoch ein feuriger Stern herab und vewandelte sich zu einer feurigen Kugel, des D. Faustus dann auch gar tief erschrak. Jedoch liebte er sein Fürnehmen und achtete es gar hoch, dass ihm der Teuffel untertänig sein sollte ...*'

A flash of lightning quickly transforms into a fiery globe that lingers in order to reveal its mysterious contents. The scene recalls the moment when God spoke to Moses through the burning bush: 'And the angel of the Lord appeared unto him in a flame of fire out of the midst of a bush: and he looked, and, behold, the bush burned with fire, and the bush was not consumed.' (*Exodus* 3:2). A reader familiar with the miracles of the Bible will conclude that a fireball that retains its flame without being fuelled indicates the presence of a spirit who is eternal and unchangeable.

Faustus demonstrates extraordinary presence of mind and concentrates his magical skills on the globe of fire:

> ... suddenly the globe opened and sprang up in height of a man: so burning a time, in the end it converted to the shape of a fiery man. This pleasant beast ran about the circle a great while, and lastly appeared in the manner of a grey friar, asking Faustus what was his request. (EFB 94)

The text resonates with biblical references easily recognisable in a Protestant environment that regarded reading the scriptures as a vital step on the road to salvation. Describing the 'fiery man' as a 'pleasant beast' is a parodic allusion to the apocalypse when the end of historical time is marked by the appearance of frightful beasts that forebode the last judgement. The 'fiery man' also recalls an episode in the book of Daniel when Nebuchadnezzar commanded that three stolid believers in Yahweh should be thrown into a furnace as a punishment for their refusal to abandon their God. The presence of an additional fiery man stopped the fire from consuming the three righteous men so that Nebuchadnezzar said, 'I see four men loose, walking in the midst of the fire, and they have no hurt; and the form of the fourth is like the Son of God.' (*Daniel* 3:25). This and other biblical passages reinforce the idea that a flame which does not consume the object at its centre is a representation of the divine.

The God of the Old Testament explicitly forbids the formation of 'any graven image'. The only legitimate representation of God in Judaeo-Christian religion, repeatedly employed by the Bible, renders God through the vehicle of the four elements. The 'angel of the Lord' appears unto Moses 'in a flame of fire out of the midst of a bush', and Yahweh himself appears in a 'pillar of fire', 'in a thick cloud', and 'answered Job out of the whirlwind'.[47] When Yahweh interacts directly with his people, he is frequently shown to be utilising an elementary force. While this allows him to disguise his true identity, it also reminds us that a theory of worship that bans representation is both very sophisticated and very basic. While resorting to archaic imagery in order to counteract anthropomorphic images, it also brings about a powerful approximation with archaic notions of the godhead. This is to say that a non-anthropomorphic God appears in response to the conjurations of Faustus, only to transform himself from an animistic deity into a common human guise. Leaving aside the gibes directed at the grey friars, Mephostophiles'

---

47 *Exodus* 3:2, *Exodus* 14:24, *Exodus* 19:9 and *Job* 38:1.

appearance as a monk marks his capacity to assume flesh, thus imitating Jesus' mystical transformation from a member of the spirit world to a human being.

The quick transformation of the fiery globe into a mystic character and a grey friar invokes a range of different genres from the sublime to the burlesque. It also gives body to quite different aspects of religion: the animistic worship of elementary forces, the adoration of an abstract power of transcendence, and representatives of contemporary religious orders. It portrays a pagan fire spirit, an anthropomorphic beast of the apocalypse as well as an ordinary human being. The act of representing them in quick sequence reminds us of the uncanny resemblances between them. It also strips Christian belief of the civilising layers that seek to conceal the elementary core of its mysteries.

Transformation plays a part not only in occult practices like alchemy and magic but is also located at the very heart of Christianity. Whether it is a literal or symbolic transformation is of course a crucial element in the fierce debate between Protestants and Catholics. A similarly heated controversy revolved around the question of whether the visual representation of the sacred amounted to idolatry. It is relevant to remember that various religious sects of the sixteenth and seventeenth centuries were severely indicted for their heretical aberrations when they tried to render a palpable image of their godhead. It was precisely the controversies over how to gain experience or even evidence of the godhead that entrenched the separation between the established church and heretical beliefs.

When Mephostophiles displays his transformational skills he dramatizes transubstantiation and thus expresses the core mystery of Christian belief. Regardless of whether it happened at the instigation of Faustus' conjuration, or whether some spiritual agency wanted to treat his audience to a dramatic spectacle, this scene enacts the mystery of the New Testament when the spirit turned flesh. The text's insistence that the devil is named as the master of ceremonies may throw an ambiguous light on its theological symbolism, but Mephostophiles' appearance is nevertheless a sublime moment. A comic dimension slips in, though, when the spectacular transformations reveal as their final product a grey friar. The clearly recognized gibe at Catholicism, however, does not undo the power of the previous mystery. It merely detracts attention from a moment of revelation.[48]

As Obermann emphasizes, it is a moot point for Lutheranism that God cannot be grasped by the human senses: 'the *omnipotent* God is indeed real, but *as such* hidden from us. Faith reaches not for God hidden but for God revealed, who, incarnate in Christ, laid Himself open to the devil's fury'.[49] By contrast with the Protestant God who exceeds both physical and intellectual understanding, the devil is a constant physical presence. In their attempts to grasp physical manifestations

---

48 The mysterious transformations that precede the anthropomorphic appearance of Mephostophiles bear resemblance to the events surrounding the creation of the philosopher's stone; cf. Lyndy Abraham, *A Dictionary of Alchemical Imagery* (Cambridge: Cambridge University Press, 1998), pp. 145–8.

49 Oberman, *Luther*, p. 104.

of contemporary cosmology, the Faust Books therefore present us with a whole variety of devils that belong to various forms of religious belief.

According to most traditions, the devil embodies the principle of evil, but except for his desire to possess the soul of Faustus, the devil of the Faust Book does not really show himself as an evil character. He may assist Faustus in some rough pranks but the story is far from describing seriously offensive deeds. It lacks downright evil and does not revel in the gory details of the devilish acts of folklore.[50] No new-born babes are dashed on the ground and devoured by the damned Faustus. Considering that he is damned and knows it, his breaches of contemporary morality are very modest. Moreover, the account of his life does not attempt to invert the standards of morality. David Pocock argues that the symbolic inversions ascribed to witchcraft and sorcery are important means by which society safeguards the moral order and symbolizes the ideal of order itself.[51] In anthropological terms, projecting gross misbehaviour and malice onto individual miscreants strengthens moral prerogatives. By contrast, Faustus is surprisingly civilized.

Mephostophiles, likewise, is essentially a well-behaved character whose roguish tricks ridicule the authority of the Pope and take revenge on petty criminals and impertinent louts. He serves his master dutifully and acts almost as a companion or confidant of Faustus. The contrast between his spectacular first appearance and his essentially human behaviour draws attention to the complex range of ambiguities associated with the devil. So who is the devil?

Lucifer, the lord of Hell, has a complex history as rival deity to or opponent of Yahweh.[52] Any other name associated with the devil draws on equally complex histories. In keeping with the devil's multiple forms and ambiguous character, the Faust Books emphasize his extraordinary ability to transform himself. He can assume the guise of a ball of fire, a dragon, animals, and even insects. In one chapter, the Princes of Hell appear in the shape of pre-Christian deities like Belial, Beelzebub, Astaroth, Anubis. The representation of the Princes of Hell parodies the nightmarish descriptions of the Book of Revelation. The literal translation of Lucifer's appearance, for instance, reads: 'Lucifer himself sat in manner of a man, all hairy, but of a brown colour like a squirrel, curled, and his tail turning upwards on his back as the squirrels use'. The English translation adds the further comment: 'I think he could crack nuts too like a squirrel' (EFB 117; GFB 52).

---

50 A telling contrast is provided in the eighteenth-century drama about Faustus by Maler Müller. The beginning of Müller's story is a meeting of devils during which they vie with each other for the favour of Satan on the strength of their power to spread evil in the world; cf. H.W. Geissler, ed., *Gestaltungen des Faust* (München: Verlag Parcus, 1974), vol. 1.

51 David Pocock, 'Unruly Evil', *The Anthropology of Evil*, ed. David Parkin (Oxford: Basil Blackwell, 1985), p. 47.

52 Cf. Forsyth, 'The Origin of Evil', *The Old Enemy: Satan and the Combat Myth* (Princeton: Princeton University Press, 1987), p. 27. Also compare John D. Cox, *The Devil and the Sacred in English Drama, 1350–1642* (Cambridge: Cambridge University Press, 2000), p. 49.

When the terrifying qualities of the monsters of Revelation are blended with those of a small furry animal, the description is reduced to a comic spectacle.

The English translation repeatedly picks up on the various traditions that converge in the portrayal of the devil, exaggerating the comic absurdity of the German descriptions. Anubis, for instance, is portrayed as a motley dog by the German version, but the English Faust Book transforms him into a most bizarre creature who 'had a head like a dog, white and black hair, in shape of a hog, saving that he had but two feet, one under his throat, the other at his tail' (EFB 117).[53] This icon of absurdity differs from the jackal-headed god of ancient Egyptian death worship. While the Anubis of the English Faust Book travesties certain fantasies, its playful attitude towards some traditions encourages us to infer that all images of the devil are imaginary projections. Both German and English Faust Books offer a summary account of human projections of supernatural beings. Or more precisely, they *almost* do. The most telling example is that of Christ. At first sight this parallel appears to be carefully excluded but, as I will argue later, they nevertheless draw attention to striking parallels between Faustus and Christ.

The Pact with the Devil

The pact, or contract, with the devil provides a seminal element of the story. As the narrative of the Faust Books unfolds, the conditions of the pact are rendered twice, which detail confirms their heterogeneous source material. Importantly, there are some striking differences between the first and second bill of fare. Faustus' first list of demands from the devil reads as follows:

1. That the spirit should serve him and be obedient unto him in all things that he asked of him from that hour until the hour of his death.
2. Further, any thing that he desired of him he should bring it to him.
3. Also, that in all Faustus his demands or interrogations the spirit should tell him nothing but that which is true. (EFB 95; cf. GFB 18)

The first demand stipulates unconditional servitude, while the second and third specify particularly relevant instances of the general agreement relating to material wealth and the possession of true knowledge. An assumption implicit in these demands is that the devil can fetch every object under the sun and that he is also infinitely knowledgeable. He is sketched as being all-powerful and all-knowing and hence possesses the two qualities commonly reserved for God. Aspiring to possess these qualities for himself, Faustus implicitly demands to become like God.

---

53 Cf. GFB: '*Anubis hatte einen Hundskopf, schwarz und weiss, im Schwarzen weisse Tüpflein und im Weissen schwarze; ansonsten hatte er Füsse und hängende Ohren wie ein Hund; er war vier Ellen lang*' (GFB 52).

The second account of the pact begins on an even grander scale: not only does Faustus ask for the benefits of his spirit's unlimited power and knowledge but he claims these qualities for himself. His first demand is: '1. That he [Faustus] might be a spirit in shape and quality' (EFB 96).[54] The remaining conditions concern the mode of existence and type of service which Faustus expects of his spirit-servant. They flesh out the key argument of the first version of the contract: 'that the spirit should serve him and be obedient unto him in all things'. The main scandal of this version of the pact, however, depends on Faustus' challenge to the hierarchies of heaven and earth through which he aims to become a spirit himself. Disregarding the conventional boundaries between spiritual and material substances he aspires not only to power and possession, but also endeavours to change the very nature of who he is. He seeks to shed the essential qualities with which he was created and by doing so aims to be the master of his own destiny rather than succumbing to divine ordinance. By claiming to become a spirit himself, then, he argues for the possibility of such a transition, or indeed, he brings about a much closer resemblance between materially embodied human beings and metaphysical beings. Such an idea, of course, radically challenges the prevailing idea of hierarchy that was supposed to rationalize the order of creation.

Transformation of base into sublime substances and spiritual essences, of course, was one of the most fundamental objectives of alchemical studies. The philosopher's stone, a metaphor for the mysterious capacity of transformation,[55] is founded on the assumption that the fluid boundaries between different substances can be overcome. The philosophy behind alchemical analyses of matter suggests that there exists a close relationship between spiritual and real substances, which intimates an ideal unity between the phenomenal and the noumenal world. Implied by this philosophy is a world of energies that differs fundamentally from the Christian idea that earthly existence is pivoted on the tension between sin and salvation. It is true that the Faust Books emphatically talk about the damned status of Satan and his devils. A force that is capable of transforming physical into spiritual matter, however, owns the same creative characteristics as the Christian God. This alternative view, then, fundamentally challenges the Christian belief system.

The Gnostic Roots of the Faust Book

The most striking divergences between the English and German Faust Books concern the astrological practices of Faustus. The second part of the narrative

---

54 An interesting detail about the otherwise less elaborate Spies version is that here Faustus demands 'firstly, that he might possess and obtain the skilfulness, shape and physique of a spirit'. *('Erstlich, dass er auch die Geschicklichkeit, Form und Gestalt eines Geistes möchte an sich haben und bekommen.')*, GFB, p. 20.

55 Cf. Abraham's entry on 'philosopher's stone' in *A Dictionary of Alchemical Imagery*, pp. 145–8.

begins along similar lines in both versions: 'Doctor Faustus having received denial to be resolved any more in suchlike questions [concerning the nature of God and his creation], forgot all good works and fell to be a calendar-maker by help of his spirit' (EFB 113). Spies' version then leads into a dialogue between Faustus and his spirit concerning nature and the objectives of astrology. This is when the spirit provides the following answer:

> The matter is this that all star-seers and sky-observers cannot practice anything for certain, for these are hidden works of God which human beings cannot fathom like us spirits, who are hovering beneath heaven ['heaven' and 'sky'] and see, measure and fathom the fateful events of God. For we are old spirits, experienced in the course of the heavens.[56]

This account challenges the implied view that the devil is the damned opponent of God. Referred to as a spirit, and not as a devil, Mephostophiles acquires an ambiguous status deriving from the suggested competition between God and devils. However, no reason is given for their longstanding disagreement. Reconfiguring the devil as a spirit challenges the morally based differentiation of the good God and evil devil and reduces both of them to the common level of non-materiality. The detail that describes devils as 'old spirits' foregrounds the heretical idea that spiritual beings are in possession of great knowledge, or wisdom, about the secret workings of both theological heaven and secular sky. Of course, the secret motive behind Faustus' calendar making is to predict 'the fateful events of God'. It embraces the wish to improve agricultural methods through a better understanding of the seasons, but it is also concerned with foretelling and interpreting the course of a human life. Indeed, Faustus does not simply want to predict the future but also seeks to unfold the true nature and hidden characteristics of a human being.

While mainstream Christianity believed that God had banned the pursuit of knowledge, his right to do so had not always been uncontested. What came to be known as the Gnostic heresy fiercely indicted the God of *Genesis* as a tyrannical demiurge who kept his creatures in slavish subjection by forbidding access to the knowledge that might lead his creatures to rival his superiority.[57] Gnosticism

---

56 GFB, p. 46: *'Es hat ein solch Judicium, dass alle Sternseher und Himmelgucker nichts Sonderliches als gewiss practiciren können, denn es sind verborgene Werke Gottes, welche die Menschen nicht, wie wir Geister, die wir in der Luft unter dem Himmel schweben und die Verhängnisse Gottes sehen und abnehmen, ergründen können. Denn wir sind alte Geister, erfahren in des Himmels Lauf.'*

57 Hans Jonas argues that the overt hostility of the most prominent Gnostic systems may be owing to the fact that they grew out of Jewish heretical traditions; cf. *The Gnostic Religion: The Message of the Alien God and the Beginnings of Christianity* (Boston: Beacon Press, 1963), p. 33.

rebelled against this tyranny and, in particular, defined the figure of Christ as the Saviour because he replaced blind ignorance with recognition and wisdom.[58]

A comment on the meanings of orthodoxy is appropriate here. It was after Constantine the Great had become emperor of Rome in A.D. 306 that the Christian religion was adopted by the Roman imperial government and in 'the course of these events the idea and reality of a single, unified, and orthodox church gradually became more established'. Bentley Layton specifies that '[a]lthough it is historically correct to speak of early Christianity as one religion, it can also be described as a complex network of individual parties, groups, sects, or denominations'.[59] Gnosticism was only one among many sects to be exterminated during the Christian church's struggle for uniformity.

According to its etymological roots, Gnosis means quite simply knowledge. By stark contrast with the warning of *Genesis*, Gnostics deeply valorized knowledge; particularly the knowledge about God and the sacred. The term 'Gnostics' can therefore be paraphrased as 'people fit to have acquaintance (*gnosis*) with god'.[60] Hans Jonas explains that '*Gnosis* meant pre-eminently knowledge *of God*' and goes on to argue that owing 'to the radical transcendence of the deity it follows that "knowledge of God" is the knowledge of something naturally unknowable and therefore itself not a natural condition'.[61] The knowledge aspired to by the Gnostic amounted to a mystic acquaintance with the creative spirit and the created world. Emphasis was on first-hand experience, rather than intellectual perception. A range of oppositional sects challenged the prohibition of knowledge and curiosity. Persecution and the suppression of Gnostic texts dispersed the adherents of the sect and, as tends to happen under these circumstances, the impossibility of establishing a formally recognized Church preserved their ideas as intellectual abstractions which, in their turn, influenced other heretical-oppositional beliefs. Allusions and implicit Gnostic statements hidden behind logical ambiguities gave impetus to a form of religion that valorized knowledge and insight and encouraged its individual believers to explore their place in the larger plan of the Creation.

My interpretation of some crucial passages will illustrate that the Faust Books reflect some crucial Gnostic beliefs. If we assume a Gnostic undercurrent, we can suddenly understand the text's insistence on exploring the origin, reason and nature of the Creation while simultaneously attacking the Christian conception of God. When Mephostophiles insists that he will not engage in further conversation on 'divine and heavenly matters' (GFB 48), he can hence be understood to object to

---

58 For a discussion of Gnostic beliefs, see Giovanni Filoramo, *A History of Gnosticism*, trans. Anthony Alcock (Oxford: B. Blackwell, 1990); *Gnosticism: A Source Book of Heretical Writings from the Early Christian Period*, ed. Robert McQueen Grant (New York: Harper Brothers, 1961).

59 Cf. Bentley Layton's introduction to *The Gnostic Scriptures* (Garden City, NY: Doubleday, 1987), pp. xvii and xviii.

60 Layton, *The Gnostic Scriptures*, p. xv; see also p. 9.

61 Jonas, *Gnostic Religion*, p. 34.

regurgitating the views of Christian orthodoxy. The rejection of traditional beliefs, however, does not deny the possibility of spiritual experiences. The Faust Books do not provide a coded message that can be unequivocally unpacked; rather, they give voice to untiring quests for the meanings of existence. The Faust Books are not directed against discussions of divine matters but against a mere rehashing of received wisdom. In other words, the subversive undercurrent of the Faust Books gestures towards a spiritual enlightenment that reflects the personal quest of an early modern believer who increasingly identifies himself (or herself?) as a unique individual.

Interestingly enough, the English translation appears to erode what might be looked upon as specific references to Gnostic belief. Far from indicating a rejection of Gnostic traditions, this appears to be the result of a more general valorisation of knowledge that had established itself among its prospective audience. Rather than identify with a specific set of beliefs, it simply offers a portrait of a strong mind in search of spiritual and worldly fulfilment.

The Origin of the World

Before Faustus and Mephostophiles embark on their journeys, they discuss the nature of the universe. Prior to his empirical exploration of the material world and its cosmology, Faustus demands a conclusive explanation of its origin. The German Faust Book discusses this question in a separate chapter that develops from its hero's preoccupation with calendar making. The English translation, however, incorporates this question into the devil's visit to the home of Faustus.

An interesting issue in this context concerns the behaviour and moral principles of the devils. The English Mephostophiles is never shown to breach his side of the contract while his German counterpart is insistently described as deceitful and malicious. A particular instance of his dishonesty concerns his account of the origin of the world:

> The Spirit then gave an ungodly and false account and said the world, my Faustus, has not been born and is immortal. The human species has likewise existed from all eternity and has not initially had an origin.[62]

The treacherous description of the German devil reflects contemporary views according to which the devil is the master of appearances and deceptions, his proper realm being chaos while order was considered to be the demesne of God. From his first appearance, the (German) devil's chief goal appears to be that of making a fool of the inquisitive scholar. But he sees through his attempt to cheat

---

62 GFB, p. 51: *'Der Geist gab Doctor Fausto hierauff ein Gottlosen und falschen Bericht, sagte, die Welt, mein Fauste, ist unerboren und unsterblich. So ist das Menschliche Geschlecht von Ewigkeit hero gewesen und hat anfangs keinen Ursprung gehabt'.*

him and plans to use him in such a manner that his victim will lose his game twice over.

The German Mephostophiles specifically denies the biblical story of creation: he gainsays the conventional role of God and rejects the idea that this God created the universe. His description of the origin of the world reads as follows:

> The earth had to nourish itself and the sea separated from the earth; they have therefore compared themselves with each other in friendly manner, as if they could talk. The earth demanded its dominion from the sea in the form of fields, meadows, woods and grass or foliage while the water demanded the fishes and everything else that is in it. But then they allowed God to create man and the heavens so that they ultimately had to subject themselves to God. From this dominion emerged four dominions: air, fire, water and earth. I cannot report it differently or more concisely. Doctor Faustus mused [speculated] on this and it would not get into his head for he had read in the first chapter of Genesis that Moses told it differently; so that he, D. Faustus, did not say much against it.[63]

This passage blends several different accounts of the creation.[64] The account of the separation of earth and water evokes an animistic worldview according to which earth and water are deities endowed with the capacity to nourish themselves and all creatures inhabiting their spheres. A competing argument invoked here is Hippocrates' theory that all matter is a composite of the primary four elements: air, fire, water and earth. These two theories of origin are contrasted with the Christian view reported in *Genesis*. Intermingled in these different accounts is a story of origins that reports the conflicts between a subjugated nature and a tyrannical god. The intermingling of these rivalling theories produces an odd result, implying a god who initially existed at a distance from the world and who first had to gain permission before he could exercize his creative capacities in order to subjugate the world. But nature is said to have given its consent and is likewise portrayed as an agent with godlike qualities.

---

63 GFB, p. 51: *'Die Erde hat sich selber nähren müssen, und das Meer hat sich von der Erde getrennt; sind also freundlich miteinander verglichen gewesen, als wenn sie reden könnten. Das Erdreich begehrte vom Meer seine Herrschaft, als Äcker, Wiesen, Wälder und das Gras oder Laub, dagegen das Wasser die Fische und was sonst noch in ihm ist. Doch dann haben sie Gott zugegeben, den Menschen und den Himmel zu erschaffen, also dass sie letztlich Gott untertänig sein müssen. Aus dieser Herrschaft entsprangen vier Herrschaften: die Luft, das Feuer, Wasser und Erdreich. Anders und kürzer kann ich dir nit berichten. Doctor Faustus speculierte dem nach, und es wollte ihm nicht in den Kopf, denn er hatte Genesis am 1. Capitel gelesen, das Moyses es anders erzählte; also dass er, D. Faustus, nicht viel darwider sagte'.*

64 Mephostophiles indeed outlines the four creation myth types, which Paul Ricoeur describes as archetypal patterns, through which human societies tried to account for the origin of evil. See *The Symbolism of Evil*, p. 172.

Christian, Gnostic and animistic traditions (familiar, for example via Classical antiquity) are freely intermingled in this passage, and the crafty German Mephostophiles makes no attempt to bring any sense into this tapestry of competing voices. This passage is heretical, first and foremost, because it does not privilege the Christian narrative, while refuting the others as false. For the gullible reader of the cautionary tale, it illustrates a 'hair-raising' example of Mephostophiles' untrustworthiness, but it also represents a comic attempt to force the competing explanations that were circulating in the late sixteenth century into one coherent whole. Yet, it is hard to imagine that Faustus would not immediately have recognized the origin of the strange brew of different traditions presented to him by his spirit. The emphasis on his insatiable craving for knowledge indeed implies that he must have possessed the familiarity with humanist scholarship required for grasping the allusions. But an unsophisticated reader would hardly have sniffed heresy here. For an educated reader the act of commingling disparate elements into one supposedly coherent narrative must have come across as a reminder that all implicitly mentioned arguments are equally the result of human projection, or speculation, and that none of them represents the ultimate truth.

The English Mephostophiles, by contrast, answers the question about the origin of the world by summarising the religious views of his period. A further liberty of the translation is that it inserts the debate into a temporary phase of despair. The beginning of chapter 19 paints a moving picture of a dejected Faustus whom Mephostophiles tries to cheer up: at first Faustus does not even respond to the question of 'what thing so grieved and troubled his conscience'. But the spirit behaves like a caring friend who 'very earnestly lay upon him to know the cause, and if it were possible, he would find remedy for his grief and ease his sorrows'. The intimate interaction between the two suggests that Mephostophiles is a spiritual adviser rather than a servant:

> 'My Faustus, thou knowest that I was never against thy commandments as yet, but ready to serve and resolve thy questions. Although I am not bound unto thee in such respects as concern the hurt of our kingdom, yet was I always willing to answer thee and so I am still: therefore my Faustus, say on boldly, what is thy will and pleasure?' At which words, the spirit stole away the heart of Faustus, who spake in this sort: 'Mephostophiles, tell me how and after what sort God made the world and all the creatures in them, and why man was made after the image of God'. The spirit hearing this, answered: 'Faustus thou knowest that all this is in vain for you to ask. I know that thou art sorry for that thou hast done, but it availeth thee not, for I will tear thee in thousands of pieces if thou change not thine opinions', and hereat he vanished away. Whereat Faustus all sorrowful for that he had put forth such a question, fell to weeping and howling bitterly, not for his sins towards God, but for that the devil was departed from him so suddenly and in such a rage. (EFB 116)

I have quoted this passage at length in order to show how closely enmeshed are personal issues and theological questions. On the emotional level, Mephostophiles is a real devil who sadistically coaxes Faustus into confessing an illegitimate desire, for which he is immediately punished. The tone of their dispute, however, is reminiscent of a quarrel between two close friends. Mephostophiles forces his master into a classic double bind: in order to reciprocate, Faustus has to tell him the truth about his most secret wishes, but if he is honest he loses his affection. The formulation 'the spirit stole away the heart of Faustus', then, implies that his spirit's kindly behaviour did not simply make Faustus open his heart but that he projected him into an impossible situation.[65] When Faustus falls to 'weeping and howling bitterly' he bewails his squabble with his companion but he also gives vent to his annoyance at having been caught in a double-bind. The most bitter pain that creeps into this moment of disillusionment may be caused by the recognition that the opponent of Yahweh is equally uncompromising in squashing the will of his adherents.

After Mephostophiles has left, Lucifer and his hellish cohorts invade the home of Faustus. At first Faustus is terrified but he gradually enters into a sociable dialogue with the prince of Hell. Lucifer comes to remind him of his contract but also shows benign forbearance, explaining 'wherefore I am come to visit thee and to show thee some of our hellish pastimes, in hope that will draw and confirm thy mind a little more steadfast to us' (EFB 117). He is an enlightened devil who prefers the use of persuasion to brute force. By giving him another chance, as it were, Lucifer shows himself to be more forgiving than Yahweh. The scene closes – in both the German original and English translation – with a pageant of different types of devils who appear with the bells and whistles of the most blatant hocus-pocus.

In the Spies version, Lucifer's appearance in the home of Faustus concludes with a further demonstration of the devil's transformational skills. The devils assume the shapes of gnats, ants, leeches, horse flies, crickets, and locusts, and begin to plague Faustus mercilessly: flees, gnats and bees sting him while countless ants urinate on him. When suffering from an onslaught of insects, caterpillars and spiders, it would be only natural to whine and lament. However, Faustus responds in a spirit of amusement: 'I believe that all of you are young devils'.[66] Rather than interpreting the devil's torments as an element of the archaic battle between good and evil, he laughs them off as the boisterous pranks of young rogues.

The response of laughing at the devil was a 'stock-in-trade' of the medieval world. However, the customary emphasis, recommended, for instance, by Luther,[67] was to remind the devil of his ridiculous inferiority to God. It was assumed that hurting his pride was an effective way of driving him away because he could not bear to be laughed at. In this passage, though, Faustus does not laugh at the devil as a means of shooing him away but he expresses a sense of being entertained.

---

65 For an explanation of the mad-making consequences of the double bind, see Gregory Bateson, 'Toward a Theory of Schizophrenia', *Steps to an Ecology of Mind* (New York: Ballantine, 1972), especially pp. 206–8.

66 GFB, p. 54: *'Ich glaube, dass ihr alle junge Teufel seid'*.

67 Luther, *Tischreden*, vol. 6.6817.

I have argued above that the English translation heightens the comic potential of the devils and, thus, exposes them as figments of the imagination. In spite of his playful fooling around, the devil's games nevertheless revolve around sadistic torment. This scene next examines the reason for the existence of vermin. The German Faust Book accounts for the origin of vermin as a consequence of the fall from grace. Vermin had been created, the devils claim, 'in order to torment and harm the human beings. Thus we can transform ourselves into a large variety of vermin as much as into other animals. D. Faustus laughed and demanded to see this'. Of course he cannot complain about having his wish fulfilled.[68]

The English Faustus demands no demonstration of the transformational skills of the devils. Instead he asks, 'And how cometh it that all these filthy forms are in the world?' To which Lucifer replies: 'They are ordained of God as plagues unto men, and so shalt thou be plagued', his speech conjuring up 'scorpions, wasps, emmets, bees and gnats, which fell to stinging and biting him'. This is also the moment when the devil mocks him for his curiosity concerning the origin of the world: 'Ho ho ho Faustus, how likest thou the creation of the world?' (EFP 119). No attempt is made to explain the existence of these 'filthy forms' as the consequence of the fall from grace in the English Faust Book. In response to Faustus' wish to learn about the secret mysteries of creation, the devil marshals its most offensive creatures in an attempt to persuade him that its maker is less glorious than he had imagined.

This episode also explores the tensions between being and appearances. The devil confronts Faustus with his mocking reply to the origin of creation:

> 'Mephostophiles, my faithful servant, where art thou? Help, help I pray thee.' Hereat his spirit answered nothing, but Lucifer himself said: 'Ho ho ho Faustus, how likest thou the creation of the world?' and incontinent it was clear again, and the devils and all the filthy cattle were vanished. Only Faustus was left alone, seeing nothing, but hearing the sweetest music that ever he heard before, at which he was so ravished with delight that he forgot the fears he was in before and it repented him that he had seen no more of their pastime. (EFB 119)

Lucifer's creations may be illusory but they are able to inflict real pain and pleasure. At first Faustus suffers from the fact that the devil's cohorts are literally all over him, but then he suffers the even more acute pains of abandonment.

The devil of the English Faust Book is a master of appearances with an acute sense of what causes psychological pain. After mockingly reducing the creation to a host of 'filthy cattle' he plays musical notes that are reminiscent of the divine harmonies. We are led to conclude that Faustus suffers a pang of misery when he hears the 'sweetest music that ever he heard' because it reminds him of being

---

68 GFB, p. 54: *'Sie sagten, nach dem Fall des Menschen sei auch das Ungeziefer erwachsen, damit es den Menschen plagen und ihm Schaden tun sollte. So können wir uns in mancherlei Ungeziefer verwandeln, wie in andere Tiere. D. Faustus lachte und begehrte, solches zu sehen; und es geschah'.*

excluded from paradise. What must weigh even more heavily is that Faustus realizes that he does not possess the magic that can take him into a state of bliss. The reminder of his powerlessness is meant to register the fact that the devil is only capable of creating a chimerical resemblance of the true and divine version of bliss. But it also draws attention to the fact that there is no objective difference between the real divine harmonies and their semblance; their experience is equally a matter of perception.

Far from simply dismissing all immaterial phenomena, the text draws attention to the very similar sensory experience of two radically opposed ideas of the universe. Of course, we may read them as parallel instances of the devil's repertoire of tortures but we can also argue that the passage contrasts a painful with a delightful account of the essence of creation. That they are both imaginary and lack material substance simply draws attention to the non-material components of reality. The real suffering caused by the seeming reality of the 'filthy cattle', for instance, is a powerful reminder that reality consists of psychological factors; this is to say, is formed by the experience of things rather than by the material conditions themselves. That it is the consequence of imaginary forces does not mean that the nature of an experience is completely unpredictable. On the contrary, the competing traditions of the narrative portray conflicting views concerning the appropriate response to sensory stimuli.

The Protestant matrix of the story suggests that when Faustus hears the 'sweetest music that ever he heard before' he is forced to think of his damned condition and must experience this acoustic experience as a painful reminder that his yearning will never be gratified. However, the passage's observation that 'he was so ravished with delight that he forgot the fears he was in before' also describes him in an ecstatic state, freed from both physical pain and mental anguish. The concluding sentence of the chapter even comments that he was so ravished that he 'repented' (i.e. regretted not being able to extend his beautiful experience). A story that is so intimately preoccupied with the conditions of damnation, however, cannot lightly use the word 'repent'. The flippant comment that 'it repented him that he had seen no more of their [the devils'] pastimes' deliberately toys with its readers' expectations.

Both the painful and blissfully delightful experiences caused by the devil are shown to be mere figments of his imagination. These two parallel creations – or projections – of the devil's art have very different status in the text. The text shows the act of conjuring the vermin of this earth as a familiar trick of the devil but only indirectly alludes to the fact that he was the originator of the divine chords. Even though we are told that Faustus hears the sweetest music imaginable, its experience is shrouded in mystery. Importantly, however, the devil does not try to mock Faustus when he is ravished by heavenly chords. What better occasion for a scoffer and enemy of God to declare that all metaphysical phenomena are illusions to deceive the gullible? But the devil keeps a respectful distance and even allows Faustus a brief moment of bliss. The moment of enjoyment is brief but its presence hints at a deeply moving experience. The question concerning the origin of creation, therefore, leaves us with a foretaste of the miseries and delights that might be experienced during Faustus' journeys through hell, heaven and earth, described in the following chapters.

The Journey through Hell

The narrative element that turns a rogue's tale into a literary work, the description of Faustus' journey through heaven and hell, is steeped in a wealth of cultural traditions. The most important allusion must be to Christ's descent into hell, a seminal, if controversial element of the Apostle's Creed that defined the core beliefs of Christianity.[69] The ultimate point of reference of the Creed is the life of Christ, as described by the New Testament, but similarly important for the Faust Books were popular beliefs about Christ's capacity to perform miracles, ranging from the miracle at the wedding of Canaan, accepted as orthodoxy when the Council of Nicea (325) decided on the list of books that would be included in the Bible, to largely discredited, popular tales that projected Christ as a kind of arch-magus. The idea that the Christ figure was in possession of magical skills would also be asserted in Milton's *Paradise Regained*. Another remarkable parallel between Milton and the Faust Books concerns the link between the possession of magical skills and the experience of space. I will return to this later. At this point I simply want to mention that the knowledge of secret arts presupposes such a profound understanding of the mysteries of heaven and hell that a journey merely renders literal the metaphorical idea of being thoroughly familiar with the mysteries of these places.

Descriptions of journeys through heaven and hell were also important in apocalyptic literature, a genre that circulated widely during early modernity. Bernard McGinn explains that:

> One group of apocalypses concentrates on the revelation of secrets about the mysteries of the universe, especially of the heavenly realm. These apocalypses often involve an otherworldly journey in which the human recipient is taken on a tour of the heavenly realms (and later also of hell). ... The God of the apocalypses is paradoxically both farther away and yet nearer than the God of the prophets. He is more distant because he cannot be attained directly but only through intermediary spirits, his angelic messengers, and because divine control over the world is not evident in the midst of the confusions

---

69 Cf., for example, *Creeds of Christendom*, accessed 16 February 2006, http://www. creeds.net/ancient/apostles.htm. Note that the descent into hell remained an integral part of the life of the Son of God (Article III) in the *Augsburg Confession* (1530), the written documentation of Luther's articles of faith: 'He also descended into hell, and truly rose again the third day; afterward He ascended into heaven that He might sit on the right hand of the Father, and forever reign and have dominion over all creatures, and sanctify them that believe in Him, by sending the Holy Ghost into their hearts, to rule, comfort, and quicken them, and to defend them against the devil and the power of sin'.

and trials of the present time when the powers of evil seem triumphant. And yet he is nearer, at least to the seers, for they achieve what no previous Jewish religious leaders had accomplished – they ascend into heaven itself.[70]

Apocalyptic descriptions of the disintegration of the entire world – society, law and order – also offer a powerful foretaste of the two alternative realms believed to be the future locations of all departed souls. Going beyond an abstract reference to the landscape and furniture of these two precincts, apocalyptical works enter into a physical description of these spaces. Although they abound with accounts of the suffering of the sinners in hell, they also offer sensuous accounts of the ultimate moment of fulfilment: the blissful union between God and believer. The Faust Books are indebted to the apocalyptical tradition in so far as they similarly explore the state of mind of the person who experiences heaven and hell, and by doing so render these realms real in the moment of experience.

Another key influence on the anonymous writer(s) of the Faust Books was Dante's *The Divine Comedy*.[71] Written in exile (between 1307 and 1321) during a time of despotism and political intrigue, this work's visionary depiction of hell, purgatory and paradise offers a striking analysis of human aspirations. It is the achievement of an individual who embarked on a flight of the imagination in order to experience the richness of his inner resources and to reassure himself that he still belonged to his contemporary culture in spite of being banished by the despotic Florentine state. Jacob Burckhardt's attempt to account for the vibrancy of Dante's writing argues that banishment 'either wears the exile out or develops whatever is greatest in him'.[72] Dante's capacity to transcend exclusion from his Florentine home in the fiction of his otherworldly journeys may have suggested the idea to the writer(s) of the first literary Faust Book that nothing is impossible for the imagination of a truly free spirit. Not even the fulfilment of intellectual curiosity and spiritual enlightenment are ultimately inaccessible.

Dante's poem is materialistically involved with the events of his time but it also undergoes a process of spiritual purification. His spiritual world is that of medieval Catholicism, according to which moderate sinners had the opportunity of shedding the taints of their past trespasses by suffering a limited period of punishment in the preparatory demesne of purgatory.[73] Dante's purgatory provides an important link between the worst misery and the highest bliss. By immersing himself in the hopes and fears of the respective inhabitants of these three realms, the hero of the

70 McGinn, *Antichrist*, pp. 11–12.

71 Dante Alighieri, *The Divine Comedy*, ed. Edmund Gardner (London: Dent, 1955).

72 For a discussion of the relationship between despotic governments and the emergence of individuality, see Jacob Burckhardt, *The Civilization of the Renaissance in Italy* (London: Allen & Unwin, 1944), pp. 81–103, p. 83.

73 CF. F. Donald Logan, *A History of the Church in the Middle Ages* (London: Routledge, 2002), pp. 287–94.

visionary tale acquires the necessary emotional and moral qualities for grasping the nature of paradise.

The Divine Comedy facilitates spiritual insight through intensely physical experiences, a feature that is reflected by the Faust Books' portrayal of heaven and hell. Interestingly, though, Faustus is not able to set foot in either of these places. He in fact sets off on his first journey when 'he dreamt and was terrified of hell'. After summoning Beelzebub he asks him 'whether he might not be able to get a spirit to lead him into hell and out again, so that he might see and fathom the quality, fundament and characteristics, as well as substance of hell'. His wish is granted but instead of truly satisfying him, the devil simply plays tricks of deception: 'Now hear how the devil dazzled and aped him so that he seriously believed that he had been in hell' (GFB 55).[74]

The adventures of Faustus in hell are a blend between nightmare and farce. The Spies edition says that '[w]hen it was night and pitch-dark, Beelzebub appeared to him who carried a chair of bones on his back that was fully closed. Faustus sat on it and set off immediately'.[75] The idea that his conveyance is literally made of bones is a gruesome reminder of human mortality, heightened by the possibility that the chair mounted on the back of Beelzebub is not simply a chair made of bones but a human skeleton. There is even a certain sense that Faustus travels enclosed in a skeletal frame, much as the human soul was believed to perform its journey through life enclosed in the body. The English Faust Book, by contrast, embellishes the scene with a thunderclap announcing the appearance of the devil. It reframes the scene as follows: 'withal came a great rugged Bear, all curled, and upon his back a chair of beaten gold, and spake to Faustus, saying: "Sit up and away with me!"' (EFB 120). The precious quality of the golden chair suggests that Faustus is treated with the respect owing to a magician and not just tossed through the air like a rag doll.

While some of the contextual details may be less gruesomely comic, he is experiencing a similar nightmare. A confrontation with a flying bull, which can be interpreted as the emblem for the Evangelist Luke, overturns the vehicle. But Faustus is saved from falling to destruction by 'a monstrous ape' and there is no suggestion that the bull, or Evangelist, should have intervened. Horrifying figures come and go until Faustus believes himself to be deserted by his hellish guides:

---

74 The English translation embellishes the appearance of the devil in this scene with great clouds of smoke, suggesting that Faustus is almost smothered. By doing so, it renders visible an abstract idea: 'But mark how the devil blinded him and made him believe that he carried him into hell, for he carried him into the air, where Faustus fell into a sound sleep, as if he had sat in a warm water or bath.' (EFB, p. 120)

75 '*Als es nun Nacht und stockfinster war, erschien ihm Beelzebub, hatte auf seinem Rücken einen beinernen Sessel, ringsum ganz zugeschlossen; darauf sass D. Faustus und fuhr also davon*' (GFB, p. 56).

I am forsaken of the devils, and they that brought me hither; here must I either fall to the bottom or burn in the fire or sit still in despair. With that, in his madness he gave a leap into the fiery hole, saying: 'Hold, you infernal hags, take here this sacrifice as my last end, the which I justly have deserved.' Upon this he was entered, and finding himself as yet unburned or touched of the fire … (EFB 121)[76]

The most tantalizing element of this passage revolves around the idea that Faustus finds himself materially unhurt in spite of physically suffering the pains of hell, a reminder that in hell, death offers no escape from even the most excruciating pains. According to prevailing beliefs of the time it is logically impossible to annihilate oneself and thus remove oneself from the pangs of the after-world by suicide: the soul, the essence of a human being, is eternal and its never-ending existence has to be spent either in heaven or hell. A rather different explanation for Faustus' inability to escape from the pains of hell is that he is experiencing them only in his imagination. He cannot extricate himself from them by suicide but he can leave everything behind by waking up.

Although the text does not explicitly state that the entire journey through hell was a dream, the narrative blurs the boundaries between waking and sleeping. Faustus' departure from hell is dramatized as follows:

Then this devil that brought him in, came to him again in likeness of a bear, with the chair on his back, and bad him sit up, for it was time to depart: so Faustus got up and the devil carried him out into the air, where he had so sweet music that he fell asleep by the way. (EFB 122)[77]

The proverbially infernal confusion and noise experienced by Faustus while gazing at the sufferings of hell confirms popular ideas about this location, but although he is confronted by a whole array of chimeras he fails to obtain any reliable information about the true nature of hell. The journey through hell described in the German Faust Book similarly emphasizes the dreamlike nature of his experience. The final part of Spies' description of hell, for example, reiterates the idea that the devil cheated Faustus and merely sent him fantasies instead of reality. It describes his experience as mere *'Wahn', 'Verblendung', 'Gauckelwerk'*, delusion and make-believe (GFB 58). As an experienced scholar and alchemist, Faustus is not the kind of person who would refrain from harbouring doubts as to

---

76 The same idea is expressed in the Spies version: *'Nun was musst du tun, dieweil du von den höllischen Geistern verlassen bist; entweder musst du dich in die Kluft und in das Wasser stürzen oder hier oben verderben. In dem erzürnete er sich darob, und sprang also in einer rasenden, unsinnigen Furcht in das feurige Loch hinein …'* (GFB, p. 57).

77 The Spies version blurs imagination and reality even more decisively and merely mentions that Faustus arrived back asleep without specifying when and how he fell asleep: *'In solchem Wahn kommt D. Faustus in der Nacht wiederum nach Haus, und weil er seither auf dem Sessel geschlafen, wirft ihn der Geist also schlafend in sein Bett hinein'* (GFB, p. 58).

the reality of what he has just experienced. The English translation dramatizes this moment as follows:

> When he awaked he was amazed, like a man that had been in a dark dungeon, musing with himself if it were true or false that he had seen hell, or whether he was blinded or not: but he rather persuaded himself that he had been there than otherwise, because he had seen such wonderful things ... (EFB 122)

We are told that when Faustus wakes up in his own bed, he persuades himself of the reality of what he saw during the previous night. That he sat down and recorded them truthfully, though, and that his detailed notes were 'afterwards found by his body in his study' simply proves the material existence of his writing, but fails to persuade the reader that this description of hell is based on reliable foundations.

The Journey through the Heavens

Hell is dismissed as a burlesque fantasy by both Faust Books, but its traditional counterpart is accorded a far more serious treatment. Following on from a discussion about the reliability of astrological studies, the English version enters into a discussion of science's access to metaphysical truths. Mephostophiles explains that:

> the practitioners or speculators, or at least the first inventors of these arts, have done nothing of themselves certain whereupon thou mayst attain to the true prognosticating or presaging of things concerning the heavens or of the influence of the planets: for if by chance some one mathematician or astronomer hath left behind him any thing worthy of memory, they have so blinded it with enigmatical words, blind characters and such obscure figures that it is impossible for an earthly man to attain unto the knowledge thereof without the aid of some spirit or else the special gift of God, for such are the hidden works of God from men: yet do we spirits that fly and fleet in all elements, know such, and there is nothing to be done, or by the heavens pretended, but we know it, except the day of doom. (EFB 114)

The passage explains that the main obstacle to a proper understanding of the cosmic system depends on the fact that scholars of astronomy prefer meaningless verbiage to clearly stated descriptions of their observations. The main problem depends on lack of inspiration; or failure to communicate with superhuman agents or spirits. These beings illustrate what William Empson has described as 'middle spirits', powerful beings in spite of their inferiority to God, who stand between man and God on the great chain of being.[78] Although they know far more than even the

---

78 William Empson, *Faustus and the Censor: The English Faust-book and Marlowe's 'Doctor Faustus'*, ed. John Henry Jones (Oxford: Basil Blackwell, 1987), pp. 98–120.

most gifted astronomer, their knowledge is limited. They may know everything about the intricacies of astrological notation but they do not know the day of doom. They are, nevertheless, described as possessing a unique understanding of the characteristics and objectives of God's works.

This description invokes a Christian God who endows some of his creatures, especially 'middle spirits', with the gift of recognising his secrets. When Mephostophiles is consequently described as possessing the capacity to 'fly and fleet in all elements', he shows himself free from any sense of imprisonment in hell, which is why he confidently asserts that it is impossible to hide any secrets from beings like him. This passage argues that knowledge of the 'course and recourse' of the planets, 'the cause of winter and summer, the exaltation and declination of the sun, the eclipse of the moon' (EFB 114) are the prerogative of Yahweh and his initiated spirits. While the understanding of the principles of the natural world is unavailable for an uninformed layman, it does not follow that these principles have necessarily been concealed. It is simply extremely difficult to grasp them. Even though human minds may be almost incapable of comprehending the intricacies of the natural world, such knowledge is neither sinful nor strictly impossible. Mephostophiles continues to praise his special skills by elaborating on the further marvels of the cosmos:

> yea, herein there is nothing hidden from me but only the fifth essence, which once thou hadst Faustus, at liberty, but now Faustus, thou hast lost it past recovery: wherefore leaving that which will not be again had, learn now of me to make thunder, lightning, hail, snow and rain: the clouds to rent, the earth and craggy rocks to shake and split in sunder, the seas to swell and roar and overrun their marks. (EFB 114)

An important dimension of this passage relates to the fact that Mephostophiles' description of his skills portrays him as a godlike figure in his own right. The text suggests that the ability to access the fifth essence requires a translation into a godlike state. If Faustus should be able to access the fifth essence, we could interpret this as a fulfilment of the first condition of the pact, when Faustus stipulated '[t]hat he might be a spirit in shape and quality' (EFB 96). If this should be so, Faustus can be seen as having acquired godlike qualities.

The wish to experience this fifth essence is the primary objective of Faustus' speculations. But what is the fifth essence? Although an answer is hinted in the Faust Books, it is only sketched implicitly. *The Oxford Dictionary of Philosophy* defines 'quintessence' as 'the fifth element, distinct from earth, fire, air and water, exempt from change and decay, and found only in celestial bodies'.[79] Since the fifth essence, or quintessence, was free from mundane contaminations, it was believed to be the element from which the superlunary regions and the empyreal heavens were composed.

---

79 *The Oxford Dictionary of Philosophy*, ed. Simon Blackburn (Oxford: Oxford University Press, 2003).

So as to understand the symbolic significance of the term, let us turn to the most striking description of the fifth essence in Dante's *Paradise*. It was readily available at the time, and must have been well known by the author(s) of the Faust Books. The narrator opens the passage by drawing a connection between Beatrice, his heavenly guide, and his own soul:

So she, who doth imparadise my soul,
Had drawn the veil from off our present life,
And bared the truth of poor mortality:
When lo! as one who, in a mirror spies
The shining of a flambeau at his back,
Lit sudden ere he deem of its approach,
And turneth to resolve him, if the glass
Have told him true, and sees the record faithful
As note is to its metre; even thus,
I well remember, did befall to me,
Looking upon the beauteous eyes, whence love
Had made the leash to take me.
… a point I saw, that darted light
So sharp, no lid, unclosing, may bear up
Against its keenness. The least star we ken
From hence, had seem'd a moon …[80]

The abstract idea of light and its physical manifestation converge here; subject and object become one at the moment of revelation, a mystery made possible by the spiritual love between Dante and Beatrice. The power of love also transforms visual experience into insight which, in turn, merges with self-recognition. Seeing the 'bared truth of poor mortality' is compared to observing the world in the mirror. So the experience of self, compared to the brilliance of the 'flambeau' in the mirror, turns into joyful awareness as the reflection of its radiance, along with the radiance of its reflection, mingles with the image of the self. And so a sober intellectual experience is turned into an emotional reality. The simile of the mirror also suggests that 'the beauteous eyes' are both his own and those of his divine guide Beatrice. Their mystical union is the precondition for seeing the originary point, or essence, of the universe. The radiance of this sharp point establishes a connection between the mystical lovers' 'beauteous eyes' and the moons and stars. The quintessence, 'the sparkle of truth' (l. 34), consists of the recognition that there is a subliminal connection between each and everything, or as Beatrice explains, 'Heaven, and all nature, hangs upon that point' (l. 38). The Divine Essence, therefore, also embraces the nature of belief, described in a previous canto: 'I in one God believe; / One sole eternal Godhead, of whose love / All Heaven is moved, Himself unmoved the while' (24, ll. 127–9). When he

---

80 Dante's *Paradise*, canto 28, ll. 1–18.

encounters the Divine Essence, the Aristotelean foundation of his belief turns into an emotionally intense experience so that his belief becomes truly real for him.[81]

The German and English Faust Books adopt different solutions to convey a comparable experience of spiritual insight. But while neither of them is unambiguous about the seeker's possibility of accessing spiritual enlightenment both versions highlight different aspects of the entanglements between the experience of metaphysical truths (heaven), and the perception of the celestial bodies (the heavens).

The Faust Books' approach to the fifth essence is a logical consequence of Faustus' imaginary journey through the material heavens. Compared to the hazy account of the journey to hell, the narrative that introduces the exploration of the heavens goes to great lengths to insist on its authenticity. It also assures us that Faustus set out on this trip in a state of wakefulness; and is therefore fully conscious throughout this journey. Addressing an old friend, he says:

> And now will I tell thee, good friend and schoolfellow, what things I have seen and proved; for on the Tuesday went I out and on Tuesday seven nights following I came home again, that is, eight days, in which I slept not, no not one wink came in mine eyes, and we went invisible of any man ... (EFB 124).

The idea that he is wide awake is emphasized so strongly that the previous paragraph prefixes the journey with the explanation that Faustus had a phase of insomnia as a result of being too preoccupied with calendar making. Within the fiction of the narrative, his experience of being 'carried through the air up to the heavens to see the world, and how the sky and planets ruled' is therefore stated as an empirical fact:

> I being once laid on my bed, and could not sleep for thinking on my calender and practice, I marvelled with myself how it were possible that the firmament should be known and so largely written of men, or whether they write true or false, by their own opinions, or supposition, or by due observations and true course of the heavens. Behold, being in these my muses, suddenly I heard a great noise, insomuch that I thought my house would have been blown down, so that all my doors and chests flew open, whereat I was not a little astonished, for withal I heard a groaning voice which said: 'Get up! The desire of thy heart, mind and thought shalt thou see.' (EFB 123)

Faustus' first-hand experience begins with the comment: '[t]hen looked I up to the heavens'. The passage is replete with verbs of vision: 'behold', 'gaze', 'look up', 'see'. The heavens are described as 'clear and shining bright as a crystal', and the sun 'shows himself over the whole world'. Clarity and the possibility for insight are emphasized. At the same time, the quintessence of the creation is also

---

81 Cf. Aristotle, *Metaphysics*, book 5.

described as a creative force that gives form to chaos and sublimates it into the beautiful harmonies of the heavens:

> It is the axle of the heavens that moveth the whole firmament, being a chaos or confused thing ... even so is the whole firmament of chaos, wherein are placed the sun and the rest of the planets, turned and carried at the pleasure of God, which is wind. (EFB 125)

The scientific foundations for the claims contained in this passage have long been disproved. But the scientific facts are less important here than the prevailing philosophies of its time, particularly the philosophical idea that the universe revolves around a continuous formation of order born out of chaos. The consequence of this interpretation of creation is that God is no longer viewed as an anthropomorphized creator, but as a creative principle that continues to keep the carefully designed rationale of the cosmos in place for all eternity.

This chapter of the Faust Book sets first-hand experience of the sensory qualities of the creation against dry, scholastic notions about its origin. It also contrasts a dynamic conception of boundless energies with a static explanation of the world as being formed during one long past creative moment. The authenticity of a genuine experience of the divine is underlined with reference to *Genesis*:

> and to prove some of my sentence before to be true, look into Genesis unto the works of God, at the creation of the world, there shalt thou find, that the Spirit of God moved upon the waters before heaven and earth were made. (EFB 126)

The reference to *Genesis* reminds us that the Faustus of the English chapbook is preoccupied less with sacrilegious transgressions than with an attempt to integrate the mysteries of the biblical sublime into his scientific understanding of the world. He approaches the divine essence in the course of studying the cosmic secrets required for calendar making, and his objective is to obtain mystical acquaintance with the secret of God's works, inspired by the biblical verse that he who studies the Heavens rightly will perceive that the 'heavens declare the glory of God' (*Psalm* 19:1).

The German Faust Book sketches a quite different moment of revelation. In the context of describing Faustus' earthly journeys, it says:

> And now let me come to the point: the reason why Doctor Faustus ascended such heights was not merely to view from there certain parts of the sea and the kingdoms and landscapes in the vicinity but he also thought that some islands had mountains as high that he should finally see paradise; but he did not and did not dare to approach his spirit because of this. And especially on the Isle of Caucasus, whose peaks and summits exceed all others in height, he thought that he could not fail but to see paradise. (GFB 76)[82]

---

82 '*Und damit ich ad propositum komme: die Ursache, dass D. Faustus sich auf solche Höhen getan, ist nit allein gewesen, dass er von dannen etliche Teile des Meers*

Interestingly enough, the English version edits out the spiritual motive for his journey through the world and simply describes him as an early explorer who travels for the sake of accumulating knowledge.

Other telling elisions of the translation turn the fact that during his visit to Britain he saw 'warm springs and a large amount of metals, also the stone of God and many others which Doctor Faustus brought back with him' (GFB 75) into the simple comment that 'he went into the isle of Britain, wherein he was greatly delighted to see the fair water and warm baths, the divers sorts of metal, with many precious stones and divers other commodities the which Faustus brought thence with him' (EFB 142). Unlike the *'formae coniurationum'*, which were claimed to have been excized from the story in order to prevent foolhardy youths from imitating them (GFB 12), the reference to the 'stone of God', or the philosopher's stone, cannot have been suppressed for reasons of censorship. What has been removed from the English translation are passages that view magic in a naively religious light.

At the end of the chapter about paradise, the German version agrees with the English translation about the inaccessibility of paradise: 'the spirit said unto Faustus, "neither thou, nor I, nor any after us, yea all men whosoever are denied to visit it, or to come any nearer than we be"' (EFB 143). Even though Faustus is forbidden to set foot in paradise, the text confirms that he is convinced of its literal existence. But both heaven and hell are nevertheless equally abstract, or symbolical, spaces whose existence and qualities are beyond human knowledge. Both versions of the Faust Book, however, posit the possibility of an experience of paradise. Although paradise is not described as a concrete space in either of them, it acquires a state of emotional reality that is neither challenged nor ridiculed. If the Faust Books wanted to describe a cosmos in which both heaven and hell are mere fantasies, they would dramatize a similarly fantastic experience of 'heaven' as that which characterizes 'hell'. Even if the experience of spiritual insight is only indirectly suggested, the Faust Books nevertheless gesture towards a spiritual interpretation of the creation that harbours a certain promise of escaping from the damning clutches of mainstream theology. While the German version proposes the existence of paradise as a literal space, the English translation advocates a much more rational experience of the creative principle of the universe. Both versions ridicule the idea of hell as a physical location, treating it as an apish invention to delude the gullible, while both allow for the possibility of metaphysical enlightenment.

There are, of course, a lot of important differences between the German Faust Book and its English translation. It has generally been recognized that the translation is a more highly developed text: it contains a lot more detail and renders the story

---

und die umliegenden Königreiche und Landschafften etc. übersehen konnte, sondern er vermeinet, dieweil etliche hohe Inseln mit ihren Gipfeln so hoch seien, wolle er auch endlich das Paradeis sehen können; denn er hat seinen Geist nicht darum angesprochen, noch ansprechen dürfen.'

more immediate by the use of direct speech. The most important differences in their respective renditions of the Faustian quest for metaphysical truth is that the German Faust Book gives a literal account of spiritual revelation while the English Faust Book offers a more abstract description; or simply gestures towards the possibility of revelation. It might be claimed that the English Faust Book is more secular, but such an interpretation fails to acknowledge that, for example, its poetic rendition of the biblical creation story makes every effort to capture its spiritual significance. Rather than erasing the idea that the spiritual quest might have a successful outcome, it redefines the literal journey through geographic space as a symbolic enterprise. It reinterprets the German Faustus' ascension of the Caucasus as a deeply human quest for meaning. As a result, it arrives at a conclusion which Sergius Golowin has observed in all cultures and all ages: that paradise does not have to be accessed from a particular location anywhere on earth; on the contrary, its porches can be found anywhere, provided that the inner capacities for its perception have suitably been developed.[83] Equipped with psychological acuity and a solid grasp of emotional subtleties, the English Faust Book takes its readers on a journey inside, encouraging them to follow the example of Faustus and to explore this realm for themselves.

The Death of Faustus

The gruesome circumstances of Faustus' death have provided the matrix for two diametrically opposed interpretations. The text's failure to mention any possibility of escaping damnation has been taken to prove the argument of the cautionary tale. Alternatively, twentieth-century deconstructive readings have interpreted the final focus on the dismembered body as, in effect, proposing an atheistic denial of any form of afterlife.[84] However, neither of these interpretations can be maintained unequivocally. The story confronts us with a bewildering multitude of meanings resulting from a heady concoction of de-contextualized quotations, subtle irony, overt mockery and heretical claims about the sanctity of human existence, sketched as it really is, rather than as it should be: passionate and endowed with an insatiable thirst for the mysteries of existence.

---

83 Sergius Golowin, Mircea Eliade and Joseph Campbell, *Die grossen Mythen der Menschheit*, Verlag Hohe, Erststadt, 2007, p. 288.

84 It is also worth remembering that according to sixteenth-century beliefs, a violent death was a very unfortunate omen. For instance, Heiko Oberman comments about the death of Luther: 'While simple believers imagined the devil literally seizing his prey, the enlightened academic world was convinced that a descent into Hell could be diagnosed medically – as apoplexy and sudden cardiac arrest. ... Thus, in their first reports, Luther's friends, especially Melanchthon, stressed that the cause of death had not been sudden, surprising apoplexy but a gradual flagging of strength: Luther had taken leave of the world and commended his spirit into God's hands.' See Oberman, *Luther*, pp. 3–4.

However, the death of Faustus puts an insurmountable barrier to subversive attempts at configuring the narrative chaos into one single coherent interpretation. Death is the ultimate aporia that cannot be overcome. The lamentations of Faustus before his death are also eloquent reminders of the crucifixion, invoking the moment when Christ gives voice to his final agony: 'My God, my God, why hast thou forsaken me?' (*St. Matthew* 26:46). The sufferings of the Faustian hero's abandonment, alienation and failure to be understood will be masterfully rendered in the last chapter of Thomas Mann's *Doctor Faustus: the Life of the German Composer Adrian Leverkühn* (1948). Mann goes to great effort in foregrounding the parallels between the final collapse of the misunderstood and alienated composer Leverkühn and the crucifixion of Christ. Fear of the Censor made it impossible for the Faust Books to draw explicit parallels between the arch-sinner and the saviour. However, Faustus' archetypically human suffering at the moment of crossing the final threshold, nevertheless, invokes the deeply human experience of the dying Christ. Faustus laments:

> have I been formed a human being in order to suffer the punishment I see waiting to suffer myself? Ah, miserable wretch, is there anything on this earth that is not opposed to me? Ah, does my wailing help me? (GFB 119)

The lamentations of Faustus dramatize the painful failure to imagine an unknowable afterworld. His sufferings are heightened by his complete inability to comprehend the contradictions of his existence. He suffers the agony of uncertainty but there is nothing to resolve him – and his readers – of his ambiguous experiences.

The Faust Books are of course unable to make any conclusive statements about life after death. However, by calling into question both the cautionary tale and the nihilistic interpretation of these fascinating works, my interpretation has explored the emotional landscape of the intellectual hero of early modernity, whose boundless curiosity and metaphysical yearning lead him to step beyond all established rules and guidelines. While my argument confirms that the portrayal of the Faustian struggle for glimpses of fulfilment leaves us with a baffling impossibility of knowing, it argues that the Faust Books reached a remarkable literary standard in their representation of the figure of the insatiable speculator.

To return to the name Faustus: regardless of the true characteristics of the person who assumed the name Doctor Faustus, this early novelistic account of his extraordinary life dramatizes his quest for the meaning and essence of the created world. Faustus searches for happiness; he wants to see and experience, with his own senses, whatever his period's world has to offer. The emphasis of all versions of the Faust Book is on first-hand experience and, as I will argue later, it is possible to conclude that Faustus practices magic mainly in order to be able to see and experience the mysteries of self and universe. In short, he not only wants to know but also to grasp with his own senses the fundamental aspects of existence. The early modern Faustus sets out to imagine and experience an alternative to the traditional metaphysics founded on the idea of the intrinsic sinfulness of human nature. If his rational capacities allow him to overcome the obstacles to a positive and pleasurable experience of self and world, he can achieve happiness indeed. But, of course, it is not possible to distil a simple happy ending from the narrative. Quite apart from pacifying the Censor, the harrowing drama of the story is more than a simple façade disguising a subversive interpretation.

Chapter 3

The Devil of Empiricism:
Marlowe's *Doctor Faustus*

During his student years, Christopher Marlowe moved in a circle of smart young men who challenged the foundational beliefs of his period. William Empson uses the evocative term 'undergraduate atheism' to characterize the intellectual climate of Marlowe's Cambridge.[1] Whilst charges of atheism were frequently laid at Marlowe's door, Nicholas Davidson reminds us that it makes more sense to describe his uninhibited investigation of the mysteries and administrative structure of Christianity as 'religious dissent'.[2] But Marlowe undoubtedly struck the majority of his contemporaries as anti-Christian in so far as most of his literary works indict Christianity for its crippling restraints on human growth and development.

Doctor Faustus, Marlowe's most frequently anthologized play, portrays its hero as a quick-witted but immature character. His intellectual brilliance is coupled with an unyielding will, but is tempered neither by wisdom nor circumspection. According to contemporary belief there were legitimate and forbidden areas of knowledge, which meant that unbridled curiosity inevitably led to disastrous consequences. Marlowe's youthful boisterousness is one thing, but the play also shows a Faustus who is indicted for the simple possession of intellectual brilliance. Owing to the constrictive morality of the vast majority of his contemporaries, his desire to discover what it means to be different was already treated with suspicion. The play therefore records a conflict-ridden quest that confronts us with the question of whether the energies of the strong-minded character can be tamed without breaking his or her spirit. It asks whether an extraordinarily gifted character can realize his or her potentials and whether he or she can achieve his or her desires without doing harm to self and environment.

---

1   William Empson, *Essays on Renaissance Literature*, vol. 1: *Donne and the New Philosophy*, ed. John Haffenden (Cambridge: Cambridge University Press, 1993–94), p. 92.

2   Nicholas Davidson, 'Marlowe and Atheism', *Christophere Marlowe and English Renaissance Culture*, eds Daryll Grantley and Peter Roberts (Aldershot: Scolar Press, 1996), pp. 131 and 142.

Spectacles of Good and Evil

Like the heroes of the chapbooks, Marlowe's Faustus is headstrong and uncompromising. Few things frighten him and he hesitates only briefly to enter into a contract with the devil. So as to discuss the issue of self-determination, he transforms a rhetorical into a real question. According to the religious dogma of the period, the proper answer to the question 'Is not thy soul thine own?' (A and B: 2.1.68) would have been a resounding 'no'. That Faustus dares to challenge this point has persuaded many critics that the play is presenting us with the self-willed damnation of a sinful character. Sara Munson Deats, for example, structures her interpretation around the question of '[w]hat drive impels the eminent Doctor Faustus to devise his own destruction?', explaining that 'within the Christian framework of the play Faustus' transgression is unequivocally condemned'.[3] But does it make sense to assume that Marlowe sought to reinstate Christian dogma? It makes much more sense to conclude that he catered to different tastes and expectations: such an outlook is reminiscent of his role as double agent, which led him to take on the guise of both the loyal servant and the subversive other.[4] As a playwright, it seems likely that he structured his dramatic version of the Faustus tale so that it would reflect back the beliefs with which a spectator would approach the play: a stolid Christian would hence see the psychological pains and ultimate damnation of the unregenerate sinner, while an atheist would see a great deal of sound and fury signifying nothing. That the latter conclusion was close to Marlowe's heart is suggested by historical descriptions of 'the playhouse as a site of anti-Christian rites and performances'.[5] However, it is important not to take for granted a too simplistic division of sixteenth-century society into mainstream Christians and their nihilistic enemies. A truly complex interpretation of the play needs to resist easy differentiations and instead explore the wider implications of Marlowe's dramatic analysis of religious belief.

Marlowe's most striking artistic feat is that he portrayed and analysed belief by means of dramatising it in the form of a spectacle, which means that he rendered illusions accessible to sensory perception. What is more, many dramatic spectacles seem to support the Christian conclusion about Faustus' steady progress towards damnation. For example, his blood is shown to congeal at the moment when he is on the point of signing his pact with the devil, which tends to be taken as an unshakeable sign that even the body of Faustus is appalled by his godless intention. His refusal to listen to even the most frightful omen is then read as evidence that he is a hardened sinner by the majority of spectators. For those who interpret the episode with the congealing blood simply as a theatrical spectacle, this scene can

---

3   Sara Munson Deats, *Doctor Faustus*: From Chapbook to Tragedy', in: *Christopher Marlowe: Doctor Faustus*, ed. David Scott Kastan (New York: W.W. Norton, 2005), p. 211.

4   Cf. David Riggs, 'Marlowe's Quarrel with God', p. 133.

5   *Ibid.*, p. 134.

examine the illusory dimensions of superstition and as such challenges established ideas about the nature of self and soul.

It is true that the introductory chorus asks us to read the play as a cautionary tale, so that Faustus is described as 'swoll'n with cunning of a self-deceit / His waxen wings did mount above his reach' (A: 20–21, B: 19–20) and the brief concluding Chorus of both A- and B-texts begins by saying that 'Cut is the branch that might have grown full straight'. The explicit indictment of his fascination for 'unlawful things' undoubtedly dominates all statements of the Chorus. While this can be interpreted as evidence that the play advocates the condemnation of Faustus, as was traditionally expressed by the cautionary tale, the Chorus is just one of many voices competing within the play.

The play itself is permeated by a multitude of voices lacking in persuasive power. For example, the Good and Bad Angels engage in a childish wrangling in which both sides are expressing trite arguments. The emphasis on the spectacle of their dispute, rather than any deeper meanings implied by it, is warranted when we keep in mind Douglas Cole's comment that '[n]owhere in the extant morality plays dated after 1500 do good and evil angels contend for the soul of man'.[6] This is to say that Marlowe revived or re-invented older traditions in order to render abstract forces visible. When Francis Quarles wished to illustrate the diverging aspects of patience and impatience in his book of Emblems, he used two winged characters who strongly resemble Marlowe's Good and Bad Angel (Figure 2). The parallels to the emblematic tradition underline the idea that both the Bad and the Good Angel are simply projections of abstract ideas. However, they are not simply abstract ideas but also embody narrow-minded attitudes about the nature of good and evil. As such they do not have any notion about the grey zones between good and evil; and furthermore, they have preconceived opinions about magic and other alternative forms of knowledge. Although Faustus seems to listen to the arguments of the Bad Angel, the burlesque quarrel between these two characters shows them to be simple stock characters – remnants of the medieval mystery play – who have nothing to offer to the hero who is caught in the complex questions of early modernity. John Cox explains that although it is not possible to tell 'whether or not Marlowe saw any of the mystery plays, they were still being staged in some places when he entered Cambridge in 1580, so his earliest audiences might well have imagined easily what Mephistopheles describes, because they had literally seen Lucifer's fall in a pageant performed within ten years of the time *Dr. Faustus* first alluded to it on the public stage'.[7] But of course Marlowe did not simply aim to immortalize these traditions in popular drama, but he utilized them as a means of rendering visible contemporary beliefs and assumptions.

---

6   Douglas Cole, *Suffering and Evil in the Plays of Christopher Marlowe* (New Jersey: Princeton University Press, 1962), p. 234.
7   John D. Cox, *The Devil and the Sacred in English Drama, 1350–1642* (Cambridge: Cambridge University Press, 2000), p. 112.

III.

Ut potiar, patior. Patieris, non potieris.

Fig. 2   Francis Quarles, *Emblemes*, London: sold at J. Marriott's shop, 1634(?), Book I, III, p. 12.

As an extension of Faustus' limited command of his period's dominant fields of knowledge, William Blackburn argues that he is incompetent also in the field of magic. Before he, for example, conjures a familiar spirit, he tried his hand at natural magic, but 'has, in short, utterly and abysmally confused the two traditions of [white and black] magic which Pico so carefully distinguishes in his *Oratio*'.[8] However, there is a marked contrast between his seeming ineptitude, which Blackburn deduces from jumbled signs and symbols that are marshalled in Act 1.3, and the Prologue's description of Faustus as 'glutted more with learning's golden gifts, / He surfeits upon cursèd necromancy' (A 1.1.24–25; B 1.1.23–24 with minute variations). The incongruity between the diabolic sinner and the inept dabbler must be a consequence of the fragmentary nature of the play. While such inconsistencies make us bemoan the absence of an authorized text, they also warn us against the dangers of closure in a field where objective knowledge is of course unavailable. Returning to Faustus' dubious practice of magic, in any case, I want to suggest that Marlowe treats arcane knowledge rather similarly as mainstream forms of learning. He leads us to conclude that magic is comparable to logic, medicine and theology, in so far as its recorded tomes only inadequately grasp the nature of language, life and God. As Blackburn points out, Marlowe puts the magician on trial.[9] He does so in an attempt to gauge why people turn to magic and what the practice of magic does to their self-perception and consciousness. But his dramatic treatment of the topic is elusive precisely because he embeds it in a general study of the nature of illusion.

What Does it Mean to Have a Soul?

If confronted with the question 'Is not thy soul thine own?', the vast majority of Marlowe's Christian contemporaries would have been horrified to hear his provocative attitude to the topics of free will and self-determination. Christian thinkers would already have been scandalized by the idea of treating the soul as a commodified property, rather than defining it as a kind of non-material substance which inhabits a human body and, through its presence, renders this body truly human. Definitions of the soul have been crucial for understanding the purpose and potentialities of human existence in all Christian traditions. More precisely, the idea that the soul constitutes the essence of human existence has given rise to a plethora of theories and social conventions while the definition of the properties and attributes of this most volatile entity came to be contested in the age of Marlowe.

---

8   William Blackburn, '"Heavenly Words": Marlowe's Faustus as a Renaissance Magician', *English Studies in Canada* 4.1 (1978), p. 5.

9   Blackburn, 'Heavenly Words', p. 12.

The Calvinist definition of the soul, which Marlowe absorbed through his early study of Nowell and Norton's *Catechism*,[10] provides the backdrop to his literary explorations of the soul. In Calvin's seminal treatise we find the following definition:

> there can be no question that man consists of a body and a soul; meaning by soul, an immortal though created essence, which is his nobler part. ... when the soul is freed from the prison-house of the body, God becomes its perpetual keeper.[11]

The human being, accordingly, is merely the temporary keeper of the soul, taking on a kind of stewardship without owning the entity that demonstrates the resemblance between man and God.

Calvin goes on to refute too optimistic interpretations that might be inferred from this resemblance. In a section that is an explicit refutation of the Manichaean error, he says:

> Because it is said that God breathed into man's nostrils the breath of life, (*Gen.* 2:7) they [the Manichaeans] thought that the soul was a transmission of the substance of God; as if some portion of the boundless divinity had passed into man. It cannot take long time to show how many gross and foul absurdities this devilish error carries in its train.[12]

For the vast majority of theologians and believers, it did not follow that a human being should gain ownership of everything that belonged to embodied existence. According to mainstream as well as oppositional Christian beliefs, the soul was the most precious, indeed the only truly valuable, element of human existence. It was understood as the divine spark or gift that resided in the human body and distinguished mankind from animals. Many strands of belief came to describe the soul as immortal and by doing so provided substance for imagining the most gruesome tortures of flawed souls. The vision of interminable suffering made it all the more urgent to preserve the soul in a condition that enabled its divine essence to remain in the fold of the saved. But this, of course, demanded painstaking and constant attention to the commandments of its maker. The task of following these instructions called into existence extraordinary vigilance and self-examination,

---

10 A. Nowell and T. Norton, *A Catechism, or First Instruction and Learning of Christian Religion* (London: printed by Iohn Daye, 1570). See David Riggs, *The World of Christopher Marlowe* (London: Faber and Faber, 2004), pp. 41–2.

11 Jean Calvin, *Institutes of the Christian Religion*, trans. Henry Beveridge (London for Bonham Norton, 1599), book I.15.2; accessed 15 August 2006: http://www.reformed. org/master/index.html?mainframe=/books/institutes/. Also compare Michael Maher and Joseph Boland, 'Soul', *The Catholic Encyclopedia* (2003 [1912]), accessed 20 August 2006: www.newadvent.org/cathen/14153a.htm.

12 Calvin, *Institutes*, I.15.5.

which gained such prominence that Michel Foucault described it as an all-important feature of post-Reformation Europe.[13]

As the Calvinist argument has shown, the soul did not belong to the person in whose body it lodged but was believed to remain the property of God.[14] So, for a conventional Christian there would have been no doubt that the soul belongs to God and that it is merely given in trust during its embodied state. Humankind gains stewardship but not ownership of its spiritual nature. The argument that Daniel Defoe adduces about the validity of pacts with the devil over the disposal of a human soul renders the conventional attitude of his as well as Marlowe's age:

... for as in our Law we punish a self-murtherer, because, *as the Law suggests*, he had no Right to dismiss his own Life; that he being a Subject of the Commonwealth, the Government claims the *Ward* or Custody of him, and so 'twas not Murther only, but Robbery, and is a Felony against the State, robbing the King of his Liege-Man, *as 'tis justly call'd*; so neither has any Man a Right to dispose of his Soul, which belongs to his Maker in Property and in Right of Creation: the Man then having no Right to Buy, or at best he has made a Purchase without a Title, and consequently has no just Claim to the Possession.[15]

The idea that we must not dispose of ourselves as we wish – body and soul – permeates western culture. Among other things, it explains why suicide was only decriminalized in the United Kingdom as late as 1961, and lingers in debates over euthanasia. Even though the overt arguments in support of euthanasia circle around the unconditional value of life, there lurks a prohibition of self-determination somewhere in the background in spite of our society's deeply rooted conviction that individualism and the rights of the individual are the most cherished values of society.

But let me return to the dramatic context of the question: 'Is not thy soul thine own?' complies with the need to write a 'deed of gift'. Faustus hence agrees to 'cut mine arm and with my proper blood / Assure my soul to be great Lucifer's' (A and B: 2.1.54–5). As he is about to write 'Faustus gives to thee his soul', he looks at his arm and exclaims 'But Mephistopheles, / My blood congeals and I can write no more' (A and B: 2.1.61–2). That his blood ceases to flow of its own volition is offered as evidence that the physical body recoils even though the

13 Michel Foucault, *The History of Sexuality*, vol. 1 (New York: Random House, 1978).

14 This feudal relationship believed to exist between God and mankind is, for instance, illustrated by the following biblical passage: 'And I will say to my soul, Soul, thou hast much goods laid up for many years; take thine ease, eat drink, and be merry. But God said unto him, Thou fool, this night thy soul shall be required of thee: then whose shall those things be, which thou hast provided?' *St. Luke* 12:19–20. The parable of the talents (*St. Matthew* 25:14–30) likewise implies a feudal relationship between God and mankind.

15 Daniel Defoe, *The History of the Devil* (London: printed for T. Warner, 1727).

intellect of Faustus has decided to proceed. The congealed blood comes across as factual evidence that points to the sinful proceedings of Faustus. But it can only be a reliable icon of sinfulness according to a Christianity which has its roots in an almost animistic understanding of the harmonious cooperation between body and soul. It gains significance simply because it panders to deeply rooted superstitions lurking beneath formal Christianity.

The religious symbolism is expanded with another stage metaphor: a chafer of coals with which Mephistopheles makes the blood flow once again. The edition of the A-text by Ormerod and Wortham glosses line 504 as follows: 'The chafer (portable grate) of coals with which Mephistopheles returns is an iconic stage representation of the Hell-fire of Faustus' new habitation'. There is little doubt that contemporary spectators would have interpreted the chafer as a reference to hell.[16] But what practical purpose does it serve? As Faustus comments, the chafer has the desired effect and 'the blood begins to clear again' (A and B: 2.1.71). Does this suggest that the prospect of hell can prevent the body from recoiling? Or does it suggest that the animal vitality of the body is simply made to yield to brute force?

There may, however, be a wider reference that develops other associations with the chafer. In its literal sense, it is a container for transporting fire, but of course there is a powerful metaphorical scope of the elementary force of fire. According to the theory of the four elements developed by the pre-Socratic philosopher Empedocles of Acragas, fire is a cardinal ingredient of all matter. The symbolic fire applied to Faustus' arm can accordingly be interpreted as saying no more than that it is in the nature of congealed blood to be liquefied by the force of fire. Of course, the fact that Mephistopheles fetches the fire would have convinced the vast majority of contemporary spectators that it possessed an association with evil. However, it might also be interpreted as a spiritual fire, an idea that resonates in the background. When Faustus exclaims '*Consummatum est!*' (A and B: 2.1.73), he quotes the last words of the dying Christ according to the text of the Vulgate (*St. John* 19.30), which came to be interpreted as 'the great formula of redemption'.[17] Although this is generally interpreted as further evidence of Faustus' sinful mind, it can also be taken to indicate that he is experiencing a spiritual ecstasy which cannot be grasped by the judgemental outlook of Marlowe's narrow-minded contemporaries.

The importance of Faustus' quotation of Christ's last words is self-evident. But what is it supposed to mean? While it seems to be an overt instance of his blasphemous perversion of the crucifixion, it also asks us to think seriously about

---

16 John D. Cox even goes so far as to argue that 'the stage miracle of blood pouring from the side of the ascended Christ in the Chester play of the Ascension has a close parallel in *Dr. Faustus* when Faustus' blood ceases to flow during the signing of the bargain'; see *The Devil and the Sacred in English Drama, 1350–1642* (Cambridge: Cambridge University Press, 2004), p. 125.

17 Cf. Blackburn, 'Heavenly Words', p. 8.

the parallels between Faustus and Christ.[18] The suggestion that Faustus should be understood as an Anti-Christ is undoubtedly in the foreground. As I have argued in the previous chapter, however, the Faustus story displays a number of telling similarities with the passion of Christ. Like Christ, Faustus ventures beyond the boundaries of common humanity. He shares his deep commitment to that which makes us human and he has the courage to die for his conviction.

If we compare the play with the Faust Books' description of the moment of signing the pact, we note that Marlowe dramatized a brief comment contained in a chapter heading: 'How Doctor Faustus set his blood in a saucer on warm ashes and writ as follows' (EFB 98: Ch.6). In the Faust Books no attempt is made to moralize about the behaviour of the blood. In their narrative context, it comes across as perfectly natural that blood congeals after it has left the body. Basic medical knowledge and simple commonsense confirm this as a law of nature. Marlowe's play, by contrast, makes much of the resistance by the substance that was believed to be the seat of life. Of course, the superficial meaning of Faustus' exclamation 'But Mephistopheles, / My blood congeals and I can write no more' is that he registers the blood's refusal to flow for an unhallowed purpose. However, sceptics amongst his audience would easily have ascribed a purely scientific reason and in keeping with this, have viewed Faustus' comment as a purely emotive response.

The Speculations of Marlowe's Faustus

Analysis of the type of sin committed when Faustus sells his soul to the devil has received a great deal of critical attention. But the question of what he aims to achieve as a result of these dealings has not been adequately answered. The first encounter between Faustus and Mephistopheles follows on from a self-congratulatory soliloquy that states the conjuror's grand goals:

> Had I as many souls as there be stars,
> I'd give them all for Mephistopheles.
> By him I'll be great emperor of the world
> And make a bridge through the moving air
> To pass the ocean with a band of men;
> I'll join the hills that bind the Afric shore
> And make that country continent to Spain,
> And both contributory to my crown.

---

18 Susan Snyder, 'Marlowe's *Doctor Faustus* as an Inverted Saint's Life', in: *Christopher Marlowe: Doctor Faustus*, ed. David Scott Kastan (New York: W.W. Norton, 2005), describes Marlowe's *Doctor Faustus* as a 'travestied saint's life' (p. 322). While the parallels between the life of Faustus and that of a conventional saint clearly exist on the surface, we should not easily interpret Marlowe's transformation of the model as a travesty.

The emperor shall not live but by my leave,
Nor any potentate of Germany.
Now that I have obtained what I desire,
I'll live in speculation of this art
Till Mephistopheles return again. (A: 1.3.103–15, B: 1.3.101–13)

This soliloquy shows Faustus as an insatiable character, who desires the unlimited power of God.[19] He wants to rearrange the topography of the earth, repeat the miracle of the Red Sea (*Exodus* 14:27) and determine imperial succession. As befits an immature and short-sighted young man, his fantasies concentrate on power and influence. In his excitement over the idea of controlling political and geological constellations, he forgets to ask for the ability to enjoy the realisation of his grandiose aspirations. Heaven is hell, Mephistopheles might have told him, if one lacks the ability to enjoy it.

Since Faustus has only started to dabble with magic and does not yet know what he can expect from it, he fills his mind with imaginary visions. When he concludes the sequence of high-flown fantasies with the comment that he will now fill his time with speculation, he might be referring to no more than projections of his future power. However, the meanings of the term 'speculation' that were current in the late sixteenth and seventeenth century go far beyond the faculty of imagining or fleshing out the future course of his life. The meaning of entry II.4 listed in the *Oxford English Dictionary*, described as a frequent usage during the seventeenth century, is paraphrased as the 'contemplation, consideration, or profound study of some subject', while the similarly revealing entry 5. talks about '[a]n act of speculating, or the result of this; a conclusion, opinion, view, or series of these, reached by abstract or hypothetical reasoning.'

Describing Faustus as a speculator, therefore, foregrounds him as a scholar who engages in profound, hypothetical and arcane reasoning. It is true that Marlowe's Faustus comes across as brash, impatient and unsuitably informed at the beginning of the first act. Critical studies of the play have indicted Faustus for his immature responses to the main tenets of the intellectual disciplines of his age. For instance, he does not seem to immerse himself in the wider context of rhetoric, medicine, jurisprudence, theology and metaphysics, but simply jumps to his conclusions. Although he seems to dismiss the authority of Aristotle, Galen and Justinian in a remarkable *tour de force* (Act 1.1), his responses are founded on serious knowledge of these sources. When it comes to his hostile response to the Bible, David Riggs comments: 'Critics rightly point out that Faustus is hideously mistaken about the Bible; but the Church he is rejecting has taught him to make precisely these mistakes.'[20] Although he neglects to explore the logical frame of reference within which the arguments of key figures of Renaissance thought make

---

19 Cf. Deats, '*Doctor Faustus*: From Chapbook to Tragedy', p. 213. Also compare Cole, *Suffering and Evil*, p. 196.
20 Riggs, *The World of Christopher Marlowe*, p. 240.

sense, Faustus is nevertheless right to draw attention to their circular reasoning and, more importantly, to indict them for their failure to satisfy the needs of the uncompromising thinker.

Faustus does not want to follow the route of the conventional scholar: rather than waste his life in exhausting debates with his fellow scholars, he wants to push ahead and discover new ground. He also wants to apply his extraordinary energy to new challenges. A side-glance into Marlowe's *Tamburlaine the Great* reveals striking parallels:

> Yet would I with my sword make Jove to stoop.
> I will confute those blind geographers
> That make a triple region in the world,
> Excluding regions which I mean to trace,
> And with this pen reduce them to a map ... (Part I: 4.4.77–81)[21]

Like Faustus, Tamburlaine is driven by an insatiable hunger to act and achieve. As military commander with the capacity for building an empire, he is in the right position to realize his aspirations. Marlowe's age was of course the time when the familiar 'triple region' of Europe, Asia and Africa began to be expanded significantly. Beyond the vast geographical areas that lay open to him, however, the intellectual map of the world was also waiting to be revised and expanded. This was the task of the intellectual and not of the military commander.

However, the close resemblances between imperial and intellectual power are demonstrated in another passage where Tamburlaine seeks to rationalize his commandeering spirit:

> Nature, that framed us of four elements
> Warring within our breasts for regiment,
> Doth teach us all to have aspiring minds.
> Our souls, whose faculties can comprehend
> The wondrous architecture of the world
> And measure every wand'ring planet's course,
> Still climbing after knowledge infinite
> And always moving as the restless spheres,
> Wills us to wear ourselves and never rest
> Until we reach the ripest fruit of all,
> That perfect bliss and sole felicity,
> The sweet fruition of an earthly crown. (2.7.18–29)

Tamburlaine's speech echoes Act 1.3 of *Doctor Faustus*. While Tamburlaine's account of bliss climaxes with the achievement of 'an earthly crown', Faustus'

---

21 Quotations are taken from *Doctor Faustus and Other Plays*, eds. David Bevington and Eric Rasmussen (Oxford: Oxford University Press, 1995).

spontaneous enumeration of the grand feats made possible by the performance of magic concludes with the ill-defined comment 'I'll live in speculation of this art.' At first sight this line seems to mean that he is planning to contemplate or imagine what he might achieve with the assistance of Mephistopheles. The context of the preceding lines certainly suggests that Faustus will envisage further opportunities that will allow him to savour his triumph. The gratifications received by Faustus immediately after signing the contract emphasize the power afforded by wealth and magic. However, the text's lack of explicitness allows us to infer that Faustus may have in mind a very different type of speculation from the fantasies of conquest described at the end of act 1.3.

So, what kind of speculator is Marlowe's Faustus? The play provides only fragmentary information about the precise nature of his speculation. But depending on whether he is seen as aspiring to some less materialist goals, the play's audience will either conclude that he deserves to be damned or challenge this conclusion. The play's overt argument concentrates on two related questions: can God forgive, and can Faustus repent? But its implicit emphasis is on the psychological motivation of the character who breaks the formalized rules of his society.

In my analysis of the Faust Books, I argued that the narrative is motivated by, and revolves around, Faustus' yearning for a first-hand encounter with God. In this chapter, I want to argue that a similar craving informs Marlowe's *Doctor Faustus*. Marlowe's notoriously heretical behaviour must at least in part have been motivated by his objection to the idea of a jealous and vengeful God. In any case, since God was the ultimate instance invoked in the organization of daily life, Marlowe's Faustus play demonstrates a powerful impulse to examine the nature of God, or indeed, to interrogate the culturally defined conception of God. At first sight, the play enacts a trial that determines the nature of the hero's sins and concludes with the confirmation of his unforgivable guilt. When we look deeper into this we encounter an investigation of sin and guilt that does not stop short of demanding a justification, or at least an account of the reason behind the creation. In this respect, it closely mirrors the *Book of Job*. Considering that Job was granted the right to demand that God justify himself, Faustus' craving to know the reasons behind laws of nature and morality cannot be offensive. Of course, he approaches his goal with arrogant insistence, while Job can only voice his demand after a great deal of suffering.

Nuttall interprets the powerful parallels between Marlowe's *Doctor Faustus* and the *Book of Job* as evidence that the play interrogates the contradictory justice of God in creating humankind with certain characteristics that will cause its damnation if they are allowed to come to the foreground.[22] Gregory Bateson's interpretation of the *Book of Job* opens up a further perspective on Marlowe's Faustus. He argues that God is willing to respond to the challenges of Job because this gives him an opportunity to confirm the connectedness between all organisms. When he speaks out of the whirlwind he does not give vent to his anger but simply

---

22 A.D. Nuttall, *The Alternative Trinity: Gnostic Heresy in Marlowe, Milton, and Blake* (Oxford: Clarendon Press, 1998).

reveals himself in close alliance with the natural elements. Bateson even claims that Job experiences enlightenment in the sense that he reaches 'a sudden realization of the biological nature of the world in which we live. It is a sudden discovery or realization of *life*.'[23] The abstract concept of *life* invokes metaphysical notions of existence and steps beyond the limits of empirical science. Bateson may here run the danger of being dismissed as unsound by those who insist that science should offer rational, verifiable explanations of nature. However, as quantum physics has demonstrated, for instance, the boundaries between the observer and the observed are ultimately blurred. There is a deep and unalienable relationship between mind and matter which exceeds the powers of human comprehension. Along with the natural scientist of the present day and age, Faustus can therefore be seen to be looking for a sense of interconnectedness between humankind and nature, organisms and mechanisms, mind and matter.

The Journey through the Heavens

The attempt to define God and the sacred in terms that do not belong to any formalized religion goes hand in hand with the deeply human wish to experience the forces which hold the universe together. The quest for this experience can be observed in the substantive additions to the B-text. A telling passage occurs in the opening of the third act. The A-text has Wagner give a summary of what happened between the moment when Faustus entered into his pact with the devil to a time when the twenty-four years of its agreed duration have almost elapsed. This text adopts a tone that fits well with the earlier emphasis on worldly power and scientific knowledge:

> Learnèd Faustus,
> To know the secrets of astronomy
> Graven in the book of Jove's high firmament,
> Did mount himself to scale Olympus' top,
> Being seated in a chariot burning bright
> Drawn by the strength of yoky dragons' necks.
> He now is gone to prove cosmography ... (A: 3.1–7)

The thirteen lines added after line six in the B-text offer a vivid description of what he sees in the course of his journeys.

The additional lines transform the narrative tone from a simple enumeration of events to the description of a potentially life-changing experience. In the B-text, Faustus does not go on his journey merely for the sake of settling cosmological disputes. Here is what Faustus sees from the safety of his magic chariot:

---

23 Gregory Bateson and Mary Catherine Bateson, *Angels Fear: An Investigation into the Nature and Meaning of the Sacred* (London: Rider, 1987), p. 74.

> He views the clouds, the planets, and the stars,
> The tropics, zones, and quarters of the sky,
> From the bright circle of the horned moon
> Even to the height of *Primum Mobile*;
> And, whirling round with this circumference
> Within the concave compass of the pole,
> From east to west his dragons swiftly glide
> And in eight days did bring him home again. (B: 3.7–14)

These additional lines hint at some fascinating moments in the course of his journey. In the previous chapter I argued that the journey through the heavens is such an essential element of the typology that it elevates the Faust Books from the status of a moderately interesting folk tale to a work that explores the depths of human psychology. When Marlowe delves into the thought processes of the magician, he concentrates on his hero's craving for power. However, the portrait of the magician would be grossly simplistic if it excluded his wish to understand the principles and rationale of the material world. It would also be incomplete if his pursuit of unlimited knowledge was not underpinned by his attempt to experience a sense of connectedness to the object of his study.

Even though Faustus' exploration of the cosmos is only briefly mentioned, it adds an important dimension to the revised B-text. The A-text treats Faustus' expedition as an act of spying into Jove's book of astronomical secrets. Although the B-text likewise describes its hero as wanting to discover astronomical secrets, the Faustus of the B-text reaches the height of *Primum Mobile*, or *empyreal orb*, the location of the first cause of motion and life, which was believed to be the dwelling place of God. Although this is mentioned almost in passing, it shows, at least for those familiar with the terminology, that Faustus achieves first-hand experience of the principles of cosmic motion. The B-text suggests that he can catch a brief glimpse into the ultimate mystery of existence.

Faustus summarises his extraordinary journey in a further additional passage in the B-text:

> Thou know'st within the compass of eight days
> We viewed the face of heaven, of earth, and hell.
> So high our dragons soared into the air
> That, looking down, the earth appeared to me
> No bigger than my hand in quantity.
> There did we view the kingdoms of the world,
> And what might please mine eye I there beheld. (B: 3.1.68–72)

This passage makes only the briefest mention of heaven and hell. No attempt is made to flesh out their characteristics. That this is so might corroborate the popular view of an atheist playwright. We might feel encouraged to concur with Faustus' conclusion: 'Come, I think hell's a fable' (A and B: 2.1.130). However, the silence about what it is that 'might please mine eye' is eloquent. Faustus is clearly excited about witnessing the diminutive aspect of the earth seen from a vast distance. In this sense he has experienced the wildest dreams of his period's science as a physical reality. On the other hand, mentioning the size of his hand might also imply that he is literally holding a small Book of Secrets supposed to comprise all important knowledge about the entire world.[24] Such a playful reference to the familiar juxtaposition between the book of nature and the book of God might then prepare Marlowe's audience to look for a religious interpretation in the cryptic comment that 'what might please mine eye I there beheld'.

Of course it is easy to read over such a brief and unspecific reference. The line's refusal to reveal what Faustus saw while spelling out that it was something truly extraordinary would have been another pointer for a member of an oppositional circle that this cryptic moment must refer to the experience of scaling the 'height of *Primum Mobile*'.

Ann Geneva reminds us that 'the seventeenth century appears to have had what amounted to an impulse towards encrypting'.[25] The prevalence of Books of Secrets[26] reminds us that before the age of Enlightenment, people were not yet accustomed to long lists of facts waiting to be remembered and applied in future researches. On the contrary, nature was imagined to harbour secrets which she would yield to those who knew how to discover them. Terms like natural magic belonged to a cosmology that sought to bridge the understanding of cosmic orbits with an explanation of their influence on human life.[27] According to the hermetic traditions that provided the melting pot of early modern science, no part of nature existed in isolation, but it was taken for granted that there were powerful links between, for example, plants and the annual cycle, or the constellations of the stars and human temperament. Neo-Platonic emblematic practices were an ideal conduit for expressing the hidden mysteries of the cosmos, while proto-scientific schemas of planetary orbs easily lent themselves to divinatory purposes.

If we return to the attempt to figure out the import of Faustus' speculations, we notice that the play is not simply silent on this head. The B-text repeatedly draws attention to the omission of a concrete description of that which pleased Faustus. But of course this accords well with the fact that the speculations of Faustus are

---

24 The historical reference might be to books of secrets, such as *The Book of Secrets of Albertus Magnus of the Virtues of Herbs, Stones and Certain Beasts, also A Book of the Marvels of the World*, eds. Michael R. Best and Frank H. Brightman (Oxford: Clarendon Press, 1973).

25 Ann Geneva, *Astrology and the Seventeenth Century Mind: William Lilly and the Language of the Stars* (Manchester: Manchester University Press, 1995), p. 17.

26 One example is *The Book of Secrets of Albertus Magnus*, though this was only one of many similar publications.

27 For a detailed explanation of concepts like 'natural magic', see Daniel P. Walker, *Spiritual and Demonic Magic, from Ficino to Campanella* (Nendeln: Kraus Reprint, 1969).

unequivocally secret. We know neither his motives for pursuing them nor what he feels in the face of obtaining his wishes.

Diverging interpretations also depend on the choice of text on which we base our interpretation. The A-text is not only more fragmentary but it also contains hardly any indications that Faustus might be engaged on a quest for metaphysical truth. By contrast, the additions of the B-text suggest that Faustus explored material phenomena in order to grasp the essence of his own existence, as well as wishing to comprehend the connections among the different material and metaphysical parts of the created world. But I will return to a more detailed comparison of the two versions.

Pseudo-sciences and the Quest for New Knowledge

It is in the nature of empiricist science to valorize experience. Observations based on the sensory impressions of individual witnesses, therefore, were the precondition for defining the matters of fact of the new science.[28] But while the empiricist ideology clearly privileged the experience of the senses over theoretical speculations, it also sought to subject sense experience to objective standards. To ensure that the observations of an individual should be valid for the assessment of scientific laws, every attempt was made to remove emotional overtones from the language that was used for the description of sense experience.[29] Calling for well-trained observers who could identify the relevant qualities of a certain thing, the new science declared it inappropriate for an observer to comment on any personal feelings associated with his or her observations. But at the same time as the new science sought to establish an empiricist practice that turned sensory observations into mechanical processes, a whole range of religious movements of the seventeenth-century listened carefully to the tremors of the soul and treated them as evidence of a close relationship between the believer and God.

While the Faustus narrative revolves around the key interests of the natural philosopher (of either hermetic or empirical orientation), it also pays special attention to the world of emotions. Rather than present the search for meaning about the creation in intellectually abstracted terms, it portrays the moral dilemmas, grand ambitions and tortured emotions of the character who searches for such meaning. The behaviour of Mephistopheles, moreover, is a deeply human issue, informed by his ambivalent dependence on several intellectual traditions. He is a

---

28 For a detailed analysis of the cultural context of empiricist observation, see Steven Shapin and Simon Schaffer, *Leviathan and the Air-Pump* (Princeton: Princeton University Press, 1985).

29 The most influential attempt to reach through the preconceptions caused by cultural conditioning and the particular set-up of the sensory organs can be found in Francis Bacon's analysis of the 'idols'; see *Novum Organum, with Other Parts of the Great Instauration* (1629), trans. and eds. Peter Urbach and John Gibson (Chicago: Open Court, 1994).

rational interlocutor who follows the principles of a Socratic dialogue but he also presents himself as a more modern spirit who challenges Faustus to discover a new account of the relationship between symbolic abstractions, such as heaven and hell, and deeply human experiences of hopes, fears, pleasures and pain.

As a point of reference, it is relevant to remember that Bacon made every effort to separate religious from secular issues, which strengthened the differentiation between emotional from rational responses. As I have argued earlier, it is no coincidence that Bacon describes as superstitious those who rely on the impressions of the senses without questioning their biased nature. So as to establish science as a purely rational occupation, he demanded that it be cleansed of religious enthusiasm and superstitious preconceptions. Marlowe's Faustus acts in the spirit of Bacon's scientific programme when he rejects all previously published explanations of nature and insists on exploring the great questions of existence for himself. He approaches his period's received wisdom with a soberly rational mind and seeks to replace flawed theories with coherent explanations that are based on his own experience. But then his goal also differs decisively from Bacon's. Faustus' attempt to question the foundations of his period's knowledge is not restricted to a scientific analysis of natural phenomena. Here is the list of delights Faustus imagines to be available as a result of devoting himself to the study of magic:

These metaphysics of magicians
And necromantic books are heavenly,
Lines, circles, signs, letters, and characters –
Ay, these are those that Faustus most desires.
O, what a world of profit and delight,
Of power, of honour, and omnipotence,
Is promised to the studious artisan! (A: 1.1.51–7; B: 1.1.49–55 with minute variants)

It is the graspable quality of the printed letters and figures which makes Faustus abandon the works of the accepted authorities. When he exchanges their wisdom for the books of magic, he commits himself to a world in which the essences of things are accessible through incantations, or ritual enunciations of their names. His thinking is affected by a heady concoction of Platonic metaphysics and hermeticism, Gnostic traditions and spiritualist confabulations. Given that the period did not yet draw a clear line between orthodoxies and heretical beliefs, the wide-ranging traditions on which he draws cannot be interpreted as a sign of his intellectual confusion. As Lyndy Abraham explains, 'the Platonic and alchemical truths were in complete harmony with the teachings of Christianity ... Sir Walter Raleigh's *History of the World* ... began with an account of the Creation which quoted Mercurius (Hermes) Trismegistus alongside St. Augustine, St. Paul, Plato, and Moses'.[30] It should also be noted that 'from the thirteenth century onwards, the Church made an important doctrinal distinction between witchcraft and sorcery.

30 Lyndy Abraham, *Marvell and Alchemy* (Aldershot: Scolar Press, 1990), p. 21.

Control of the forces of nature for magical purposes was not necessarily prohibited unless coupled with heresy'.[31] The mere practice of alchemy was not, in itself, cause for damnation. As is illustrated by Johannes Trithemius, Abbot of Sponheim, the ability to understand and command over the forces of nature was even acceptable in an esteemed man of the Church. However, Faustus is not satisfied with the demesnes of natural magic,[32] and his crime consists of dealing with the 'metaphysics of magicians'. When he does so, he oversteps the line between magic and witchcraft, and hence incurs the wrath of Christian thinkers.

Two eminent alchemists appear on stage in response to the line '[c]ome, German Valdes and Cornelius' (A: 1.1.100; B: 1.1.99): the name Cornelius appears to be an indirect reference to Cornelius Agrippa von Nettesheim, while Valdes cannot be identified with any historical figure.[33] Contemporary audiences stood in awe of eminent alchemists, and this may be why the play remains unclear about the true identities of these two figures. Popular belief, or superstition, as Leah Marcus reminds us, went so far as to credit the theatrical performance of magical rituals with their full efficaciousness.[34] Although the play obfuscates an overt identification with an existing alchemist, Faustus' invocation of Valdes and Cornelius nevertheless resembles the act of conjuring spirits.

When we study the historical significance of astrological beliefs and practices, we have to bear in mind that they had a well-established bearing on the philosophical, intellectual, cultural and scientific spheres of life.[35] Ann Geneva reminds us that '[m]odern astrology generally bears little resemblance to earlier practices, and often the less one knows about modern methods the easier it becomes to penetrate the early modern mentality'.[36] In any case, the Renaissance was an age in which magical formulae were culturally central. Owing to the period's political and intellectual instability, magical knowledge was also utilized as a means of exerting control over the ever-present experience of change and uncertainty. The alchemical study of transmutation and transformative processes (from base substance to high substance, from iron to gold, from poor to rich) nurtured aspirations for growth, development and advancement on the social hierarchy.

For these reasons, those with interest in natural magic also tended to stir the atmosphere of political unrest. Historical examples consist of the circles formed

---

31 Leslie Shepard's Foreword to *the Philosophy of Natural Magic by Henry Cornelius Agrippa von Nettesheim* (Seacaucus, NJ: University Books, 1974), unpaginated.

32 Cf. John Baptista della Porta, *Natural Magick*, ed. Derek J. Price (New York: Basic Books, 1957).

33 Gareth Roberts, 'Necromantic Books: Christopher Marlowe, Dr. Faustus, and Agrippa of Nettesheim', in Darryll Grantley and Peter Roberts, eds., *Christopher Marlowe and English Renaissance Culture* (Aldershot, Hants.: Scolar Press, 1996), pp. 148–71.

34 Cf. Leah Marcus, 'Textual Indeterminacy and Ideological Difference: The Case of *Doctor Faustus,*' *Renaissance Drama* 20 (1989).

35 Cf. Keith Thomas, *Religion and the Decline of Magic* (London: Weidenfeld and Nicolson, 1971).

36 Geneva, *Astrology*, p. 3.

around John Dee, Edward Kelly and Thomas Harriot. These three knew each other well and they established networks for the propagation of medical recipes as well as critical responses to contemporary theology and politics. We also need to keep in mind that the investigation of matters of belief was always political. Both Frances Yates's study of early seventeenth-century Rosicrucianism and Margaret Jacob's study of Freemasonry during the early Enlightenment concluded that radical politics could be traced back to religious splinter groups that disagreed profoundly with mainstream beliefs.[37]

An important aspect of 'alchemical magic' is that it elevates the one who practices it into a position of almost supreme power. The secular rulers, as well as some bishops and other dignitaries of the Church, had alchemists in their service (that the quarrel between Elizabeth I and Rudolf II at Prague concerned the right to claim Edward Kelly as court astrologer illustrates the significance of these alchemists).[38] Contemporary potentates might boast about an alchemist at their courts in order to glorify their position. However, an alchemist was also a potential source of danger, since he might end up wielding more power than those in whose service he was employed. James I, in any event, preferred the sober Francis Bacon, who refused to engage with spiritual matters, over John Dee, who struck most contemporaries as an uncanny character. Ironically enough, it is now assumed that Bacon was impeached in 1621 because he too was thought to possess a dangerous amount of power, and was therefore deposed in order to curb his influence.

We must approach Marlowe's *Doctor Faustus* with an awareness of the intrinsic relationships between power and knowledge. The first act of both the A- and B-texts begins with a lengthy soliloquy in Faustus' study. His first words are:

Settle thy studies, Faustus, and begin
To sound the depth of that thou wilt profess.

We first meet him when he has completed his studies, having already absorbed all the learning available at the period. Since there is no additional knowledge to be mastered he decides that this is the right time to investigate the meaning of what he 'professes'. The verb 'profess' has come to be coloured by its morphological link to 'profession', but the twentieth-century meaning of a 'career' misses the contemporary resonances of the term. The term nevertheless describes the character of Faustus through a reference to his knowledge and skills. As such, the term is sketching a dimension of human existence that, in the course of the eighteenth and nineteenth centuries, would come to be described as professional identity. What Faustus 'professes', of course, powerfully influences his beliefs about himself and his intellectual abilities.

---

37 Frances A. Yates, *The Rosicrucian Enlightenment* (London: Routledge, 1972) and Margaret C. Jacob, *The Radical Enlightenment: Pantheists, Freemasons and Republicans* (London: George Allen and Unwin, 1981).

38 See Abraham, *Marvell and Alchemy*, pp. 5–6.

Although Faustus owns up to the empirical method, his investigation of 'what he professes' focuses not on the physical but on the metaphysical dimension. He explores the spirit (or meaning) behind the words and delves into the emotional dimension of beliefs. It is telling that he picks up one tome after another written by the key figures of his cultural tradition, *reads* a representative line and puts these texts behind him with the gesture that he has intellectually outgrown them. His approach is superficial and he fails to engage seriously with the terms of reference of the most important intellectual traditions of his period. He is nevertheless justified in his dissatisfaction with their arguments. One reason why he is attracted to the ritualistic text of magical incantations can be explained by his attempt to grasp the relationship between the investigator, language and the world. Faustus acts true to the Paracelsian conviction that meaning is the consequence of a rapport among all of these three participators, and his bent towards magic suggests that he believes in an intrinsic connection between knowledge of the self and knowledge of the world.

The prologue describes Faustus as possessing extraordinary skills of disputation:

> Excelling all, and sweetly can dispute
> In th' heavenly matters of theology;
> Till, swoll'n with cunning of a self-conceit,
> His waxen wings did mount above his reach,
> And, melting, heavens conspired his overthrow.
> For, falling to a devilish exercise,
> And glutted now with learning's golden gifts,
> He surfeits upon necromancy;
> Nothing so sweet as magic is to him,
> Which he prefers before his chiefest bliss. (B: 17–26)[39]

The comment that he possessed 'waxen wings' with which he 'did mount above his reach' compares Faustus with Icarus, and the text's emphasis on his limitless aspirations presents him as an anti-hero. The warnings against the damaging consequences of an insatiable appetite for knowledge are rendered by a host of terms related to eating and over-eating: 'falling to', 'glutted with', 'he surfeits', 'nothing so sweet'. Because his rhetorical disputations do not satiate him, Faustus oversteps his limits. He commits hubris and initiates his own downfall, or so the voice of the Prologue would have us believe.

Our first encounter with Faustus is overshadowed with a harsh judgement of his behaviour, prejudicing the spectator-reader to the first appearance of the hero: 'And this the man that in his study sits' (A: line 27; B: line 28). When the Prologue describes the 'heavenly matters of theology' as the goal of his studies, the underlying

---

39 The main variant in the A-Text is that it qualifies 'necromancy' with the judgemental adjective 'cursed' in line 25.

physical metaphor equates heavenly theology with wholesome food. Even though he is 'glutted with' the legitimate food of 'learning's golden gifts', he turns to illegitimate sources of nourishment. The implied conclusion of the Prologue is that his spiritual-intellectual body is bound to destroy itself on this superabundance of food. If we turn to the opening of the first act, though, we notice that neither 'heavenly theology' nor any other legitimate tradition of learning satisfies him. He exclaims against the limitations of knowledge on account of summarising the key points of his age's most influential authorities: Aristotle, Galen, Justinian and the Bible. It has been pointed out that he is lacking in scholarly stamina when he, for example, quotes Aristotle via the essentially anti-Aristotelian Peter Ramus, rather than going back to the original text.[40] But even if Faustus had read all of Aristotle, his maybe rashly conceived conclusion about the limitations of knowledge would have been confirmed. We only need to go to the propositions of twentieth century science and their more recent applications to cultural analysis as further evidence for this point.[41]

Lawrence Danson takes Faustus to task for reading out of context and distorting the theological points of his age: 'According to the spiritual lawyer St. Paul, all men are condemned to death under the law but saved by Christ who fulfils the law'.[42] Of course, Faustus' much quoted rendition of this passage omits the second part of the argument:

If we say that we have no sin
We deceive ourselves, and there's no truth in us.
Why, then, belike we must sin and so consequently die.
Ay, we must die an everlasting death.
(A: 1.1.43–6; B: 1.1.41–5 with minute variations)

All those who indict Faustus for his headstrong omission of the Christian account of redemption disregard the gist of his question: rather than trying to explain the cornerstones of Christian dogma, he is examining the ethics of a religious theory that describes human nature as sinful. Although he does not undertake a detailed analysis of the theological discourses of his period, these lines invite us to imagine the crippling impact on the growth of the human mind of an all-pervasive idea of sin. In the course of his own education, Marlowe must have experienced the emotional pains that are instilled by Calvinist fears of one's sinful nature. The process of growing up with such convictions is a form of damnation in its own right. When we return to the fictional character Faustus, his dismissive behaviour

---

40 Cf. Lawrence Danson, 'The Questioner', *Christopher Marlowe: Modern Critical Views*, ed. Harold Bloom (New York: Chelsea House, 1986), pp. 197–9.

41 As a representative work that outlined the vagaries of cultural relativism, I refer to Jean François Lytard's *Le différend* (Paris: Minuit, 1983).

42 Danson, 'The Questioner', p. 200.

is an understandable response to the stifling intellectual climate in which religious doctrine was taught.

The play will repeatedly remind us of the similarities between appearance and reality. An amusing instance consists of the wish by the German Emperor to 'prove' the hear-say story that the paramour of Alexander the Great had a little wart or mole on her neck by going up to the ghostly apparition and checking her skin from close distance. Even though Faustus emphasizes that 'These are but shadows, not substantial' (B: 4.1.103), the Emperor immediately stumbles back into his deluded assumption that the appearing shadows really and truly *are* Emperor Alexander and his paramour. The make-believe of the spirits who embody the deceased characters is so accurate that the empirical method of going up to them and touching them with one's own hands fails to yield reliable proof of their existence. In the world of ontological uncertainty conjured up by Marlowe's *Doctor Faustus*, sensory experience cannot offer unequivocal evidence. While Faustus may not even have reliable scientific techniques to prove his own existence, the physical metaphors of the Prologue suggest that the only facts he can determine with certainty concern his physical well-being. If magic can provide the fulfilment which orthodox theology cannot, Faustus can at least extricate himself from the damnation pronounced by those who are unable to understand the differences between being and appearances.

The Hell of *Doctor Faustus*

As was customary in the period, the intellectual dialogues in *Doctor Faustus* are livened up by low comedy and carnivalesque pageants. The appearance of the Seven Deadly Sins (A and B: 2.3.106ff), for instance, introduces physical grotesqueness into the prosaic conversations between the scholar Faustus and a devil in the habit of a Franciscan monk. This element of folk lore injects a ritualistic substance into the discussion of contemporary Christian doctrine while it also renders visual the idea that Faustus fathoms the full extent of his transgression. However, the dramatic presentation of the scene develops its own dynamics. As in folk rituals associated with, for instance, winter solstice, where people assume the guise of evil forces, dramatic embodiment is ambiguously pitched between exorcism and an acceptance that the forces play an integral part in human existence. Morris dancing and other noisy expulsions of life-endangering forces like frost, darkness and infertility invoke pagan deities in an attempt to contain their power within boundaries. Given that annual rites recur again and again at certain times of the year, they both exorcise evil forces and perform certain forms of worship. But of course, the ritualistic performances around such figures are contradictory and overdetermined; they instil fear of frightening forces at the same time as they seek to defuse their destructive potential.

The theatrical display of Faustus' dealings with evil forces is also steeped in folkloristic elements. It is during a period of regret that a group of devils comes to chasten him for breaking his pact. After threatening him with severe punishments if he should be tempted to breach it again, they remind him of the attractions of hell: 'we are come from hell in person to show thee some pastime. Sit down, and thou shalt behold the Seven Deadly Sins' (B: 2.3.98–100),[43] to which he replies, 'That sight will be as pleasant to me as paradise was to Adam the first day of his creation.' (B: 2.3.102; A: 2.3.102). The line that says that the sight of the Seven Deadly Sins should please Faustus is normally spoken with ironic groans. This means the appearance of these characters is taken as a frightful reminder of his damned condition. Unfortunately, we lack detailed stage directions and therefore do not know what kind of spectacle they offer. There is a tacit assumption, however, that the Seven Deadly Sins must be an ugly train of ghouls to whom Faustus responds with the deepest revulsion, even though he asserts that this sight delights his soul (A: 2.3.157; B: 2.3.154).

Of course, Faustus might have expressed his enjoyment under coercion, but it is also conceivable that he enjoyed the spectacle because it revealed these figures as empty stereotypes. Alternatively he might be pleased by the idea that hell will allow him to indulge in all kinds of sinful behaviour without having to fear further reprisals.[44] In any case, the spectacle afforded by the Seven Deadly Sins inspires a powerful craving in Faustus to experience hell from an uninvolved vantage point. It is possible that he wants to find out whether hell is just an empty pretence, or he might even want to discover whether there is enjoyment for the damned souls. According to Christian dogma, hell is certainly the place of punishment for the sensory pleasures of this world. But is it possible, rather, that hell should be a place of enjoyment?

Lucifer's assertion that 'in hell is all manner of delight' opens up a whole range of possible interpretations. Faustus' eager response to Lucifer's portrayal of hell's delights is certainly telling:

FAUSTUS
O, might I see hell and return again safe, how happy were I then!

LUCIFER
Faustus, thou shalt. At midnight I will send for thee. [*Presenting a book*] Meanwhile, peruse this book, and view it throughly, and thou shalt turn thyself into what shape thou wilt. (B: 2.3.156ff; A: 2.3.159 with minor variations)

---

43 The equivalent passage in A: 2.3.98ff is preceded with an outspoken commitment by Faustus that he 'vows never to look to heaven, / Never to name God or to pray to him, / To burn his Scriptures, slay his ministers, / And make my spirits pull his churches down.' The corresponding passage in the B-Text has him say no more than 'Faustus vows never to look to heaven.'

44 I owe this idea to Neil Ramsey.

In the immediately following Chorus that opens Act 3, two of the traditional journeys are mentioned: Faustus travels through heaven and earth. But the Chorus makes no mention of a visit to the devil's realm. The fragmentary nature of the play may explain that an important piece is missing here or it is possible that Marlowe deliberately refrained from a reference to hell. Another possibility is that Lucifer's promise that Faustus may see the delights of hell is not simply forgotten but that the play suggests that there is no such thing as hell. The delights mentioned at the beginning of the act would therefore refer to the secrets of the astronomical cosmos. On the other hand, the phrase chosen by the Chorus to describe the object of interest as 'Jove's high firmament' might not simply be a randomly chosen allusion to classical mythology, but imply a creator of the universe who diverges from the Christian conception of God.

The play here again confronts us with questions concerning the whereabouts and nature of hell. They tie in with the dialogue at the beginning of the play, when Faustus asks Mephistopheles why he is not in hell and receives the answer, 'Why, this is hell, nor am I out of it' (1.3.74). In another passage, Faustus explicitly asks his spirit, 'where is the place that men call hell?' (A: 2.1.117; B: 2.1.116). He impatiently demands a more detailed account and is told that it is 'Under the heavens':

> Within the bowels of these elements,
> Where we are tortured and remain for ever.
> Hell hath no limits, nor is circumscribed
> In one self place, but where we are is hell,
> And where hell is there must we ever be.
> And, to be short, when all the world dissolves,
> And every creature shall be purified,
> All places shall be hell that is not heaven.
> (B: 2.1.119–26; A: 2.1.119–26 with minor variations)

Except for mentioning the conventional idea of hell being the place of torture, this passage gives no indication as to the concrete location of hell. 'Within the bowels of these elements' alludes to the folk belief according to which hell is underground. Assuming that Mephistopheles points downwards, he appears to confirm traditional assumptions. What exactly is implied by 'within the bowels of *these* elements', however, remains ambiguous. The reference to elements might very well be to the four elements believed to constitute the entire material world: fire, water, air and earth. As such, Mephistopheles' spatial identification might amount to saying that hell is a part of everything. The ensuing comments, then, elaborate on the idea that hell is an amorphous space that is coextensive with the creation. Mephistopheles may therefore be suggesting that hell exists wherever evil is done, but he might also be saying that hell is inside; that it is a part of our inner reality rather than some subterranean place.

Faustus has no ear for subtleties. When he hears the seemingly inconclusive explanations by his spirit, he provokes him with the comment, 'I think hell's a fable' (2.1.127). But what exactly does he mean by the term 'fable'? A figment of the imagination? An invention? Or an allegory for something that exceeds human understanding? Mephistopheles does not engage in a sophist controversy. He simply rejoins: 'Ay, think so still, till experience change thy mind' (A and B: 2.1.128), warning Faustus against bold conclusions that are divorced from the realm of experience. When Mephistopheles counters Faustus' audacious claim with the empiricist argument, he reminds him that imaginings about hell can have palpable dimensions even if they do not describe a physically real place.

At this point, it is also important to discuss the graphic portrayal of hell in the B-text. Towards the end of the play, the Bad Angel confronts Faustus with the goriest colours of suffering:

> Now, Faustus, let thine eyes with horror stare
> Into that vast perpetual torture house.
> There are the Furies tossing damnèd souls
> On burning forks.
> …
> But all these are nothing. Thou shalt see
> Ten thousand tortures that more horrid be. (B: 5.2.116–27)

When Faustus replies, 'O, I have seen enough to torture me!', the Bad Angel sadistically reinforces his point, 'Nay, thou must feel them, taste the smart of all. / He that loves pleasure must for pleasure fall.' (B: 5.2.128–130). While the Bad Angel confirms the message of the cautionary tale, his physically grotesque portrayal of suffering dramatizes long-established beliefs about the quality of hell, but we should also be aware that we are primarily witnessing the anguish conjured up by ideas of physical pain. Since the play stages traditional views of hell, it forces the audience to share the mental tortures of the hero. The dramatic spectacle of hell, however, also draws attention to itself as a spectacle of hell that is a product of theatrical machinery, reflecting fantasies and beliefs without realistic foundations.

However imaginary these visions of suffering may be, Faustus experiences real pain when he contemplates them. He states himself that he is tortured by the thought of hell. His anguish in the face of conventional ideas about the punishment of worldly transgressions, however, does not prove that he is about to encounter such punishment himself. The physical spectacle of hell merely proves the physical reality of agony, showing us that his fears torture him while he is still alive. Although hell may be real in the imagination of Faustus, and the majority of Marlowe's early audience, the theatrical spectacle cannot make any conclusive statements about the afterlife of Faustus.

The play concludes with the death of Faustus. In spite of the statement made by the Chorus that '[c]ut is the branch that might have grown full straight' (A and B: 5.3.1), the play does not go beyond the fact of its hero's death. It is true that the Chorus invites us to '[r]egard his hellish fall' (A and B: 5.3.4) and gestures towards all kinds of punishments, but it cannot do more than present us with the spectacle of a dead body. Even the gruesome display of Faustus' mangled body cannot overrule the simple fact that death is the inevitable termination of every life and that it is therefore impossible to know what happened after Faustus breathed his last.

The Value of Human Existence

Christian belief treated the body as the evil and corrupt part of human existence. In spite of giving voice to the warnings at the beginning of the play, good and evil cannot be as easily distinguished as the authoritarian voice of the Prologue suggests. The character of Mephistopheles, then, presents us with transformations that challenge received ideas about the devil. His changeability has always been taken as evidence of the devil's unreliability and dishonesty. A key instance of Mephistopheles' changing behaviour relates to his treatment of Faustus as an equal, suggesting that once Faustus has overstepped his period's boundaries of legitimate knowledge, he can indeed become 'a spirit in form and substance' (A: 2.1.97; B: 2.1.96), the most important demand identified in the pact.

Faustus' decision to leave the fold of common humanity does not guard him against remorse and he is ravaged by doubt about whether he has chosen the right route. Mephistopheles tries to revive his spirits, telling him:

> Think'st thou heaven is such a glorious thing?
> I tell thee, 'tis not half so fair as thou
> Or any man that breathes on earth. (A and B: 2.3.5–7)

In response to the eager demand by Faustus that he should prove this point Mephistopheles replies: 'It was made for man, therefore is man more excellent' (A: 2.3.9). The edition by Ormerod and Wortham argues that Marlowe intended to parody the familiar Renaissance eulogy on the glory of man, adducing as evidence that Marlowe 'gives this perverted form of its expression very properly to a devil.'[45] Mephistopheles, however, is not simply exaggerating the humanists' view. He plays a rhetorical game with unspoken beliefs about God's motives for forming the creation, and by doing so introduces a purpose into the original void of creation (*Genesis* 1:2). Mephistopheles exchanges the product of the creative process for its cause and rationale. In support of the special significance of the human being he can, of course, quote the line that God gave mankind dominion 'over every living thing that moved upon the earth' (*Genesis* 1:28). He is taking this claim to its logical conclusion when he argues that since the world was made

---

45 Cf. David Ormerod's and Christopher Wortham's commentary to lines 633–8: *Doctor Faustus: The A-Text*, eds. David Ormerod and Christopher Wortham (Nedlands: University of Western Australia Press, 1989), p. 64.

for man, it is only reasonable to assume that heaven, earth and hell have also been made for man.

Mephistopheles is devil enough to oppose contemporary views about the position of humankind within the creation. Rather than fashion himself as a crude opponent of God, he takes on the role of a spiritual guide whose arguments are founded on a commitment to human dignity. A telling contrast can be found in Shakespeare's *Hamlet*, where the special qualities of the human mind and body are eulogized in order more decisively to trample them into the dust:

> What a piece of work is a man! How noble in reason! how infinite in faculties! in form and moving, how express and admirable! in action, how like an angel! in apprehension, how like a god! the beauty of the world! the paragon of animals! And yet, to me, what is the quintessence of dust? Man delights not me ... [46]

For Hamlet, description of the extraordinary qualities of the human being is a rhetorical ploy for emphasising his disappointment at finding an evil disposition inhabiting an angelic form. Mephistopheles, however, refuses to couch his praises in misanthropic contempt for the ultimate shortcomings of mankind. He is far from sharing Hamlet's frame of mind, and does not reject the entirety of mankind in response to a personal trauma. For all his hellish origins, Mephistopheles does not judge humanity by concrete actions and shortcomings, but accepts its dignity without further qualifications.

Another contemporary example that highlights the discrepancy between the body's physical excellence and the sinful components of the human mind is John Donne's Holy Sonnet V:

> I am a little world made cunningly
> Of Elements and an Angelice sprite,
> But black sinne hath betraid to endlesse night
> My worlds both parts, and (oh) both parts must die.[47]

Donne's admiration for the marvellous design of body and soul pays tribute to the skill and dexterity of God, the craftsman, who created a complete little world from a myriad of parts. The paradoxical conceit of Donne's sonnet offers tribute to the clever plan of human existence, but his moralising subverts the accolade. The examples quoted here show that contemporary writers strove to give expression to a joyful spirit of existence at the same time as they experienced a powerful sense of unease, explaining why both Shakespeare and Donne undercut their eulogies. But while the moralising habits of the poets hampered their imaginative reach,

---

46 Cf. *Hamlet* in *William Shakespeare: The Complete Works*, ed. Peter Alexander (London: Collins, 1987), 2.2, 305ff.

47 John Donne, 'Holy Sonnet' (1635), *The Poems of John Donne*, vol. 1, ed. Herbert J.C. Grierson (Oxford: Clarendon Press, 1912), p. 324.

early scientists found it easier to praise the beauties of the physical world. William Harvey, the anatomist who discovered the circulation of the blood, for example, wholeheartedly praised the beautiful and wise organisation of the human body in his ground-breaking essay 'Movement of the Heart and Blood in Animals' (1628). Invoking a Copernican comparison between macrocosm and microcosm, he argues that the heart 'deserves to be styled the starting point of life and the sun of our microcosm just as much as the sun deserves to be styled the heart of the world'.[48]

When Mephistopheles tells Faustus that heaven is 'not half so fair as thou' he therefore refuses to play the role of the contemporary moralists. Though spoken by a devil, we cannot necessarily assume that this claim for the grandeur of human beauty must be evil or perverted.

The Magic of Doctor Faustus

Faustus famously demands that his spirit should 'resolve me of all ambiguities' (A: 1.1.82; B: 1.1.79). In other words, he aims to use magic to sound the 'depth' of his burning questions. But what kind of magic does Faustus use?

Beneath the semblance of the cautionary tale, the play explores the cultural significance of magic. Act 1.2 begins with a dialogue between some fellow scholars of Faustus: 'I wonder what's become of Faustus, that was wont to make our schools ring with "*sic probo*"'. The Latin for 'I prove it thus' shows Faustus to have delved into countless problems and to have possessed the wit to formulate many answers. This amounts to saying not only that he made daring speculations, but also that he knew how to offer evidence in support of his claims. From the dialogue between the scholars we also learn that they did not simply come to enquire after the well-being of Faustus, but wanted to confirm their suspicions that his unbridled curiosity must have caused him much misery.

The play describes him as an outstanding scholar even at the time when he possessed no magic. So, what does he want magic for? As he says in the first scene of the play, he wants it to resolve ambiguities. And his dialogues with Mephistopheles show that the most irksome ambiguities reside in moral concerns and are to be found in the cosmology on which are founded moral decisions.

This is why Faustus likes to talk with his spirit about 'who made the world' (A and B: 2.3.65). For the most part, though, the magic performed on stage is trivial and burlesque. Faustus knocks the Pope's company round the ears, dramatizes a bawdy joke by punishing a scoffing knight with a pair of horns, and takes advantage of a crooked horse-courser by selling him a phantom horse. Even Faustus' necromantic demonstration amounts to a trivial display of his skills. The appearance of Darius, Alexander and his paramour certainly feature as sensational spectacles but their

---

48 Cf. William Harvey, *The Circulation of the Blood*, trans. Kenneth J. Franklin and Andrew Wear (London: Everyman, 1990), pp. 46–7.

appearance bears no comparison, for instance, to the ghost of Hamlet's father. As Faustus explains, 'These are but shadows, not substantial' (B: 4.1.103).[49] That his necromantic spectacles are not in the least frightening might be interpreted as a sign that they are simply theatrical make-believe. Alternatively, we might conclude that ghosts are essentially chimera of the mind and as such are only frightening if they instil feelings of guilt or fear. Be this as it may, the act of conjuring the phantoms from Greek mythology, along with the horns sprouted by the contemptuous knight, are instances of stage magic, designed to entertain a noisy crowd rather than satisfy anybody's yearning for metaphysical truth.

Stage hocus-pocus is prevalent throughout the play; so much so that it almost buries the existence of a more subtle type of magic. As I have argued, Faustus' quest for metaphysical truth is only adumbrated alongside his performance of coarse feats. However, it is important to be aware of the existence of different types of magic: there is a powerful balance between the wish to experience 'what might please mine eye' (B: 3.1.74) and sensational spectacles. As a result, the play compares the wish for control over the minds of the gullible with a yearning to experience and be a part of that which holds the universe together. Bateson uses respective categories to differentiate between magic and religion. Using the behaviour of nomadic tribes as an example, he argues:

> If the hunter performs a ritual imitation of an animal to cause that animal to come into his net, that surely is magic; but if his purpose in imitating the animal is perhaps to improve his own empathy and understanding of the beast, his action is perhaps to be classed as religious.[50]

Bateson goes on to explain that religious spirituality, based on the empathetic experience of natural phenomena (what is sometimes referred to by the name 'natural magic') is an archaic, deeply human character trait. The wish to exploit and exert control, by contrast, mars the possibility of enjoying the simple pleasures of natural religion. So even if Faustus is to be interpreted as an initiate of a hermetic subculture, he is nevertheless prone to self-aggrandizement. In so far as he prefers the adulations of a crowd to the solitary experience of the sacred, he may have fallen pray to a temptation more subtle than the one which supposedly induces him to sell his soul.

The play dramatizes its arguments at a variety of levels. For example, the Good and the Bad Angel not only engage in a theological dispute, but wrangle with each other like two children fighting over a toy. The cheap tricks performed by the two low characters Robin and Dick offer a parallel that throws further doubt on the dramatized examples of Faustus' magical skills. Regardless of whether Act 2.2 is

---

49 The Faustus of the A-Text explains: 'But if it please our grace, it is not in my ability to present before your eyes the true substantial bodies of those two deceased princes, which long since are consumed to dust.', A: 4.1.43ff.

50 Bateson and Bateson, *Angels Fear*, p. 56.

interpreted as a direct parallel or as a contrast to the quest for sublime knowledge, the play's low comedy scrutinizes the motivations behind breaches of moral and religious taboos.

Wagner, the servant of Faustus, similarly sheds light on the magician's wish for control over his admirers and enemies. The rhetorically brilliant rudeness with which he treats the scholars who have come to enquire after his master smacks of a fantasy of revenge familiar to anyone who has ever suffered at the hands of small-minded pedants:

> Yet if you were not dunces, you would never ask me such a question. For is he not *corpus naturale*? And is not that *mobile*? Then, wherefore should you ask me such a question? But that I am by nature phlegmatic, slow to wrath, and prone to lechery – to love, I would say – it were not for you to come within forty foot of the place of execution, although I do not doubt but to see you both hanged the next sessions. Thus, having triumphed over you, I will set my countenance like a precisian and begin to speak thus: Truly, my dear brethren, my master is within at dinner with Valdes and Cornelius, as this wine, if it could speak, it would inform your worships. (A: 1.2.17–28; B: 1.2.17–25 with minor changes)

Wagner derides his interlocutors by switching between different modes of address. He thrusts his linguistic skills into their faces in order to make a fool of them. More than that, his insolent power game challenges social decorum and propriety. He begins with a parodic imitation of Aristotelian logic. The comic effect of his misapplication of philosophical reasoning depends on his wilful disregard for context, pretending that their social visit concerns a philosophical moot point. By doing so, however, he also reminds them that they are not simply paying Faustus a social visit but want to spy on his moral probity.

When Wagner asks the scholars, 'wherefore should you ask me such a question?', he ridicules their ignorance on the abstract level of his argument. However, his subsequent outburst, when he calls them criminals who deserve to be hanged, is also motivated by observing their mean-spirited goal of confirming that he 'is fall'n into that damned art'. By running through a whole spectrum of personae, from the pedantic philosopher to the churlish fellow and the obsequious servant, Wagner gives them to understand that his language skills are a form of magic. His deceptive changeability, then, turns him into a semblance of the devil who admits to, and even boasts of, his deceitful handling of conversational registers. Wagner is not simply ridiculing a couple of dunces, but is also interrogating the distorting dimensions of representation. His mastery of representation, then, also reveals itself as the basis for the abuse of gullible crowds.

At this point I want to come back to Mephistopheles' claim that experience changes one's mind. If viewed as a general comment on how thought is affected by the context of a concrete situation, this appeal to experience invites us to examine the relationship between material living conditions and beliefs. A striking example of this occurs in the scene where Wagner asserts that Robin, the poor clown, is 'so hungry that I know he would give his soul to the devil for a shoulder of mutton, though it were blood raw' (A and B: 1.4.7). Robin's objection that he would insist on its being 'well roasted, and good sauce to it, if I pay so dear' dramatizes his brutish indifference to salvation. By staging the simple fellow's crude responses, the play asks us to think about the use of a convoluted theory of salvation for the uneducated masses. The figure of Robin, moreover, does not simply belong to the poor, but also personifies the claims of the body, indicating that theological ideals tend to be disregarded in conditions of physical distress. The play establishes a parallel between the Faustus persona, who is figuratively hungry for meaning, and Robin, who is literally starving. While the audience may easily despise Robin for his materialist craving for sauce, the spectacle of this starving character also draws attention to the inhumanity of rules and laws that condemn those deprived of physical and spiritual sustenance, rather than endeavouring to appease their hunger.

Low comedy offers a telling parallel to Faustus' magical experiments in another scene in which Robin and Dick are dabbling in magic. In act 3.3 Robin stumbles across the formula that forces Mephistopheles to appear. These two comic characters are playing around with formulae that remind us of the hocus-pocus that might be encountered on a fairground. That Mephistopheles appears in response to their magical formulae seems to prove their effectiveness, and implicitly settles the ambiguity as to whether Mephistopheles originally appeared in response to the conjurations of Faustus, or whether he was prowling in his vicinity because he sensed Faustus' sacrilegious intents. Alternatively, the appearance of Mephistopheles in response to the two servants' use of magical formulae suggest that he is no more than hocus-pocus himself. Even his genuine ability to hurt them may be interpreted as damage they do themselves because they believe themselves to be moving on forbidden ground.

The play shows that magic is primarily about the manipulation of appearances. From the beginning, the devil is presented as a master of appearances who can become invisible, or transform himself into any and every creature. The scene in which Mephistopheles first materializes demonstrates his skills in changing his appearances. Faustus shoos him out of his initial guise with the sarcastic comment:

> … change thy shape.
> Thou art too ugly to attend on me.
> Go, and return an old Franciscan friar;
> That holy shape becomes a devil best. (A and B: 1.3.23–6)

The fun poked at the Catholic Church clearly overshadows the more serious question concerning the nature of spirits. When Mephistopheles introduces himself by performing extravagant transformations of his outward appearances, we are presented with various understandings of the nature of a devil, ranging from an ugly monster to a Catholic monk. Implied by his capability for transformation is that devils are non-material beings that can randomly make use of material bodies. On the face of it, the dramatically emphasized changeability of the spirits supports their ultimate immateriality, but it also relegates them to a narrative realm in which reality and unreality merge. Magic resides in imaginings and in narrative. This means that the play is essentially about a character who asks for magic as an instrument for mastering the creative potentials of the imagination.[51] The play shows that a creative intellectual can only satiate his hunger by intuiting, and feeling, the magic that stands behind his experience of the world.

Conclusion

Any interpretation of Marlowe's *Doctor Faustus* which aims to draw attention to the play's sympathies with hermetic beliefs needs to comment on its dramatic techniques. Nuttall's incisive analysis of its Gnostic elements emphasizes its experimental approach to dramatic conventions and genre:

> In both the 1604 and 1616 editions the work is called a 'tragical history'. This, we may say, is a warning shot fired across the bows of the Historicist. It signals, 'Not a morality, but this new, exciting thing, a tragedy'. In a rough and ready way it is fair to say that tragedy is distinguished from the older morality-drama in having moral ambiguity at its centre.[52]

That the type of narrative by which the life of Faustus is told is described as a 'tragical history' can hence be read as an indication that the Faustus story was a vehicle for the self-definition of contemporary society. If we remember that the question of whether or not Faustus is damned remains unresolved, we gain a new perspective on the moral and intellectual uncertainties of a period of dramatic change.

Not surprisingly for an age that was riven by competing interpretations of salvation, the play dramatizes a struggle between Gnosticism and other arcane-hermetic branches of knowledge, on the one hand, and a repressive theology most easily identified with Calvinism, on the other. This conflict primarily concerns freedom of conscience, along with the ability to take one's destiny into one's own hands. This is why Nuttall argues that 'Agrippa's man has unbounded freedom to ascend. Calvin's man is totally depraved, predestined to damnation, in bondage to sin, destitute of all freedom.'[53] Alan Sinfield summarizes the dilemma of Faustus according to a Calvinist reading: 'Faustus is damned because he sinned ... but

---

51 Cf. Ian McAdam, *The Irony of Identity: Self and Imagination in the Drama of Christopher Marlowe* (Newark: University of Delaware Press, 1960).

52 Nuttall, *Alternative Trinity*, p. 23.

53 *Ibid.*, p. 28.

… Faustus sinned because he is damned'.[54] The question that sustains the tension to the end of the play is whether Faustus can escape from this fateful dilemma. But the main issue, I argue, is not whether God can forgive him for his fling with magic but whether Faustus can escape from a world view that denies him the right to ascend.

The final agony of the play is normally taken as evidence that the Calvinist interpretation wins out over competing beliefs about life after death. The agonized shrieks during the midnight hour imply the divine verdict on Faustus' life. But on the other hand, the B-text adds a telling scene following on from the death of Faustus. The scholars' decision to 'give his mangled limbs due burial' in hallowed ground demonstrates that they at least have decided to accept the unconventional and seemingly sinful behaviour of Faustus as a by-product of his intellectual greatness; what they describe as practicing 'wondrous knowledge in our German schools' (B: 5.3.13–19).

Witnessing Faustus' final agony, followed by the stage metaphor of seeing his mangled body lying on the stage, in any case, is not conclusive proof for the final damnation of Faustus. The possibility of a facile closure that sees the traditional ban on curiosity and self-determination reinstated would indeed sit very strangely at the end of a play that emphasizes the pervasive nature of ambiguity. The gripping language of his agony at the very least strengthens the bond between Faustus and the spectator while also alluding to contemporary culture's most evocative account of the moment of death: the agony of Christ. While the transition from life to death is undoubtedly accompanied by physical pains, as well as psychological terror about a frightening discontinuation of ego and identity, it is impossible to make any predictions on the basis of these agonies. All we can say is that at the moment of death, the ambiguities of life metamorphose into an absolute ignorance about that which comes afterwards.

The impossibility of gaining any certain knowledge is a deeply disturbing feature of the play. However, it is also the basis for a necessarily sympathetic response of the audience towards Faustus. Angus Fletcher describes how we might recognize ourselves in this rebellious character as follows: '[i]t is less his specific desire for knowledge, or riches, or power that make Faustus appealing than his need to see past his humanness, to find the peace of mind that lurks always in the beyond. Indeed, the triumph of *Faustus* is that the play forces us to participate in the doctor's state of mind, so that we are drawn into sympathy with him even if we do not recognize why.'[55]

Finally, some comments concerning the textual traditions of Marlowe's *Doctor Faustus* are in place. The introduction by David Bevington and Eric Rasmussen

---

54 Alan Sinfield, 'Reading Faustus's God', *Critical Essays on Christopher Marlowe*, ed. Emily Bartels (London: Prentice Hall, 1997), p. 192.

55 Angus Fletcher, '*Doctor Faustus* and the Lutheran Aesthetic', *English Literary Renaissance*, 35 (2005), electronic section VI.

reminds us how strongly the choice of source text affects the general mood of a modern interpretation:

> The excessive reliance until recently on the B-text has had the unfortunate effect of giving us what Michael Keefer aptly calls 'a general relapse from the tragic ironies of the A-version in the direction of the more grotesque features of the Faustbook'.[56]

What Bevington and Rasmussen call 'grotesque features' also positions the drama more immediately within the popular tradition and therefore underlines the play's interrogation of fantasies and projections which thus become recognisable as imaginary entities rather than unshakeable facts.

My interpretation has heavily drawn on the textual revisions and additions of the B-text, conserved in printed form at a time when Marlowe had been dead for over twenty years. Since it is generally assumed that these changes had been made by another hand, I am certainly not trying to claim that the B-text is closer to Marlowe's original intents. When it comes to the attempt to uncover his motivations and artistic design, the uncertain history of textual transmission leaves us no other choice but to speculate. If we should assume that the A-text was indeed closer to Marlowe's heart, Faustus can be interpreted as a Tamburlaine figure, a military conqueror transposed into the field of magic and metaphysics. The Faustus play, then, is primarily a study of power; it is founded on make-believe and tricks of the imagination rather than military weapons.

In this chapter I have argued that the additions of the B-text are more explicit in their reference to the quest for metaphysical truths. In their absence, the play might be seen to dismiss the quest for the sacred as a figment of the imagination that makes people vulnerable to exploitation. However, if drawing the portrait of a power-monger who cannot but destroy himself had been the goal of the play, the fall of Faustus could have been painted in more flamboyant colours. Mephistopheles could have tempted him to extraordinary abuses of his power and he might have been depicted as overreaching himself spectacularly and with great stage-effect. However, already the A-text suggests that metaphysics plays an important role.

Lynn Thorndike reminds us that magic had its origins in scientific curiosity as well as in attempts to gain control over the elements and other human beings.[57] When Marlowe's *Doctor Faustus* explores the nature of magic, therefore, the play portrays a whole range of different types of superstitions and metaphysical abstractions. Rather than arguing that they are all equally founded on deceit and pretence, the play invites us to pay tribute to their intriguing qualities.

------

56 See the introduction to David Bevington's and Eric Rasmussen's edition of *Doctor Faustus* (Manchester: Manchester University Press, 1993), p. 47; the reference for Michael Keefer is to his 'Verbal Magic and the Problem of the A and B Texts of *Doctor Faustus*', *Journal of English and Germanic Philology* (1983): 324–46.

57 Lynn Thorndike, *A History of Magic and Experimental Science during the First Thirteen Centuries of Our Era* (New York: Columbia University Press, 1923).

First and foremost, the play is a study of human motives, appearances and representations. Or as David Riggs argues, 'Marlowe captures the paradox of a culture that taught men not to believe in its own ultimate values'.[58] This is the setting for staging magical rituals that aim to understand the meanings of life and death. The impossibility of knowing any ultimate truths is clearly in the centre of the play. However, if we draw parallels between Faustus and historical investigators of spiritual cosmology, such as Paracelsus or Copernicus, Marlowe's Faustus sheds the garb of a headstrong young man in order to turn into a brilliant scholar capable of challenging the world view of his period. If we therefore read *Doctor Faustus* as a study of the moral dilemmas of an ingenious scholar and his period, the play largely justifies its hero's behaviour. His character demonstrates many weaknesses, but his transgressions do not deserve the eternal damnation demanded by traditional morality.

---

58 Riggs, *The World of Christopher Marlowe*, p. 241.

Chapter 4

The Alternative Worlds
of the New Science:
Burton, Milton and Fontenelle

The changing attitudes of the seventeenth century towards scientific enquiry generated a great deal of uncertainty about the social relevance of new methodologies and new topics of investigation. This study will draw attention to the human motives behind the emergence of these changing attitudes towards discovery and exploration. At issue are the expectations and emotional energies invested in the study of nature. The desire to expand knowledge has been described as the most prominent objective of this century. Such a grand commitment to progress could only be formulated in hindsight, though. It fails to take account of a myriad of individual initiatives that converged into a far-reaching transformation of the period's intellectual landscape. What has subsequently come to be described as the new science of the early modern period therefore harboured promises for people from a vast range of backgrounds.

The desire to see and experience the mysterious facts of nature was a powerful incentive driving the period's scientific investigations. Such explorations were largely conducted in the spirit of secularization, but they could also be regarded as a vehicle for achieving metaphysical insights. This is why Richard Yeo reminds us that although curiosity was treated with a good deal of suspicion in this period, 'the quest for knowledge of the natural world [was] a crucial part of man's attempt to be again at one with God'.[1] The contemplative study of nature had never been banned in the first place. But since the interpretation of observed facts and phenomena could come into conflict with contemporary beliefs about man's place in the universe, scientific scholars continued to be treated with reservation. The philosophical musings of the medical practitioner Robert Burton, therefore, assert the religious and moral integrity of the scientific scholar so that he can embark on the analysis of controversial issues without incurring the accusation of heresy.

Scientific inquiry increasingly offered itself as a rational investigation of human needs. The secularizing tendencies of science, however, were not necessarily its chief recommendation. Many simply resorted to the new science as an instrument for investigating topics that were not permitted by traditional theology. While

---

1 Richard Yeo, *Encyclopedic Visions: Scientific Dictionaries and Enlightenment Culture* (Cambridge: Cambridge University Press, 2001), pp. 2–3.

the daring intellectuals of the seventeenth century no longer had to defend their scientific curiosity, they were nevertheless accused of promoting heterodoxies or even downright heresies. The desire to discover the secrets of nature was theologically acceptable but the attempt to make sense of new observations could still run into difficulties. Although caught up in serious dogmatic controversies, Church authorities retained a great deal of influence over the definition of human nature. The overarching significance of the Scriptures explains the emergence of, for example, Thomas Burnet's *Sacred Theory of the Earth* (1684),[2] an energetic attempt to reconcile the biblical creation story with the most advanced scientific theories of the period. But many early modern intellectuals felt discomfited by the incongruities between religious and scientific attempts to reveal meaning and purpose behind natural phenomena. In the course of the seventeenth century, this task really became more, rather than less, difficult. When William Harvey's *The Circulation of the Blood* (1628) described the heart as the 'sun of our microcosm',[3] he could give vent to a spontaneous fascination for the beauty and intelligence of the body's interior design without pondering the dogmatic implications of his metaphor. As is instanced by Robert Hooke's cautious use of figurative language in his *Micrographia* (1665), scientific writers became increasingly self-conscious about the implications of their revisionary descriptions of organic processes.[4]

Many of the new scientific discoveries and inventions revised or even overturned theories about the functioning of the body or the cosmos that had been established by antique authorities. The attempt to assess the cultural significance of the new theories therefore inspired an imaginary competition between the aims and objectives of the ancients and the moderns. In his *Dialogues of the Dead* (1683), Bernard le Bovier de Fontenelle, for example, stages a fictional dialogue between the antique physician Erasistratus and William Harvey, during which the early modern pioneer is asked to assess his achievements in the light of his period's responses. He says:

> Since I have found out the Circulation of the Blood, 'tis now a matter of Emulation who shall find out a new Conveyance, a new Canal, or a new Reservatory: It appears as if the whole Man were new cast.[5]

---

2   Thomas Burnet, *Sacred Theory of the Earth: Containing an Account of the Original of the Earth, and of all the General Changes which It Hath Already Undergone, or is to Undergo, Till the Consummation of All Things* (London: printed for John Hooke, 1719).

3   William Harvey, *The Circulation of the Blood* (1628), trans. Kenneth J. Franklin and Andrew Wear (London: Everyman, 1990), pp. 46–7.

4   Cf. Christa Knellwolf, 'Robert Hooke's *Micrographia* and the Aesthetics of Empiricism', *The Seventeenth Century* 16.1 (2001): 177–200.

5   Bernard le Bovier de Fontenelle, *Dialogues of the Dead*, trans. John Hughes (London: printed for Jacob Tonson, 1708), p. 86.

As the fictional Harvey is made to admit, his discovery has not simply fired the zeal of enthusiastic imitators, but has actually encouraged modern anatomists to expect that organic bodies contain additional circulatory systems. Far from being an isolated discovery, Harvey's work represents a turning point in contemporary beliefs about the body. Scientific explorers had learnt to think differently. They had changed beliefs about the very nature of the human body, hardly considering themselves to be examining the same object as their predecessors.

Although the act of exploring the secrets of nature had managed to discard any vestiges of sinfulness, the pursuit of scientific questions encountered many objections. It was claimed that large amounts of financial resources were squandered for no real reason. Scientific investigation of, for example, the minutiae of living organisms, was also thought to incapacitate a commonsensical assessment of the nature and purpose of different beings. In an *Essay Concerning Human Understanding* (1689), John Locke objected to the use of the microscope because it duped scholars, such as Marcello Malpighi, who used the microscope to prove that the body is 'an ensemble of micromachines whose true structures and operations are invisible to normal vision'.[6] Locke claimed that the microscope did not necessarily expand the optical capacities of its users but instead disturbed the customary perspective of human experience.[7] Discussion of the enlightening or obfuscating potential of optical instruments illustrates some of the difficulties encountered when early modern society tried to come to grips with its period's dramatically changing ideas about knowledge and progress. The most widespread objection to the cognoscenti of the new science must have been that they occupied themselves with trivial matters. When viewed in the light of the moral imperative of the period, waste of time was tantamount to a failure to ponder the issues that would enable their moral progress.

It was common through the period for parodic criticism and ridicule to be levelled at the new science. For the most part this was the response of an intelligent but otherwise ignorant lay audience who failed to see any deeper sense in the practical investigations of scientists and scientific organisations, such as the English Royal Society. This attitude was not altogether unjustified since scientific explorations had not yet yielded much useful and reliable information. Not even the intelligentsia of the period were sure about the course of scientific progress, even though it was convinced that ground-breaking transformations were under way.

There was a great deal of optimism about the benefits of a disciplined investigation of the natural world but there was also concern that the new science challenged established interpretations of nature. Bernard le Bovier de Fontenelle,

---

6   Catherine Wilson, *The Invisible World: Early Modern Philosophy and the Invention of the Microscope* (Princeton: Princeton University Press, 1995), p. 97. For John Locke's comments on the problematic benefits of the microscope, see *Works* (Aalen: Scientia Verlag, 1963), vol. 2: 3.6.24, p. 223.

7   For a discussion of the controversies over the microscopic discoveries of the seventeenth century, see Knellwolf, 'Robert Hooke's *Micrographia*', pp. 192–3.

the spokesman for the French Academy of Science, devoted most of his later life to making the new theories of the cosmos accessible to a wider audience. His most widely read popularisation of Cartesian physics, *Entretiens sur la pluralité des mondes* (1686), describes these theories' frightening claims about the insignificance of the earth. Although offering a challenging intellectual outlook, he does not adopt the voice of a prophet of doom. His recommended solution to the problem is to instil a profound curiosity about the concrete facts of a cosmic system that had been shown to consist of planets and stars revolving on infinitely complex orbits.

The scientific developments of the seventeenth century would no doubt have been to the taste of Faustus, had he been resuscitated in a fictional form as a witness of the period. But no attempts were made to re-invent the Faustus figure for the main part of this century. It nevertheless retained its presence in contemporary imagination, but did so mainly through the continuing performance of Marlowe's play. That William Mountfort concluded a century that saw the rise of the new science with *The Life and Death of Doctor Faustus Made into a Farce* (1697), however, is a telling coincidence. I will discuss Mountfort's Faustus play in the context of other comic adaptations of the topology in the next chapter. Here I want to concentrate on fictions that encouraged the inquisitive minds of the period to persevere in their investigations. At first sight the absence of contemporary versions of the Faustus legend might suggest that its concerns had lost their relevance. The fact that the Faustus theme not only resurfaced but indeed turned into a major theme of early eighteenth-century popular culture suggests that the Faustus typology never lost its salience. But I will return to this later.

This chapter examines some prominent literary examples from the seventeenth century that utilized the imagery and theoretical support of the new science. Robert Burton's carefully argued justification of the new approaches to studying the nature of life allows us to consider him as a historical version of Faustus. Contrasted with the seventeenth-century scientist are two diametrically opposed literary figures. It may appear a random choice to contrast the poetic visions of John Milton with Fontenelle's polite but rational portrayal of the social reception of new theories in astronomy, but doing so highlights some striking parallels in their respective representations of the principles that hold the cosmos together. While Milton scholarship has recognized that his work embraces Gnostic portrayals of mankind's place in creation,[8] Fontenelle is committed to a consistently rational interpretation of mystical and otherwise hard-to-explain phenomena. Milton's drama about the forces of creation goes to great length to convey both the rational and metaphysical dimensions of heaven and the heavens. By contrast, Fontenelle's illustration of Cartesian astronomy describes the planetary and stellar revolutions as if they were beautiful machinery. Although frighteningly vast, it is reassuring

---

8   See for example A.D. Nuttall, *The Alternative Trinity: Gnostic Heresy in Marlowe, Milton, and Blake* (Oxford: Clarendon Press, 1998).

because it lacks superhuman agents that threaten to destroy the rationale of the creation.

However strongly they might have been opposed in their views about the significance of the new science, most prominent scholars of the seventeenth century shared the conviction that scientific studies opened up new intellectual perspectives and new opportunities, for individuals and society as a whole. Although the personages chosen to represent the spirit of their age did not engage in a direct dialogue, my contrastive analysis of their arguments and aesthetics allows us to grasp some of the period's changing self-perception and visions for the future. Analysis of their representations of what constitutes progress and advancement of knowledge, then, helps us understand the controversies behind the establishment of the Enlightenment as a major period in western thought.

Thomas Browne's Self-definition as a Scientist

The seventeenth century brought forth many scurrilous thinkers who welded together idiosyncratic interpretations of a wide range of materials and physical phenomena. One of the most remarkable intellectuals to muddle himself through contemporary controversies and conflicts was Thomas Browne, a mature and confident thinker who sought to understand how his own beliefs fitted into the traditional outlook of Christianity. Many scholars fondly remember Browne's description of the minutiae of creation: 'Who admires not *Regio-Montanus* his Fly beyond his Eagle, or wonders not more at the operation of two souls in those little bodies, than but one in the trunck of a Cedar?' (I.15).[9] The heterodox nature of his beliefs is disguised by the warmth with which he expresses his views on the beauty and perfection of God's creation.[10] While he openly committed himself to Christianity, his circuitous formulations played hide and seek with those who tried to identify his precise beliefs. When he claims that '[a]t the sight of a Crosse or Crucifix I can dispence with my hat, but scarce with the thought and memory of my Saviour' (I.3) he is making sure that no religious faction can find fault with his argument. But he also emphasized his generally devout submission to Christian dogma as a justification for transgressing it in some particular respects. We will never find out to what extent he used Christianity as a convenient façade. His circuitous and indirect formulations, however, suggest an uncomfortable attitude towards Christian belief while his heterodox claims show him to have wavered between scepticism, natural religion and the formal conventions of Christianity.

---

9   All quotations from *Religio Medici* are from Thomas Browne, *The Prose of Sir Thomas Browne* (Garden City, NY: Anchor Books, 1967).

10 For a discussion of how Browne managed to escape from accusations of heresy, see Don Cameron Allen, *Doubt's Boundless Sea: Skepticism and Faith in the Renaissance* (Baltimore: Johns Hopkins University Press, 1964), pp. 7–8.

The contradictory quality of Browne's treatise is typical of early modern self-analytical prose. Writing in a landscape of fierce religious conflict, Browne may have been particularly careful to remain within Christian perimeters. In spite of his circumspection, there are parallels between his treatise and the chapbooks and dramas about Faustus, which likewise examined the nature of belief. My analysis of his fragmentary and frequently contradictory treatise will shed light on the preconceptions of those early modern intellectuals who were exploring the nature of reality and struggling to understand the self at a time when traditional religious and social practices were being challenged.

The contrast between Browne's frank admiration for the perfect little body of '*Regio-Montanus* his fly' and his indirect, almost grudging affirmation of Christian practices shows that he is arguing along at least two different lines. Borrowing Francis Bacon's differentiation between the book of nature and the book of God, he explains:

> Thus are there two books from whence I collect my Divinity; besides that written one of God, another of his servant Nature, that universall and public Manuscript, that lies expans'd unto the eyes of all: those that never saw him in the one, have discovered him in the other: This was the Scripture and Theology of the Heathens: the naturall motion of the Sun made them more admire him, than its supernaturall station did the Children of Israel; ... surely the Heathens knew better how to joyne and reade these mysticall letters, than we Christians, who ... disdain to suck Divinity from the flowers of nature. (I.16)

Browne's descriptions of nature are pervaded by a pantheistic spirit that squares ill with the received wisdom of Christianity. However, this passage also highlights some intrinsic parallels between all forms of beliefs, particular in so far as their spiritual truths are based on sensory observation. Browne's voice burgeons with passion and his language conveys a palpable sense of how metaphysics manifests itself in the physical world. Although his treatise embraces a detailed study of his beliefs, it refuses to remain on the purely argumentative level but proposes a need for knowing the emotional foundation or manifestation of belief.

The rhetorical polish of *Religio Medici* indicates that it was intended for an audience. It was nevertheless conceived as a private meditation in which Browne identified and justified his beliefs to himself. First published in 1642 without the author's knowledge and re-published in 1643 in corrected form, it turned into an immediate bestseller in which his period recognized some of its most urgent concerns.[11] Its popularity must be the consequence of its courageous commitment to answering the following question: how can the pioneers of natural history identify with a religion that is at odds with the scientific interpretation of the world? Browne's

---

11 For a discussion of the book's reception and contemporary relevance, see Andrew Cunningham, 'Sir Thomas Browne and his *Religio Medici*: Reason, Nature and Religion', *Religio Medici: Medicine and Religion in Seventeenth-Century England*, eds. Ole Peter Grell and Andrew Cunningham (Aldershot: Scolar Press, 1996), pp. 12–61.

discourse advocates religious tolerance. But it also goes further. By contrast with the slightly later philosopher John Locke, whose medical background did not enter into his philosophical reasoning, Browne is clearly exploring his period's religious controversies as a doctor of medicine. Hence his annoyance that his first-hand knowledge of life and death is derogatively referred to as 'the generall scandal of my profession' (I.1). While arguing for the moral integrity of his profession, he also insists that it is not acceptable to escape into one's own private thoughts. At a time when the entire population of his country was embroiled in religious conflicts, it was imperative to make a stand. The natural philosopher's familiarity with the mysteries of creation, he suggests, were an invaluable background for re-introducing a cool-headed approach to spiritual matters.

The stated objective of *Religio Medici* is to refute the world's suspicions that practitioners of the medical profession have no religion (I.1). Browne accordingly commits himself to the core tenets of Christianity and says: 'I desire to exercise my faith in the difficultest points, for to credit ordinary and visible objects is not faith, but perswasion' (I.9). When he delves into arguments concerning the reasons and causes of creation, he freely accepts and rejects dogmatic points and openly subscribes to hermetic traditions: 'The severe Schooles shall never laugh me out of the Philosophy of *Hermes*, that this visible World is but a picture of the invisible, wherein, as in a pourtract, things are not truly, but in equal shapes, and as they counterfeit some more reall substance in that invisible fabrick.' (I.12). Does it surprise us that he believed in the existence of witches and spirits (I.30)?

Browne also ruminates on the nature of the devil: 'I am halfe of opinion that Antichrist is the Philosophers stone in Divinity, for the discovery and invention whereof, though there be prescribed rules and probable inductions, yet hath hardly any man attained the perfect discovery thereof' (I.46). His terminology recalls the empiricist method and his use of 'discovery and invention' reflect the contemporary desire to expand the existing perimeters of knowledge. 'Probable inductions' is a clear allusion to Bacon's scientific terminology. When Browne qualifies 'induction' by the adjective 'probable', he admits that the formulation of axioms in the spiritual world is unorthodox, but he clearly thinks that doing so is a step towards the discovery of important truths.

In the above quotation, Browne freely mingles scholastic theology, alchemy, magic and Baconian induction. He also shows himself to have been exposed to a whole range of badly digested arguments coming from a range of different sources. While this demonstrates a lack of argumentative rigour it also marks his attempt to pin down exactly what he believes. His descriptions can enmesh modern scientific practice with alchemical traditions precisely because the separation between science (in the modern understanding of the word) and other forms of enquiry have not yet taken place. In the course of the eighteenth century, the new science would achieve an increasingly rigid separation from the more emotional aspects of human existence, but Browne's argument shows that a seventeenth-century intellectual was still greatly puzzled by the relevance of the new philosophy for moral and theological questions.

Even though his stated aim is to demonstrate himself as a good Christian who does not question the basic articles of faith, his meditations bring forth a motley race of heterodoxies. He certainly hedges his bets and introduces his claim by 'I am halfe of opinion'. Not only does he emphasize that he is merely speculating here, but he is consciously utilizing the act of writing as a heuristic process that should help him make up his mind. The provocative claim that 'Antichrist is the Philosopher's stone in Divinity' is therefore presented as an experiment of the imagination. Given that alchemical traditions define the philosopher's stone as a spiritual substance that can bring about the transformation of a base into a valuable substance, Browne's claim boils down to defining the devil as an indispensable element whose existence guarantees the logical cogency of religious arguments. Browne's seemingly random juggling of logical conundrums is therefore motivated by the wish to reveal a coherent and meaningful view of the creation. Rather than a simple agent of evil, the devil becomes a necessary element in an immensely complex tapestry of reasons and causes.

Although Browne is far removed from the soul-searching confessions of a Jean Jacques Rousseau, he allows us a glimpse into the inner landscape of a historical character who was intensely aware of the dangers of religious controversies. Since the accusation of heresy continued to be a real danger during the religious struggles of the seventeenth century, Browne hides behind various rhetorical ploys. When he investigates his beliefs about miracles, he invokes the devil in the material guise of folk tradition and concludes the section with the following image: 'Thus the Devill played at Chesse with mee, and yielding a pawne, thought to gaine a Queen of me, taking advantage of my honest endeavours; and whilst I laboured to raise the structure of my reason, hee striv'd to undermine the edifice of my faith' (I.19). The image of the devil as trickster and shrewd opponent in a real contest positions Browne's philosophy within stereotypical views about the nature of transgression. But while he describes himself as having been insecure about his own beliefs, he refuses to remain silent about his doubts and queries. Like the Faustus figure, he insists on exploring exactly where he stands in relation to his period's competing beliefs.

While the Faustus stories purport to punish an inquisitive mind which crassly breached his period's prohibitions against meddling with superhuman powers, Browne justifies minor transgressions that are consistent with the rules of reason. In spite of its evasiveness and indirection, *Religio Medici* implies that outdated rules need to be replaced with guidelines appropriate to human nature as it is and not as it should be. Browne therefore argues that 'there are no Grotesques in nature' and that all creatures show the wisdom of the creator (I.15). He also takes for granted an essential goodness underlying the creation of man and world, which is why the wish to know comes to be treated as a tacitly accepted form of natural piety.

The unauthorized edition embellished the title page with an engraving that Browne chose to retain in his corrected version of 1643 (Figure 3). Andrew Cunningham comments that the image 'shows what is probably an Icarus-figure seeking to reach the heaven by his own efforts, and in his fall being rescued by the hand of God'.[12] The positive conclusion to this classical myth documents Carlo Ginzburg's argument that significant changes were taking place in the emblematic representation of intellectual curiosity during the seventeenth century.[13] Modelling his images on Andrea Alciati's collection of emblems published in 1535, Geoffrey Whitney still represented the old view and showed Icarus falling miserably to his doom. The accompanying verse gives the following moral:

> Let such beware, which paste theire reache doe mounte,
> Who seeke the thinges, to mortall men deny'de, ...
> Least as they clime, they fall to theire decaye.[14]

While Florentius Schoonhovius still punishes the sacrilegious Icarus-Phaëton for his hubristic aspirations with a pitiable fall into the sea in 1618, intellectual curiosity comes to be valorised and *'sapere aude'*, dare to know, is turning into the motto of the age. So in 1686, Anselme de Boot is showing an Icarus who is peacefully gliding over the sea, entitling his image with a bold variant of the familiar phrase: *'Nil linquere inausum'*: leave nothing un-risked, or dare everything.

In the light of this development we can make better sense of the frontispiece to Browne's treatise. It shows a falling figure whose right hand is stretched out towards the abyss in expectation of perishing. But at the same time the hand of God is extended from above, clasping his left hand firmly and securely in order to save him from destruction. Further important elements of the image are the complete isolation of the intellectual. Cunningham argues that the iconography of 'falling from the rock has an ancient Stoic meaning: to plummet from tranquillity, steadfastness and self-control into the storms of tempestuousness and despair'.[15] But although the rock in the background is rugged and isolated, it does not express inevitable destruction. The trajectory of the Icarus-figure, therefore, was not from tranquillity to despair. The symbolic mountain he abandoned may have provided physical safety but it also signified the lonely miseries of a troubled mind. Although unable to leap into heaven by his own strength, he encounters God when he risks falling to his doom. When Browne prefixes his work with the idea of an uncompromising thinker who gains support from above, he speaks in favour of all those who struggled and stumbled on their quests for meaning.

---

12 Cunningham, 'Reason, Nature and Religion', p. 20.

13 Carlo Ginzburg, 'High and Low: The Theme of Forbidden Knowledge in the Sixteenth and Seventeenth Centuries', *Past and Present* 73 (1976): 28–41.

14 Geoffrey Whitney, *A Choice of Emblemes* (Leyden: Francis Raphelengius, 1586), p. 28.

15 Cunningham, 'Reason, Nature and Religion', p. 20.

Fig. 3   Frontispiece of Thomas Browne's *Religio Medici*, in *The Prose of Sir Thomas Browne*, Garden City, NY: Anchor Books, 1967.

Knowledge and the Inner Light: Milton's *Paradise Lost*

Doctrine was a seminal concern of Milton's life: as a young man his conscience rebelled at the tyranny that had invaded the church, and he could not but conclude that 'he who would take orders must subscribe slave and take an oath withal, which ... he must either straight perjure, or split his faith'.[16] Although his late work *Christian Doctrine* (rediscovered in manuscript form only in 1823) sought to formulate a dogmatic position based exclusively on scriptural precedent, he also opposed the crippling influence of prescribed formulae for most of his life. In particular, he sought to refute the religious views about the natural depravity of human nature and hence attacked the foundation of Protestant theories of salvation. As a Protestant who embraced Reformed theology as a means of following the call of his inner light, Milton particularly objected to the anti-humanistic bent of Presbyterian theology and sympathized instead with mystic beliefs that God manifests himself in each and every one. From an early age, Milton committed himself to the humanist notion that there was an 'ideal humanity to which mankind might be educated'.[17]

The idea of the essential goodness of the human soul informed Milton's conviction that a careful questioning of religious tenets brings to light spiritual truths, which is why he was outraged at the threat of censorship. In *Areopagitica* (1644), he sketched a vision of personal growth and public justice emerging from the religious controversies of a troubled decade:

> Methinks I see in my mind a noble and puissant nation rousing herself like a strong man after sleep, and shaking her invincible locks; methinks I see her as an eagle mewing [renewing] her mighty youth, and kindling her undazzled eyes at the full midday beam; purging and unscaling her long-abused sight at the fountain itself of heavenly radiance; while the whole noise of timorous and flocking birds, with those also that love the twilight, flutter about, amazed at what she means, and in their envious gabble would prognosticate a year of sects and schisms.[18]

What comes across as chaos and disintegration, argues Milton, is indeed a phase of renewal. He would undoubtedly have agreed that the 1640s were a difficult time and that a great deal of political and personal integrity were required to master its challenges. But he was also convinced that during this decade it had become possible to establish the idea that both political and religious relationships required the consent of the individual. Both church and state came to be understood as

---

16 Milton, *Church Government*, in *Prose Works: Miscellanies*, 3 vols. (London, 1909), vol. 2, p. 482.

17 Cf. Margaret Lewis Bailey, *Milton and Jacob Boehme: A Study of German Mysticism in Seventeenth-Century England* (New York: Haskell House, 1964), p. 64.

18 All references to *Paradise Lost* are to John Milton, *Complete English Poems, Of Education, Areopagitica*, ed. Gordon Campbell (London: Everyman, 1993), pp. 611–12.

organizations founded on a set of contracts between individuals. And most importantly, these contracts were believed to be subject to revision.

Elsewhere in *Areopagitica*, Milton argues that 'God is decreeing to begin some new and great period in his church, even to the reforming of Reformation itself: what does he then but reveal himself to his servant'.[19] Following on from his rejection of anybody or anything that could mediate between the individual and God is Milton's belief that it is impossible to prescribe the modalities of the encounter between the human being and God. Awareness of Milton's wholehearted acceptance of the belief in an inner light, along with its implications for a radically personal experience of spiritual truths, adds another dimension to Milton's portrayal of the creation in *Paradise Lost*. It has frequently been pointed out that his vision of a rational and controlled universe belongs to the sphere of the anthropomorphized God of Christianity, who is challenged by alternative belief systems. While questioning the stereotypical figure of Yahweh, however, Milton would have been the last person to oppose order and rationality. This also means that although *Paradise Lost* dramatizes a clash between different dogmas,[20] Milton would not have wanted to do away with dogma. His daily experience during the decade of civil war and the ensuing Interregnum vividly illustrated the chaos resulting from the absence of a shared code of beliefs and religious practices. The poem's descriptions of spiritual insight nevertheless escape from any clearly identifiable religious denomination. It manifests a palpable sense of order and expresses a tacit notion that, though metaphysical issues are accessible to scientific investigation, there is something at the core of rationality that radically escapes from its dictates. My interpretation of the poem examines the portrayal of knowledge and divine rationality. By concentrating on the spiritual potentialities associated particularly with the poem's symbolism of light, it seeks to explain the cross-fertilizing influences between the period's new scientific theories and its attempts to legitimate the emotional subjectivity of mystical experiences.

Order and Creativity in *Paradise Lost*

It is generally accepted that Milton's imagination was strongly affected by the new science of the seventeenth century.[21] It is no surprise, therefore, that his cosmology is dramatized in a space that is both vast and clearly structured. Although it begins at a time that significantly antedates the biblical story of origin, the setting of Milton's *Paradise Lost* (1667) is always subjected to the unalterable laws of nature. Every act of creation is rigidly controlled and nothing is left to chance or simply allowed to unfold at random. The creative act required to bring

---

19 Milton, *Complete English Poems*, p. 609.

20 Cf. Nuttall, *Alternative Trinity*.

21 Cf. Dennis Richard Danielson, ed., *The Cambridge Companion to Milton* (Cambridge: Cambridge University Press, 1989).

into existence the world of Adam and Eve, for example, gives material shape to a carefully designed scheme. The anthropomorphic figure of God is imagined to be a craftsman whose acts of creation follow the principles of the new science, but whether he calls these principles into existence himself or simply applies them is not quite clear.

Even Pandemonium, the imitated world of Satan, adopts the same cosmic laws and is built according to the most accurate principles of neo-classical architecture:

Anon out of the earth a fabric huge
Rose like an exhalation, with the sound
Of dulcet symphonies and voices sweet –
Built like a temple, where pilasters round
Were set and Doric pillars overlaid
With golden architrave ... (1.710–14)

Pandemonium is Satan's arrogant imitation of God's kingdom, but Satan can only construct his realm with the help of tricks. But this idea renders it conceivable that the process of building God's world required similar tricks:

... from the arched roof,
Pendent by subtle magic, many a row
Of starry lamps and blazing cressets, fed
With naphtha and asphaltus, yielded light
As from a sky. (1.727–30)

Satan's word is enfolded within Yahweh's universe like a small copy *mise-en-abîme*. It comes across as a small model that permits insight into the principles of construction. The explanation that Satan needs to obtain fuel for the light of his 'starry lamps', indeed, offers a scientifically informed perspective on the nature of all cosmic bodies. From undefined entities, the stars come to be defined as celestial bodies whose light is the result of an ongoing process of combustion.

Pandemonium is both a parallel and a rhetorical antithesis, or inversion, of the authentic creation by Yahweh: Satan encloses in an interior space what originally was the exterior of a vast universe. Although it is taken for granted that the creative ingenuity of Satan is inferior to Yahweh's, both of them equally have to deal with the laws of nature. The forces of gravity, first described by the young Isaac Newton in 1665 (two years before the publication of *Paradise Lost*), apply as rigidly to Pandemonium as to the design of Yahweh's new 'pendent world ... hanging in a golden chain ... close by the moon' (2.1051–3). The poem's reformulation of the biblical story of creation (3.708–34) is closely modelled on the words of *Genesis*.[22] By contrast with *Genesis*, however, *Paradise Lost* does not equate the earth with

22 Also compare Raphael's more detailed narrative of Creation, VII, 216–547.

the entirety of the created universe. As a backdrop to the familiar narrative about the separation of order from chaos, and light from darkness, there is an already created universe. So the poem begins with the moment when its space is subdivided into the realms of Heaven and Pandemonium. The existence of gravity, however, antedates both the creation of the heavenly cosmos and its hellish imitation.

The contrast between God's laws and the laws of nature strengthens the frequently observed tensions between the poem's stated objective 'to justify the ways of God to men' (1.26) and a deep yearning to celebrate the mysterious forces of nature. Although unacknowledged as a conscious intention, descriptions of the divine brilliance of the sun sparkle with overwhelming beauty while they also express a type of natural rationality that challenges Yahweh's power of control.[23] Portrayals of the archaic forces of nature reflect almost magical precision but they are also opposed to a certain sense of order and control.

The kind of knowledge, which features as the single prohibition in the world of Adam and Eve, is closely connected to the pervasive presence of control. The inhabitants of the new world are not initially privy to the knowledge about the old conflicts between Yahweh and Satan. Adam and Eve are nevertheless always aware that they live in a tightly controlled world. They admire God's ingenious design of plants, rocks and animals and they spend countless hours appreciating the colour, shape and light effects that embellish their paradisiacal world. The narrative voice of the poem repeatedly asserts that the entire space of Paradise was created for their needs and pleasures. And although only the Tree of Knowledge is forbidden, not even knowledge as such is absent from their world. They are indeed encouraged to explore and admire the intricacies of Paradise because the examination of its ingenious features will reveal the superior craftsmanship of the Creator. But however beautiful and noble Paradise may be, they are confined to its circumference. The knowledge that is forbidden to them is therefore intricately linked to their equally forbidden access to the remaining spaces of the universe.

Paradise is also otherwise incomplete. When Adam describes the first moment of existence to Raphael, he talks about his initial query as to his own nature and origin and reports that he naturally concluded that he must have been called into existence by the hand of 'some great maker' (8.288). He explains that the act of addressing the sun and the paradisiacal landscape (8.273–4) was his first gesture of being and reports that his first speech consisted of a request that they should:

> Tell me how I may know him, how adore,
> From whom I have that thus I move and live,
> And feel that I am happier than I know. (8.289–91)

The piousness of his first desire is answered with a dream that presents him with a guide:

---

23 Cf., for example, the opening of Book III.

... by the hand he took me, raised
And over fields and waters, as in air
Smooth sliding without step ... (8.300–302)

The spiritual journey experienced during his dream turns out to be reality, which confirms that it must have been a spiritual revelation. His first moment of consciousness liberates him briefly from the forces of gravity. Although the blissful union with his guide, who can be nobody else but his creator, is brief, its fleeting presence suggests that such a union continues to be a real possibility and not simply an irrecoverable memory.

During Adam's visionary dream, Yahweh 'mildly' describes himself as 'author of all this thou seest / Above, or round about thee, or beneath' (8.316–17), but the ecstatic moment is cut short by the introduction of the forbidden tree. Yahweh explains that it embodies:

Knowledge of good and ill, which I have set
The pledge of thy obedience and thy faith   (8.324–5)

The God of *Paradise Lost* does not encourage his creatures to indulge in a spontaneous overflow of powerful emotions but demands strict obedience and submission. A loving relationship between creator and creature appears to be out of the question because this would put them on an almost equal footing. Adam therefore remembers it as a frightful moment when '[s]ternly he pronounced / The rigid interdiction, which resounds / Yet dreadful in mine ear' (8.333–5). When the paradise of this loving union between creator and creature is broken, Adam finds himself abandoned and lonely. Adam's narrative hardly dares to refer to his disappointment. But it is a telling coincidence that it is only after God has rebuffed Adam's wish for closeness that he requests a companion to share the experience of Paradise (8.363ff). In other words, it is the moment of rejection that gives rise to Adam's wishes and desires. The acute pain of being severed from his creator only establishes his fundamental humanity, defined by what Margaret Lewis Bailey describes as the 'two eternal, elemental passions of the self, the desire for love and the desire for knowledge'.[24]

In spite of its emphasis on order and rationality, the world of *Paradise Lost* is not devoid of emotion and Raphael poignantly confirms in his dialogue with Adam that 'without love no happiness' (8.621). In his theoretical work on Christian dogma, Milton likewise emphasizes the overarching significance of love. For example, he explains that Christ's statement that 'I and my Father are one' mean that they are so 'not in essence, but in love, in communion, in agreement, in charity, in spirit, in glory'.[25] Love characterizes the relationship between God and Christ. The

---

24 Bailey, *Milton and Jakob Boehme*, p. 6.
25 John Milton, *Treatise on Christian Doctrine*, 2 vols. (London, 1904), vol. 1, p. 92.

rigid distance between God and Adam, and, of course, between God and Satan, conversely, is a source of pain that stirs sparks of discontent and rebellion.

Although Adam receives a deserving female companion, he is constantly reminded that he lives in a world of order and control, which, to make matters worse, bars him from the knowledge that could overcome the distance to his creator. The rules of Paradise deny self-consciousness, and leave him unable to understand and judge himself and his surroundings. Most importantly, he remains incapable of experiencing moments of mystic union that might enable him to grasp that 'God is both subject and object' and understand that because God is inborn within us all, there is 'the spirit or "inner light" from Him, we can know Him and all things as well'.[26] As is demonstrated by Raphael's detailed accounts of the history and nature of Adam's world, knowledge as such is not forbidden. Raphael admits, '[t]o ask or search I blame thee not, for heaven / Is as the book of God before thee set' (8.66–7). Adam is indeed to rule over the inhabitants of Paradise 'with such knowledge God endued' (8.353), meaning that he is given an abundance of factual knowledge but he is not given what he wants. Raphael admonishes him to 'be lowly wise' and tells him:

'Dream not of other worlds, what creatures there
Live, in what state, condition, or degree –
Contented that thus far hath been revealed
Not of earth only, but of highest heaven.' (8.173–8)

When Raphael reminds Adam that he must be satisfied with the store of knowledge granted to him, he confirms the ban on 'matters hid' (8.167). His cautioning speech, however, is embedded in an enticing account of the revelations waiting to be seen if Adam should disregard the prohibition. Although he emphasizes the irrelevance of cosmic phenomena for Adam's existence, the archangel adopts the voice of the seducer, knowing full well that his hints about the gendered sympathies between 'male and female light' and the attractions between sun and moon must whet the appetite of Adam's vibrant intellect (8.150–67).

Although Copernicus's cosmic system is depicted as a hypothesis and declared as an unsuitable concern of the newly created human being, Raphael nevertheless takes Adam on a similar journey through the heavens as that which 'pleases the eyes of Faustus'.[27] It is true that Milton portrayed no 'compendious method of natural philosophy',[28] but he nevertheless shows extensive familiarity with the Copernican theory, which had established itself as general knowledge by the

---

26 Bailey, *Milton and Jakob Boehme*, p. 14.

27 'And what might please mine eye I there beheld.' Marlowe, *Doctor Faustus*, B: 3.1.68–72. Also compare the passage in the English Faust Book: 'The desire of thy heart, mind and thought shalt thou see', EFB, p. 123.

28 Kester Svendsen, *Milton and Science* (Cambridge, MA: Harvard University Press, 1956), p. 43.

mid-seventeenth century. But he is not concerned mainly with the attempt to elucidate Copernican astronomy and instead aims to explore why it captivated the imagination of the period's intellectuals. In this sense, Adam resembles Faustus; both crave knowledge about what exactly it is that keeps the planets and stars on their orbits. Scientific facts, however, are less important than the attempt to grasp the meaning and feel of the vastness of space. Adam also wants to know

> How nature, wise and frugal, could commit
> Such disproportions, with superfluous hand
> So many nobler bodies to create,
> Greater so manifold ... (8.26–9)

Adam identifies nature as the originator of the material world and takes for granted a female creative principle that rivals the traditional figure of the Creator. He therefore draws attention to the superabundance of objects called into existence: the 'many bodies' created by 'her' ambiguously refer both to the numerous celestial bodies that could be identified by the contemporary telescope and their hypothetical inhabitants. Adam is therefore rebuked for his interest in the spaces beyond the precincts of Paradise, not only because he wants to know whether there are creatures like him anywhere else in the universe but because he is pondering the possible existence of other gods, or spirits, besides Yahweh, who might likewise possess the power to create.

Adam opens a can of worms when he examines the rationale of nature. In particular, he demonstrates that he has sensed the paradox between the idea of the single godhead and its/his separation into different creative principles or agents, which can both act in mutual understanding (as with Yahweh and nature), or aim to subvert each other's achievements (as with Yahweh and Satan). When *Paradise Lost* asserts that 'God and nature bid the same' (6.176) and 'God shall be all in all' (3.341), it adumbrates the existence of a transformative power that brings about a convergence between the anthropomorphized figures and the abstract principles. But the why and how of such mystical-symbolic transformations remains unexplained.

A related puzzle is the question of why Adam is forbidden knowledge of the inhabited worlds, yet is given a lengthy description of the original clash between Satan and Yahweh. The present state of the universe clearly belongs to that which 'concerns [Adam] and [his] being' (8.174). But anything beyond the limited pale of Paradise is withheld from him. The reason for this is that knowledge of beings like him, or more noble and therefore godlike, would leave him no rest until he had fashioned means of reaching out to them. By specifying some forbidden activities and warning him against the construction of machinery for reaching other beings, Raphael gives him a few hints about the tasks to which he might devote his intellect and imagination: 'nor let thine own inventions hope / Things not revealed' (7.121). The choice of the verb 'hope' describes the act of exploring secret matters and inventing solutions (or machinery) that remove the obstacles.

'Hope' also introduces arguments concerning the salvation of the soul. This convergence confirms the idea that the prohibitions concern Adam's own creative capacities. They are treated as potentially dangerous because they might help him take his spiritual fate into his own hands. Such demonstrations of his intellectual independence are offensive because they challenge the uniqueness of God.

Adam's only permitted companion is Eve. *Paradise Lost* is emphatic that although noble, she is inferior to her husband and, for example, retires with 'lowliness majestic' when he and Raphael embark on 'studious thoughts abstruse' (8.40–2). As a result, Adam experiences an all the more powerful hankering for communications with intelligent creatures. Adam's elated gratitude to Raphael expresses his deep craving for a superior, godlike creature, who satisfies his need for both intellectual stimulation and emotional warmth, which is why Adam says: '[f]or while I sit with thee, I seem in heaven' (8.210). Although Raphael reminds him that his yearnings are akin to a desire for the forbidden fruit, the wish to understand the rationale of the universe comes across as secondary to the wish to experience and become a part of its essential forces. However, the most painful lack in his world is not knowledge but emotion. Adam already possesses remarkable knowledge of the Copernican theory of the cosmos. When he talks about 'this earth a spot, a grain, / An atom' (8.17–19), he shows himself capable of imagining what it might be like to gain sensory experience of Copernican space. His familiarity with the new astronomy is so extraordinary that his level of understanding almost equals that of Raphael. However, Adam is not primarily interested in astronomical facts but aspires to grasp the metaphysics behind them.

Adam's request for information about the cosmos concludes with a description of light and speed:

> '... while the sedentary earth,
> That better might with far less compass move,
> Served by more noble than herself, attains
> Her end without least motion, and receives,
> As tribute, such a sumless journey brought
> Of incorporeal speed, her warmth and light:
> Speed, to describe whose swiftness number fails'. (8.35–8)

Adam takes on the role of the philosophizing poet who has confidently judged, and approved of, the value of the existing solution. His fascination for the cosmic laws leads him to praise the sublime harmony of the universe. Even though his account of the precise movements of the cosmic bodies is still heavily indebted to the inaccurate Ptolemaic theory, the feudal relationship foregrounded by his imagery grasps the idea of a boundless universe traversed by the mysterious entity of light. Raphael's response corroborates Adam's awe about the sublime beauty of the cosmos. While Adam's perspective is concerned with the cosmic bodies of sun and earth, Raphael's reply clearly focuses on the 'maker's high magnificence' (8.101). This means that Adam's question remains unanswered, and the only explanation given is that space was created 'for uses to his Lord best known' (8.106). When describing his own method of moving between heaven and earth, however, Raphael explains that he travelled at a 'Speed almost spiritual' (8.110) and further consolidates the idea that the universe is the material expression of spiritual and hence ungraspable principles.

Much scholarly interest has been devoted to the scientific theories behind Milton's portrayal of the universe. When examining the role of science in *Paradise Lost*, therefore, it seems crucial to keep in mind that the early modern meaning of science was more or less equivalent with the concept of knowledge. Adam's speculations about the whys and wherefores of cosmic design are aimed not so much at the establishment of a systematic description of the mathematics and physics of the universe (what we would now understand by science) but at a first-hand grasp of its metaphysical space. It is self-evident that Adam cannot rival Raphael's performance of 'speed almost spiritual', and his physical inferiority to Raphael remains unchallenged. When it comes to his intellectual and imaginative scope, it becomes more difficult to determine whose knowledge is superior. Raphael is undoubtedly advantaged, because he is not handicapped by prohibitions and does not have to move within confined boundaries of knowledge. If Adam's imagination was not restrained to the physical boundaries of his little world, though, his capacities would be hard to differentiate from those of the angelic spirit. But the wish to reach beyond the boundaries of Paradise would only be proof of his hubris.

Whenever the argument of *Paradise Lost* returns to 'this one, this easy charge' (4.421), the lightness of the burden is emphasized. Its seriousness becomes more pronounced when we realize that 'this easy charge' (4.422) makes it impossible for Adam to grow and develop. It also confirms his insurmountable separateness from the world of God. Although Adam's last question concerning the love of spirits counts as legitimate, it shows that he cannot refrain from exploring the existence of an unconditional union between two beings. Raphael's reply that:

> Easier than air with air, if spirits embrace,
> Total they mix, union pure with pure
> Desiring, nor restrained conveyance need
> As flesh to mix with flesh, or soul with soul. (8.624–9)

What Raphael describes here is a mystical union, a blending and mingling of substances that knows no limits. Adam's physical existence, however, bars him from such an experience. He is also prevented from attaining it because of the prohibition on that kind of knowledge which goes beyond the immediate requirements of earthly inhabitants. Adam's God is distant and aloof and there is no mystical union between believer and godhead. William Empson has argued that Milton's God is tyrannical because he metes out draconian punishment for a minor offence.[29] He also impresses us as tyrannical because he is distant, unapproachable

---

29 William Empson, *Milton's God* (London: Chatto and Windus, 1961).

and refuses to have his true nature known by his creatures. The poem's endless argumentative tug of war between free will and rigid control sketches a sadistic godhead who replaces a loving interaction with his creatures with a pedantic insistence on obedience.

Such is the anthropomorphized God around whom revolves the poem's dogmatic views about the creator and single source of being. Interpretations of the more mystical passages of the poem as expressions of Gnostic or alchemically inspired heresy have argued that Milton is challenging the very idea of the all-powerful and all-knowing God.[30] But is the sense of order ousted along with a certain idea of Yahweh? Contrasted with the all-knowing but unknowable God is the portrayal of light, the enchanted, godlike source of life. Book Three begins with an address suited to a god:

> Hail, holy Light, offspring of heaven first-born
> Or of the eternal coeternal beam
> May I express thee unblamed? Since God is light,
> And never but in unapproached light
> Dwelt from eternity – dwelt then in thee,
> Bright effluence of bright essence increate. (3.1–6)

Milton describes the enchanted nature of light as a means of portraying the exterior correlative to the inner light.[31] Although he goes on to say that light had to perform its magic in response to the voice of God, the passage also says that light existed before the sun came into being. Addressing light as if it were a person, the passage insists: 'Before the heavens thou wert' (3.9).

The magnificent opening of Book Three traces a relationship between the heavenly source of light and a heavenly spark supposed to exist within each and everyone:

> ... celestial Light,
> Shine inward, and the mind through all her powers
> Irradiate; there plant eyes; all mist from thence
> Purge and disperse, that I may see and tell
> Of things invisible to mortal sight. (3.51–5)

Described in this passage is a light that is beyond sensory perception and also beyond the reaches of empirical science. Unlike Adam, the poetic voice is not limited in its understanding of the divine mysticism that connects physical with metaphysical phenomena and truths. The poetic voice also claims for itself a deep understanding of the nature of inner light. That it exists and shapes the inner life

---

30 Cf, for instance, Nuttall, *Alternative Trinity*.
31 Bailey, *Milton and Jakob Boehme*, p. 139.

of human beings is beyond any doubt. It also manifests itself, for example, in the unconscious experiences of the newly created couple.

But the inner light is also closely enmeshed with the idea of temptation. Eve prefaces the narrative of her dream of seduction and transgression with the comment that it dealt with 'offence and trouble, which my mind / Knew never till this irksome night' (5.34–5). She is baffled and confused and therefore expresses herself in disjointed style: 'I this night – / Such night till this I never passed – have dreamed, / If dreamed' (5.30–32). Was it really a dream, she asks herself, and if so, what are dreams, and where do they come from? A further question addresses the issue of whether she can be held responsible for an imaginary transgression. Of course misogynist interpretations of this passage can conclude that her receptivity for sinful thoughts demonstrates that a grain of sinfulness had been planted in her even before she is first tempted to breach Yahweh's command. However, the deeply ingrained sinfulness of human nature is counterbalanced by the idea that the inner light functions as a natural propensity for connecting with the sacred.

Milton himself was in close contact with Samuel Hartlib and the scientific community that began to meet regularly during the Interregnum and came to be established as the Royal Society at the Restoration of Charles II. Sharing their interests in the borderlines between material matters and metaphysics, he must have been familiar with this group's pantheistically inspired belief that material bodies consisted of the four elements but also contained 'a small amount of the quintessence, which connects them to the higher, spiritual world'.[32] If Eve was therefore born with an inner light, her unconscious mind cannot be interpreted as a pure source of danger but must be allowed to possess a mediating capacity between the spiritual world and the divine spark inside her.

Intertextual references to the Bible suggest that the figure who guides her to the Tree of Knowledge cannot be anybody else but Satan. The context of this passage in *Paradise Lost*, however, renders the situation more ambiguous. In her dream, Eve had the impression of waking up on her own. She gets up to find Adam:

> To find thee I directed then my walk;
> And on, methought, alone I passed through ways
> That brought me on a sudden to the tree
> Of interdicted knowledge ... (5.49–52)

Eve's attempt to find her companion, and in symbolical terms attain a hitherto lacking degree of closeness, takes her to the threshold of forbidden knowledge. Her subconscious quest for true closeness makes her aware just how much she desires the kind of knowledge that enables a more complete union with Adam. That the tree suddenly looked '[m]uch fairer to my fancy than by day' can here be interpreted as a sign that something is telling her to overcome fears of dangers and

---

32 Rober Schuler, *Alchemical Poetry 1575–1700: From Previously Unpublished Manuscripts*, ed. Robert M. Schuler (New York: Garland, 1995), p. xxi.

interdictions.[33] It is in keeping with this idea that she sees the traditional figure of the tempter not as an ugly apparition but as

> One shaped and winged like one of those from heaven
> By us oft seen: his dewy locks distilled
> Ambrosia; and on that tree he also gazed ... (5. 53–7)

That she describes this figure as 'like one of those from heaven', rather than identifying him explicitly as an angel, tends to be taken as an indication that Satan treacherously assumed angelic form. When she wakes up with Adam besides her, her choice of words confirms her conclusion that it must be impossible for an angel to encourage her to breach God's outspoken interdiction. This comment is normally read as a rhetorical question that draws attention to the devil's great skills in seducing gullible victims. However, there is also a certain sense that the figure who appears in Eve's dream is as honest a character as the one who appears in Adam's dream-like awakening to life.

The tempter's key arguments target Eve's spiritual side. They do not concern influence and power, but revolve around the idea that she might be capable of leaving behind her human guise and achieving a divine state. She is told that she could be even happier than she already is (5.75–6) and that she will no longer be

> '... to earth confined,
> But sometimes in the air, as we; sometimes
> Ascend to heaven, by merit thine, and see
> What life the gods live there, and such live thou'. (5. 78–81)

According to established dogma, the tempter presents her with a sacrilegious violation of the monotheistic world picture of Christianity. If 'gods' was interpreted as a hyperbolic paraphrase for 'spirits', however, her promised future condition also resembles the realm inhabited by those who have been saved. The idea of turning into a spirit is also reminiscent of the seminal condition demanded by Faustus when he sells his soul to the devil: 'that he become a spirit in form and substance'.[34]

Of whatever provenance he may be, Eve's tempter or spirit guide plucks the fruit and holds it 'even to her mouth' (5.83). The imaginary act of tasting it takes her on a remarkable adventure:

---

33 Note a telling parallelism to John Bunyan's slightly later *Pilgrim's Progress* (1678) which presents in allegorical form the Christian need to dedicate oneself undauntedly to the spiritual path.

34 Cf. Marlowe, *Doctor Faustus*, A: 2.1.97; B: 2.1.96; also compare the formulation in the English Faust Book: 'That he [Faustus] might be a spirit in shape and quality', EFB, p. 96.

'... Forthwith up to the clouds
With him I flew, and underneath beheld
The earth outstretched immense, a prospect wide
And various; wondering at my flight and change
To this high exaltation ...' (5.86–90)

The forbidden fruit liberates Eve from the constraints of the human body and, in esoteric terminology, allows her to experience astral travel. Matching Adam's imaginary journey through the ether (8.300–32), Eve similarly tastes the joy of overcoming gravity. The context of Adam's experience makes it clear that it was God who took him by the hand and inspired his physical elation. However, Adam's dream tends to be read as a legitimate experience because it rapidly moves from a moment of bliss to regulating his indiscriminate desire for the 'fairest fruit, that hung to the eye / Tempting' (8.307–8). When he wakes up he accordingly finds that the enticing fruit of his dream is at his disposal, except for the fruit of one single tree. Eve's dream, by contrast, does not rouse indiscriminate desire but focuses her yearning immediately on the one forbidden tree. What is more, the guide of her nightly experience boldly advises her to disregard the interdiction in order to reach a higher plane of existence. Biblical precedent condemns the contents of her 'dream', but it features as sinful also by reason of symmetry. If the male human being has a spiritual experience inspired by God, misogynist traditions find it tempting to conclude that the woman's supposedly more feeble imagination must give rise to an evil experience. Although Milton drew attention to Eve's inferiority, there is no reason to take for granted that her character must have been innately flawed.

As a consequence of his sympathies for mystical ideas, it is likely that Milton shared the mystical belief that 'there is in God an eternal contrariety or opposition of forces, through the interaction of which "eternal nature" or the universe evolves'.[35] Embodied evil is therefore perceived to be the logical complement of embodied good. Mystical studies, then, seek to overcome the contradictions of the created world. Such an outlook adds a whole new dimension to our interpretation of Eve's behaviour. Since the physical body was thought to have been created from a blend of contrary forces, it stands in the way of an enduring union between Eve and her maker. As a result she can be thought to treat death as a necessary precondition for shedding her physical existence. Her transgression can then be seen, not as the manifestation of her sinful nature, but as the free decision to surrender her immortal but separated condition in order to become one with the abstract source of being. Coming from God, the inner light within Eve cannot but strive to return to its origin. Although not developed in his doctrinal analyses, the mystical framework of Eve's dream gives voice to this alchemical-mystical theory of the human soul.[36]

---

35 Bailey, *Milton and Jakob Boehme*, p. 146.
36 Cf. Bailey, *Milton and Jakob Boehme*, pp. 119–25, esp. 122. See also Margery Purver, *The Royal Society: Concept and Creation* (Cambridge, MA: Harvard University Press, 1967).

Eve's experience concludes with the remark: 'suddenly / My guide was gone, and I, methought, sunk down, / And fell asleep' (5.90–92). The idea of her sinking alludes to the fall but it is rendered as a gentle descent instead of a rapid act of plummeting, followed by a lethal crash. Eve is not actually saved from destruction by waking up but her experience terminates when she falls asleep, recalling another seminal detail of the description of Faustus' journey through the heavens, which I have identified as a crucial component of the Faust Book. As in the Faust Book, *Paradise Lost* similarly insists that the experience just recounted was something other than a dream. Eve says that 'methought' she fell asleep at the conclusion of her experience and therefore describes impressions, rather than irrefutable facts. The text nevertheless presents us with an ambiguity about whether Eve might have been asleep, unconscious or in a state of heightened consciousness.

It is true that the conscious moment of seduction emphasizes her ruthlessness: the text talks about her 'rash hand in evil hour' (9.780) and says that 'greedily she engorged without restraint' (9.791). Visual representations of the moment when Eve eats the apple show that this act sends shudders of horror through Paradise, which further underlines the conventional view that her yearning for knowledge can only be an act of transgression (Figure 4). Eve's selfish behaviour also finds expression in her unwillingness to allow Adam to proceed in a state of innocence:

'And Adam, wedded to another Eve,
Shall live with her enjoying, I extinct;
A death to think.' (9.828–30)

These details seem to illustrate the dreadful consequences of her sinful disobedience. On another level, though, the text also insists that the fruit from the forbidden tree is special precisely because it awakens latent spiritual powers:

'... from the tree her step she turned,
But first low reverence done, as to the power
That dwelt within, whose presence had infused
Into the plant sciential sap ...' (9.834–7)

The 'power within' can here be interpreted as a simple indication that there is power 'within' the fruit, but it can also refer to the newly experienced power within Eve. Whether this is taken to be an awakening of her latent powers or an inappropriate experience of evil powers remains unresolved.

Milton's Spiritual Speculations

Nuttall argues that by the time Milton began working on *Paradise Lost*, 'Francis Bacon had, so to speak, tamed Luciferan science by abolishing secrecy, by insisting on shared scientific results, and by inventing the scientific committee.

Fig. 4   'Eve Eating the Apple', frontispiece for Book IX: *Paradise Lost*, vol. 2, London: printed for J. and R. Tonson et al., 1754.

But for Milton the astronomer remains heroically isolated in his viewing tower, alone with dangerous freedom.'[37] The liberty to explore the secrets of nature was intricately linked with the right to examine the meanings, or metaphysics, behind the physical phenomena. Milton argued not only for the right of every individual to

---

37 Nuttall, *Alternative Trinity*, p. 85.

examine theological questions, but he also proposed that the careful investigation of religious issues should be a cornerstone of daily life. One of the state papers which Milton prepared for publication after the termination of his secretaryship eloquently recommends the study of Jakob Boehme's mystic writings:

> This study rightly attained, would confute and confound the pride and vaine glory of outward humane learning, strong reason, and high astral parts, and would shew men the true ground and depth of all things; for it would lead men into the true nothing, in which they may behold and speculate all things, to a clear satisfaction and contentedness.[38]

This passage describes the object of spiritual study as a 'true nothing' and thus demonstrates Milton's intrinsic belief that spirituality deals with parts of human existence that are immaterial, and are, therefore, beyond the ken of conventional knowledge. The divine spirit ordains the encounter between the believer and the sacred but, similarly as in the Buddhist notion of nirvana, rules and commands are suspended at the moment of insight.

Spiritual experiences challenge and transcend all other descriptions of the relationship between God and the believer. Such mystical passages invalidate all previous descriptions as projections of the human mind, and even the Bible loses its otherwise supreme authority. When considering *Paradise Lost* in its entirety, it strikes us that only a few passages portray spiritual insight. They almost disappear in terms of bulk when compared to the drawn–out descriptions of, for example, the battle between the legions of God and Satan (Book 6). When trying to fathom the dominant message of the poem, it therefore seems that Milton was undecided himself. He was painfully aware of the contested nature of spiritual beliefs and must have dreaded the theological chaos resulting from religious freedom while he also opposed the strictly ordered precepts of the Presbyterian Church. The sheer length of *Paradise Lost* appears to document his almost superhuman attempt to resolve the contradictions at the heart of Christian belief. But ultimately he could not but fail in this endeavour. While treating the formulation of competing views as a fertile intellectual breeding ground, he was worried about the political consequences of such a theological position. But this did not stop him from resorting to the rational mysticism of contemporary science (especially Newtonian physics). God is light and light is God, emerges from the mystical passages of *Paradise Lost*. But God also manifests himself through the contradictory channels of sensory perception. Unless reduced to a supersensory, 'true nothing', sensory perception is always biased, or flawed. Since such a true nothing is not available as

---

38 Quoted in Bailey, *Milton and Jakob Boehme*, p. 135; although this state paper represents an address to Parliament by Mr. Samuel Herring, Bailey emphasizes that Milton must have felt that his own ideas were expressed in this paper. Reference is to *Original Letters and Papers of State, addressed to Oliver Cromwell, Found among the Political Collections of Mr. John Milton* (London, 1743).

an instance for the resolution of practical controversies, a mundane sense of rigid order is preferred over creative chaos.

As the bulk of Milton scholarship documents, radically opposed interpretations can be gleaned from *Paradise Lost*. My interpretation has concentrated on moments that escape from the rigid control of Yahweh's world. Drawing attention to some vital ambiguities has allowed me to identify an argumentative subcurrent that demands the liberation of spirituality from formulaic prescriptions. The arguments for such an interpretation are overburdened with numerous statements that justify God's explicit demand for obedience and unconditional subjection. But once the anthropomorphic projections and traditional images of God have been dismantled, the inner life of each and everyone can reach out and discover its own connections to the essence of the creation. But this is a deeply personal act and as such distances itself from the political chaos resulting from the period's attempt to agree on a shared system of beliefs.

The Cosmic Machinery of Fontenelle's Scientific Romance

Like many scholars of his period, Bernard le Bovier de Fontenelle, the long-term secretary of the French Académie des Sciences, was interested in the borderlines between physical and metaphysical phenomena. But rather than respond with the occultist's enthusiasm for this sphere, he focused a book-length study of divination and inspiration on an analysis of what constituted our perceived sense of reality. His *Histoire des oracles* (1687) concentrates on the modalities of belief and argues that oracular mysteries are heavily influenced by circumstantial factors. Illustrating his view with Classical examples, he says that when Alexander decreed that Ephaestion should be venerated as a God, the force of habit was so powerful that Alexander himself soon 'believed it to be true, and found a great deal of Pleasure, in thinking not only, that he himself was a God, but that he had also the Power of making *Gods*'.[39] His discussion demystifies oracular stories, explaining them to be the consequence of deceptive practices, ambiguities, dreams and the perennial wish to believe in the mysterious.

While Fontenelle's study of supersensory phenomena unsettles his period's theological universe, his popularising account of Cartesian cosmology confronts his audience with the implications of the new science. Far from exploiting the vertiginous nightmare of a new astronomy, he embeds potentially disturbing facts in a charming environment. The ideas communicated through Fontenelle's *Entretiens sur la pluralité des mondes* emerge from a sociable scene. As is shown in the illustrations in Glanville's translation (Figure 5), a natural philosopher and a society lady are positioned on the edge of a baroque garden landscape. While the lady faces her philosophical interlocutor, his head is turned towards the heavens

---

39 'The History of Oracles', trans. Aphra Behn, in: *The Works of Aphra Behn*, vol. 4, ed. Janet Todd (London: William Pickering, 1993), p. 219.

where the orbits of planets and comets are displayed. The reader is presented with two images merged into one: the schematic representation of the orbits of celestial bodies is superposed on the realistic portrayal of a landscape framed by the sky. The scientific image undergoes some transformations before it is allowed to converge with a charming garden scene: rendering the sun as a smiling face reduces cosmic facts to a human scale. Such a ploy emphasizes the idea that science is both pleasant and beneficial for society.

This is how Fontenelle's popularization takes the pursuit of scientific questions into the world of fashionable society. By disseminating the most striking discoveries of science to the educated fraction of society, he solicits support from the non-scientific intelligentsia of the period. Such a spread of information of course also facilitated the institutional foundation of scientific practices.[40] The formal establishment of the English Royal Society in 1660 was followed by the French Académie Royal des Sciences in 1666. Harth may be overstating her case when she says that the state institutionalised the 'new philosophy'.[41] At this historical moment, the success of science was not yet guaranteed. But while the discovery of reliable factual knowledge had not yet become a regular research routine, 'science', the systematic analysis of important questions, came largely to be seen as a morally rewarding project. In the second half of the seventeenth century, it was nevertheless still necessary to explain why science was important to state and society. It is with this objective in mind that Fontenelle set out to negotiate between the *beau monde* and the 'serious' practitioners of natural philosophy. Through his fictional dialogue between a marchioness and a male scientist, he simultaneously participated in the contemporary debate concerning the extent and quality of women's education.

One of Fontenelle's major concerns, argues Harth, was to define the boundaries between scientific investigation and religious enthusiasm, magic and amateurish dabbling. An important background text can be seen in the third *entretiens* of the Abbé de Gérard's *Philosophie des gens du cour* (1680) in which a learned marchioness serves as philosophical muse. She appears alongside another 'learned lady, a witch who spends night after night on her rooftop peering at the moon through a telescope'.[42] By contrast, Fontenelle's marchioness is intrigued by the idea of the world's continuous and rapid movement, but she is by no means given to enthusiastic protestations.[43] Although 'the astronomy lessons take place in her

---

40 Larry Stewart, *The Rise of Public Science: Rhetoric, Technology, and Natural Philosophy in Newtonian Britain, 1660–1750* (Cambridge: Cambridge University Press, 1992).

41 Erica Harth, *Cartesian Women: Versions and Subversions of Rational Discourse in the Old Regime* (Ithaca: Cornell University Press, 1990), p. 152.

42 Harth, *Cartesian Women*, pp. 150–51.

43 The philosopher invokes the Indian myth according to which 'the Earth is supported by four Elephants' and he playfully remarks, 'And I dare say, if these Indians thought the Earth in any danger of falling, they wou'd quickly double the number of Elephants. ... And, Madam, we will add as many as you please to our System for this Night, and take them away by degrees, as

DISCOURSE OF THE PLURALITY OF WORLDS

Fig. 5   Frontispiece from Bernard le Bovier de Fontenelle, *A Plurality of Worlds*, trans. John Glanvil (London, 1702).

garden, she speaks to her teacher, as it were, from the depths of the salon, as a worldly-wise but unschooled woman'.[44] What is more, her responses are guided by reason and not by emotion.

The subtext of Fontenelle's *Entretiens* sketches an erotic attraction between the marchioness and the philosopher and their nightly conversations are narrated through the lens of romance. However, romance remains a titillating possibility. The moon is deprived of its poetic resonances and any emotional responses to the objects of empirical observation are firmly held in check. The sexual attractions between the marchioness and the philosopher are likewise restrained by stylized formulas and it appears to be a mere tribute to convention that the philosopher remarks that 'the Presence of a Person of her Wit and Beauty hindered me [the philosopher] from giving up my Thoughts intirely to the Moon and Stars'.[45]

The nightly encounters between the marchioness and the philosopher, however, are by no means devoid of passionate tensions. While engaged in a conventional comparison of the respective merits of night and day, they toy with the *doubles entendres* that define the ritual of gallantry:

> Do not you believe, Madam, said I, that the clearness of this Night exceeds the Glory of the brightest day? I confess, said she, the Day must yield to such a Night; the day which resembles a fair Beauty, which though more sparkling, is not so charming as one of a brown Complexion, who is a true Emblem of the Night. You are very generous, Madam, said I, to give the advantage to the brown, you who are so admirably fair your self: Yet without dispute, day is the most beautiful thing in Nature; and most of the Heroines in Romances, which are modelled after the most perfect *Idea* fancy can represent by the most ingenious of mankind, are generally described to be fair. But, said she, Beauty is insipid, if it want the pleasure and power of charming; and you must acknowledge that the brightest day that ever you saw could never have engaged you in so agreeable an Ecstasie, as you were just now like to have faln into by the powerful attractions of this Night.[46]

Enumerating the comparative merits of night and day appears to be a rhetorical exercise by which the marchioness and the philosopher demonstrate their oratorical skills: their voices harmoniously respond to each other's statements and cautiously propound their reasons for being more interested in the secrets of the dark than in the apparently more easily accessible features of the day. This passage incorporates the discursive convention of the apology, but, while it gives some explanation for what is being talked about and why, it is also evasive and expends more energy on stimulating interest in the characters than appealing to the

---

you get more Assurance. Really, said she, I do not think they are needful at present; for I have Courage enough to turn round'; Behn, 'A Discovery of New Worlds' (1688), *The Works of Aphra Behn*, 5 vols., ed. Janet Todd (London: William Pickering, 1993), vol. 4, p. 107.

44 Harth, *Cartesian Women*, p. 156.
45 Behn, 'Discovery', vol. 4, p. 93.
46 Behn, 'Discovery', pp. 93–4; author's emphasis.

intellect of its readers. Both marchioness and philosopher state their preference for the night but, by reading the night in anthropomorphic terms, they confirm their fascination with natural philosophy through the conventions of romance. But they do so according to firmly prescribed rules, rather than letting themselves be carried away by the moment.

This concatenation between different genres makes us wonder whether the gestural apology refers to the subject matter or the formal structure of the *Entretiens*. Even while it is not presented as an explicit apology, it also serves the purpose of attracting its readers' attention. Far from explicitly stating the benefits and rational advantages of astronomical enquiries, it tackles the issue from the perspective of sketching how pleasurable such activities are. Fontenelle's work, therefore, investigates the suitability of natural philosophy for fashionable conversation. By commingling an exposition of the Cartesian system with the conventions of romance, moreover, he adds a special edge to a potentially dry subject. He also demonstrates the dependence of scientific arguments on codes of linguistic representation.

Far from trying to ignore the distorting effects of linguistic representation, Fontenelle implies that the demise of an illusory congruence between form and content opens a vast potential for reconceptualizing knowledge. By bringing knowledge into relation with desire, he confirms the legitimacy of conducting a scientific argument in the guise of romance, a genre explicitly invoked when he says that 'most of the Heroines in Romances, which are modelled after the most perfect *Idea* fancy can represent by the most ingenious of mankind, are generally described to be fair'. When the dialogue concludes that the heroines of romance lack charm or sexual seductiveness, and are generally insipid, it does not simply dismiss romance as a superficial generic category but instead calls for a more sophisticated method of joining the representation of knowledge with desire.

Fontenelle sketches an alternative romance which yields to the passion for the unknown and which cheerfully exploits the tensions between social conventions and the act of expanding the boundaries of knowledge. That the scientific is also a social drama is by no means accidental. The scientific romance, the generic form produced by linking an abstract desire for knowledge with sexual desire, foregrounds the conclusion that knowledge is not only sexualized but that sexual interest is itself cast as a desire for knowledge. This, then, explains the cerebral conception of sexuality in this work and helps us to understand why the attraction between the marchioness and the philosopher cannot be allowed to proceed to its logical conclusion, after the pattern of, for instance, the Heloise and Abelard narrative.[47] The sterile relationship between Fontenelle's figures is indeed a result of the story following the patterns of romance. Fontenelle may have wanted to suppress the attractions between the two figures because this would

---

47 For the analysis of the Heloise and Abelard topos, see Peggy Kamuf, *Fictions of Female Desire: Disclosures of Heloise* (Lincoln: University of Nebraska Press, 1982); see also Betty Radice's translation of *The Letters of Abelard and Heloise* (Harmondsworth: Penguin, 1974).

have marginalized his desire to gain approval for the new science. This is not the whole story, though. By reconfiguring the attractions between a male teacher and a female disciple as the 'powerful attractions of this Night', Fontenelle reintroduces as a literary element the mystery which he sought to dispel through his rational approach to the cosmic worlds. The scientific romance, therefore, is an attempt to negotiate between the scientist's endeavour to reduce the cosmos to the rigid grid of reason and the writer's desire to preserve a sense of wonder about the possibility of their being countless other worlds.[48]

The Alternative Worlds of the Copernican Cosmos

The contests and conflicts resulting from the transition from the Ptolemaic to the Copernican theory of the universe chiefly concerned the question of what it meant for contemporary epistemology if a stationary and determined model of the universe gave way to a dynamic one. The major threat of the new theory related to the dissolution of a single perspective and the subsequent impossibility of imagining that the universe was controlled by a system which had the earth as its centre and rationale.

Kepler and Galileo, above all, made evocative attempts to describe, explain and imagine the exact nature of the far-off and alien territories that had been brought closer by the help of mathematical computations and the technical assistance of the telescope. Even while enclosed in the narrative framework of a dream, Kepler's *Somnium* offers a scientifically accurate account of the surface of the moon, thus offering an eloquent instance of the technique of describing its landscape, as he had learnt it from Michael Maestlin and Tycho Brahe.[49] For all its imaginative novelty in allowing its readers to set foot, as it were, on alien territory, Kepler's *Somnium* presents a nightmare scenario rather than a sympathetic description of a site that has always stimulated the imagination. By the help of his recently developed telescopic lenses, Galileo's *Sidereus Nuncius* (1610) not only described a variety of new planets, moons and stars, but also confronted its readers with

---

48 For a discussion of Fontenelle's engagement with the idea of possible worlds as a semantic concept, see George Van den Abbeele, '"Fabula est mundus": on the plurality of Fontenelle's worlds', *Actes de Colombus: Racine; Fontenelle: entretien sur la pluralité des mondes; histoire et literature* (Paris: Papers on French Seventeenth-century Literature, 1990), pp. 165–80. For a discussion of the role of wonder for the history of science, see Lorraine Daston and Catherine Park, *Wonders and the Order of Nature, 1150–1750* (New York: Zone Books, 1998).

49 For an account of the background theories which informed Kepler's scientific story about the moon, see Patricia Frueh Kirkwood's introduction to *Kepler's Dream* (1609) (California: University of California Press, 1965).

such a vast conception of space that Marjorie Nicolson has described it as the most influential scientific publication of the period.[50]

Fontenelle was deeply aware of the disorienting capacities of Cartesian cosmos. He wrote in order to popularize the theory and thus allay the fears that may have developed, if the full significance of Cartesian astronomy had been grasped. During the first night, the marchioness is therefore heard to confess that she is discomfited by the idea of 'inhabiting such a little Humming-Top'.[51] When she expresses her concern at the implications of such an arrangement, the philosopher gently calms her down and dispels her fears, so that she can finally declare, 'I feel I have Courage sufficient to turn round'.[52] Her dialogues with the natural philosopher, therefore, not only enlighten her but they also abate her fears so as to render harmless what Blaise Pascal described as 'the abyss of infinity'.[53] The comic dimension of *Entretiens*, interestingly enough, functions as a means by which Fontenelle seeks to regain control over spatial imagination.

Cyrano de Bergerac's *Histoire comique des Etat et Empire de la Lune* is one of the most significant points of reference for Fontenelle: not only is it a scientific popularization that was similarly written in the comic mode but it is also one of the first scientific works to be written in the vernacular. The period under discussion was fascinated by imaginary worlds which appeared exactly to reverse the customs and laws of nature on earth. In Bergerac's 'Monde renversé', therefore, people's behaviour is explicitly labelled 'burlesque'.[54] While, for instance, Richard Brome's play *The Antipodes* (1640) uses the idea of a world upside-down to throw light on existing customs, Bergerac enhances his description by speculating whether animals might have reason, plants instinct, and metals feelings.[55] Bergerac begins his story by telling us that he let himself be carried away with imagining the moon to be a world like the earth. But then, in a blend of satire and utopian speculation, he sketches his ideas of what this other world might be like. Like Bergerac before him, Fontenelle made use of the carnivalesque element to whet his readers' appetite. His awareness of Bergerac's use of comic elements to challenge stable meanings taught him of the need to keep laughter under control, since laughter is an element that can bring about an easy transition from a static and stable to an unpredictable

---

50 Marjorie Hope Nicolson, *Science and Imagination* (Ithaca, NY: Great Seal Books, 1956).

51 Behn, 'Discovery', p. 107.

52 Ibid.

53 Blaise Pascal, *Pensées* (New York: Viking Press, 1966), pp. 87–95.

54 Cf. Cyrano de Bergerac's *Histoire Comique des État et Empire de la Lune* (Paris: Club des Editeurs, 1961), p. 76. In his introduction, Charles Nodier (p. xvi) points out that it is uncertain when Bergerac wrote this work; particularly whether it predates the French translation of Wilkins's *The World in the Moon* (1638), translated into French by la Montagne in 1653 (Delmar, NY: Scholar's Facsimiles & Reprints, 1973).

55 The idea of comic inversion had established itself as a familiar category through carnivalesque customs; see for example B. A. Babcock, *The Reversible World: Symbolic Inversion in Art and Society* (Ithaca: Cornell University Press, 1978).

and dynamic system. What Bakhtin calls a dialogic discourse, consisting of ironic parallel voices that question and subvert linguistic meaning, therefore, would be a most suitable means with which to represent the Copernican theory. But such a solution gave way to chaos, which is why Fontenelle may have made every effort to restrain the use of comedy.

Paula Findlen points out that as secretary of one of the leading scientific societies, Fontenelle was strictly opposed to 'ludic accounts of nature, relegating them to more popular publications such as his well-known *Conversations on the Plurality of Worlds*'.[56] But in *Entretiens*, he restrained laughter along with the attitude of wonder from the practice of science.[57] A certain ludic element is no doubt present in this work, but it is far removed from the playfulness of Bergerac's narrative. It simply intersperses his sober account with charming comments and sociable episodes. The philosopher, for instance, refers to the Copernican cosmos as if Copernicus had been its architect, rather than the one who discovered its logical principles. Fontenelle may have used this linguistic ploy, as it were, to reconstruct the theory. By allowing the marchioness (and his readers) to watch its development, he leads them to accept the theory gradually:

> Know then, that a certain German, named *Copernicus*, does at one blow cut off these different Circles, and the Christalline Spheres, invented by the Antients; destroying the one, and breaks the other in pieces; and being inspir'd with a Noble Astronomical Fury, takes the Earth, and hangs it at a vast distance from the Centre of the World, and sets the Sun in its place, to whom that Honour does more properly belong ...[58]

By imagining that Copernicus is rearranging the orreries and cosmic models, as if they were the cosmos itself, Fontenelle gives an evocative account of the transition from the old to the new theory. At the same time his account also ridicules those who fail to differentiate between theory and reality, and thus creates a tacit complicity between the philosopher and the marchioness, or between Fontenelle and those among his readers who think they are capable of understanding that a model differs inevitably from the thing represented.

When Fontenelle's narrator reports news from the moon, he sketches a literary scenario according to which such an idea can be imagined without problems. The marchioness is curious about the nature of such communication and the philosopher replies that these news are 'such as are brought us every Day by the Learned, who travel daily thither by the help of long Telescopes: They tell us, they have discover'd vast Countries, Seas, Lakes, high Mountains, and deep Valleys'.[59]

---

56 Paula Findlen, 'Between Carnival and Lent: The Scientific Revolution at the Margins of Culture', *Configurations*, 6.2 (1998): 243–67, p. 266.

57 For a discussion of his life-long endeavour to subject science to the order of reason, see Daston and Park, *Wonders*, pp. 324 and 352.

58 Behn, 'Discovery', p. 102.

59 Ibid., p. 117.

The act of looking through a telescope is metaphorically described as making a journey to the far-off regions espied by the glass. Almost immediately, though, we note that the news is not *from* the moon or *from* its inhabitants but that it is *about* the moon. The formulation, indeed, almost literally quotes Galileo's title *Sidereus Nuncius* ('messenger from the stars'), and thus places Fontenelle on a par with the principal authority in astronomy. The age-old desire to communicate with beings who are utterly different is thereby suppressed in favour of a discourse of discovery which circumscribes the boundaries of scientifically accessible knowledge.

The hallmark of Fontenelle's methodology is to introduce new ideas circuitously. His narrator, therefore, camouflages the new theory of the cosmos as if it was a flight of the imagination. E.D. James claims that when he draws 'imaginative analogies' between the earth and the moon, he reconceptualizes imagination itself.[60] The imagination not only plays a vital part in determining the mode of representing new and daring theories but it is a means for the self to position itself in a world that has become radically unfamiliar. The narrator first broaches the issue of whether there are other worlds apart from the earth in the following terms:

> I am sorry that I must confess I have imagined to my self, that every Star may perchance be another World, yet I would not swear that it is so; but I will believe it to be true, because that Opinion is so pleasant to me ...[61]

Why is this opinion so pleasant? A simple answer is that it has sprung out of the 'world' of his imagination and that it is pleasant because it is his own. At issue, therefore, is a demarcation of the identity of the human observer. If we understand discovery, or the imaginative projection of an idea, as an instance of intellectual proprietorship, we can conclude that the reason for this pleasantness is to be found in the fact that the speaker is conscious of his extraordinarily powerful imagination. He is pleased, therefore, not so much by the idea itself, or the product of his imagination, as by the self-conscious experience of his own mind. In this sense his own creating mind takes over the role of the biblical God who is not otherwise mentioned in the work. This celebration of the superiority of his intellectual and imaginative capacities, therefore, reestablishes man, or the male mind (represented by the figure of the philosopher), in the hub of the universe from which the Copernican theory had expelled him.

The significance of the imagination is further emphasized in a metaphorical comparison between the cosmos and the theatre:

> I fansy still to my self that Nature is a great Scene, or Representation, much like one of our *Opera*'s; for, from the place where you sit to behold the *Opera*, you do not see

---

60 E.D. James, 'Fontenelle: Scepticism and Enlightenment', *Seventeenth-Century French Studies* 9 (1990): 133–50, p. 143.

61 Behn, 'Discovery', p. 95.

the Stage, as really it is ... ; but that which makes the difficulty incomparably greater to Philosophers, is, that the Ropes, Pullies, Wheels and Weights, which give motion to the different Scenes represented to us by Nature, are so well hid both from our sight and understanding, that it was a long time before mankind could so much as guess at the Causes that moved the vast Frame of the Universe.[62]

When the narrator talks about nature as a 'representation' he draws attention to the illusory nature of scientific theories. Not only do the 'Ropes, Pullies, Wheels and Weights' required for a dramatic performance have specific associations with make-believe and deception, but they are needed for the projection of a particular point of view rather than for the simple representation of truth. In spite of its mechanical nature, the theatre cannot produce a strict correspondence between its own meanings and the 'meanings' it purports to represent. So in presenting nature as if it was a theatrical set, Fontenelle indicates that an understanding of how representations (or theories) work is more important than knowledge of the true nature of things. When, therefore, a brief history of natural philosophical enquiry begins with the narrator's remark that he 'need only draw the Curtain, and shew you the world',[63] he is legitimating his own perspective rather than offering a conclusive theory about the nature of the universe.

Fontenelle's scientific romance originally consisted of five *entretiens*. One year after it was published, he added a sixth (1687), in which the philosopher's tone had changed from playfully experimenting with the implications of the new discoveries to a clear assertion of his superiority. Even after the elapse of one year, Fontenelle's public reputation and self-confidence had been greatly enhanced. In the interim he had also been reluctant to acknowledge the subversive potential of his theories about the cosmos. He did not revoke the treatise but simply explained it in an attempt to caution his readers against taking for granted a licence for social experimentation evolving from Cartesian astronomy. The work now concludes as follows:

> Really I am more and more of opinion that Europe is in possession of a degree of genius which has never extended to any other part of the globe, at least not to any distant part. It is not perhaps able to diffuse itself over a great proportion of the earth at once, and some invincible fatality prescribes to it narrow bounds. Let us then make use of it while it is in our possession: and let us rejoice that it is not confined to science and dry speculations, but equally extended to objects of taste, in which I doubt whether any people can equal us. Such madam, are the things that should engage your attention and constitute your philosophy.[64]

---

62 Behn, 'Discovery', pp. 96–7.

63 Ibid., p. 98.

64 Bernard le Bovier de Fontenelle, *Conversations of the Plurality of Worlds*, trans. W.D. Knight (Dublin, 1803), p. 150. Note that Aphra Behn did not translate the final *entretien*. It is likely that it did not reach her before her translation went into print in 1688, but it is also tempting to think that she may have rejected it.

The cultural relativism that can be inferred from the Cartesian de-centring of the traditional core of the universe is rejected as an outright impossibility. Although he is forced to grant that there is no scientific reason why Europe should be more privileged than other parts of the world, he resorts to the old argument that nurture overrides nature. It is the cultural achievements of Europe, along with the generally accepted superiority of men over women, that warrant their respective predominance. As a representative of the establishment, Fontenelle feels called upon to impose control on the liberating potentials of the new science. The fact that he does so allows us to speculate that the first readers of his dialogues may have recognized in their argument a far more stringent abandonment of existing standards and beliefs than Fontenelle was aware himself.

Rather than seeing the new science as a basis that provided the tools for satisfying emotional or spiritual needs, Fontenelle's revised version of the *Entretiens* concludes with the sober remarks that Europe is in possession of a unique genius that is 'not confined to science and dry speculations, but equally extended to objects of taste'. The kind of genius invoked here, however, bears little resemblance to the metaphysical guide of the sensitive intellectual but invokes a sober judgement. The flights of the imagination that traverse the universe of possibilities at 'speed almost spiritual', as Milton's Raphael describes it, have been excluded from Fontenelle's guided tour through the laws of nature.

Conclusion

The representative works of the seventeenth century discussed here were published at intervals of approximately two decades. While the mentalities and political outlook of the three chosen authors diverged significantly, they also reflected the intellectual outlook of their respective periods. When Burton published his *Religio Medici* in the 1640s, he clearly wished to defend himself against suspicions of heresy but he also benefited from his age's tolerance towards homespun attempts to make sense of his experiences as a scientist and Christian. Although published in the decade after the Restoration of the monarchy, Milton's *Paradise Lost* interwove arguments from the radical sects of the Interregnum period into his confirmation of an authoritarian godhead. By Fontenelle's time, a scientific speculator could toy with the liberatory potentials of the new science as long as he relegated them to the realm of a thought experiment and refrained from drawing links between scientific and political theories.

An interesting phenomenon is that once the scientific facts of Copernican cosmology had established themselves, the speculative freedoms of the early periods were curtailed dramatically. It all began in the 1590s which, as Empson demonstrates, was a time 'full of discussion of new discoveries and ideas, though people were careful not to let it get into print'. A remarkable example of literary production is the 'science-fiction Utopia of Francis Godwin' (1562–1633): 'The Man in the Moone: Or a Discourse of a Voyage thither by Domingo Gonsales, the Speedy Messanger' which was, according to Empson, drafted in 1597.[65] That period of insatiable hunger for innovation and intellectual discovery was followed by a general feeling of frustration, of the blocking of progress, which set in about 1615 and lasted till the eruption of the Civil War.[66] Very soon the almost religious enthusiasm for imagining life forms that were different from conventional patterns became suspect. Government censors were keen to expunge ideas about the changeability of the universe because utopian projections of different identities and social structures might be followed by calls for political and theological change.

Empson shows that the Copernican theory was a serious political threat because it presented the cosmos as a dynamic and constantly changing system. The idea that God had placed humankind at the centre of creation had been closely linked to the divinely sanctioned rule of the monarch. Its loss went hand in hand with a new understanding of political sovereignty. When Empson talks about the significance of Thomas Digges (1532?–95), an important figure in the Renaissance intellectual scene, he says:

> He thought that Copernicus regarded the 'sphere' of the fixed stars, not as a smooth firm surface with spangles on it, but as an immensely deep 'outer space' carrying stars at random intervals.[67]

The idea of randomness threatened all traditional notions of stability. But it offered the mind an infinite range of imaginative conceptions of alternative identities and alternative systems of government.

Not only the unknown, far-off realms had turned into objects of speculation but the advances in microscopic technology also subjected the existing realm of experience into an extraordinary plurality of worlds. The idiosyncratic female philosopher Margaret Cavendish is one of many seventeenth-century thinkers to utilize the imagery of the new science to articulate a new understanding of the self and its place in the world. In the preface 'To Naturall Philosophers' Cavendish describes herself as follows:

> ... so shall I remaine an unsettled *Atome*, or a confus'd heape, till I heare my *Censure*. If I be prais'd, it fixes them; but if I am condemn'd, I shall be *Annihilated* to nothing: but my *Ambition* is such, as I would either be a *World*, or nothing.[68]

---

65 William Empson, *Essays on Renaissance Literature*, vol 1: *Donne and the New Philosophy*, ed. John Haffenden (Cambridge: Cambridge University Press, 1993), p. 242, p. 220 and p. 226.

66 Cf. Christopher Hill, *Intellectual Origins of the English Revolution* (Oxford: Clarendon Press, 1965), p. 11.

67 Empson, *Renaissance Literature*, vol. 1, p. 217.

68 Margaret Cavendish, *Poems and Fancies: Written by the Right Honourable, the Lady Newcastle* (Menston: Scolar Press, 1972 [1653]), p. xi.

What was considered to be so small as to be almost nonexistent has now been discovered to be the building block of everything solid and material. The new scientific perspective not only permits a more positive valuation of what had thus far been ignored but also questions the most basic assumptions about solidity and matter. Cavendish's ambition to be a 'world', above all, expresses the wish to be viewed as a self-contained entity that possesses its own integrity. While the atomic perspective endangered those who had been privileged by the old theories, it benefited those who had been excluded by the old system: women and social adventurers could benefit significantly from the act of unsettling long-established theories that excluded them. It is in this spirit that Cavendish argues, 'I have made a world of my own: for which no body, I hope, will blame me, since it is in every one's power to do the like'.[69] The act of speculating about the consequences of particular experiments undoubtedly posed a threat to stability and order, but it also opened up new perspectives and offered imaginative escapes from social control.

This new world of intellectual liberty posed a whole range of new questions about the moral implications of a liberated imagination. They mapped out a constellation that closely fitted the thematic framework of the Faustus legend. It is no surprise, therefore, that the Faustus character made his appearance in a wide range of new adaptations of the old story. The intellectual background to these seemingly trivial new versions of the Faustus story will be discussed in the final chapter of this book.

---

69 Margaret Cavendish, *The Description of a New World Called the Blazing World and Other Writings*, ed. Kate Lilley (London: William Pickering, 1992), p. 124.

Chapter 5

Comedies, Farces and
Harlequin Doctor Faustus

In eighteenth-century aesthetics, laughter and satirical derision were considered to be crucial vehicles for the correction of misguided and wrong behaviour.[1] Neoclassical writers of satire, such as Swift and Pope, emphatically styled themselves as judges of their contemporary culture. The moral significance attributed to wit, the period's most cherished form of linguistic dexterity, demonstrates that verbal comedy was thought to be more than simply a vehicle for entertainment. While it frequently concentrates on mocking what it considers to be offending behaviour, wit rises to its best when it explores the mysteries of human existence. That the comic mode became an important vehicle for the exploration of religious beliefs and practices is demonstrated by the fact that the late seventeenth century saw the emergence of a whole range of literary hybrids between comedy, tragedy and history. The humour of, for example, the mock-heroic mode is ambiguously pitched between glorification and derision. It therefore is an ideal vehicle for the portrayal of the period's mixed feelings about the religious and moral implications of the new science.

At the threshold to the age of Enlightenment, the secrets of nature had largely been established as legitimate topics of investigation. The Enlightenment period indeed assigned the highest priority to the process of collecting information. However, a great deal of uncertainty about the moral and practical impact of the new knowledge remained. As I have already mentioned, John Locke objected to the microscope on the grounds that it distorted the customary or commonsensical perspective required in daily life.[2] Comic as well as downright satirical attitudes surfaced in literary portrayals of scientific curiosity, reflecting the popular discomfort with the uncertain consequences of new discoveries and technological advancements.

Even while they were hailed as legitimate or indeed laudable, intellectual explorations and speculations continued to be associated with problems. The Faustian theme of intellectual transgression may have shed its tragic garb, but

---

1   For an overview of early modern attitudes towards laughter, see Max Byrd, *Visits to Bedlam: Madness and Literature in the Eighteenth Century* (Columbia: University of South Carolina Press, 1974).

2   John Locke, *An Essay Concerning Human Understanding*, in: *Works* (Aalen: Scientia Verlag, 1963), vol. 2: 3.6.24, p. 223.

the nature and implications of the pursuit of knowledge continued to be urgent concerns. The wish to come to terms with ambiguous feelings about the moral and social implications of experimentation therefore turned Faustus into a hero of popular comedy and farce. This chapter unravels the fantasies about the value and usefulness of knowledge engendered by the comic transformation of the Faustus myth.

A History of the Devil

In an age of progressive secularization, comedy was the ideal avenue for an experimental approach to re-thinking and re-defining the borderlines between religion, magic and science. Comedy was also an ideal instrument for investigating traditional personifications of evil in an age that wavered between a staunch adherence to the Bible and a comprehensive rejection of all non-material concepts. For instance, Joseph Glanville, a reputable member of the Royal Society, used his scientific skills to prove the existence of evil spirits.[3] When the journalist and novelist Daniel Defoe undertook to write a history of the devil some forty years later, he adopted a light-hearted tone but did not challenge the idea that the devil is a factual entity. He gives the following explanation for writing a history of the devil:

> ... seeing we are not to expect he will write his own History for our information and diversion, I shall see if I cannot write it for him: In order to this, I shall extract the substance of his whole story, from the beginning to our own times, which I shall collect out of what is come to hand, whether by revelation or inspiration, that's nothing to him ...[4]

Martin Luther would have shuddered at the idea that an account of the devil's origin and activities should be a subject of diversion. But Defoe shows no signs of being terrified about the contamination that might result from contact with the devil. He reflects on the controversy between himself and his divine opponent from a distanced vantage point. Though writing in prose, Defoe demonstrates an intense awareness of the theatrical potentials of the age-old conflict between good and evil. Defoe's tone also reflects familiarity with the harlequinades about hell and damnation that had taken the London audiences by storm when different versions of Harlequin Faustus were played in both playhouses in 1723.

Defoe does not simply enumerate all instances of the devil's interference in human affairs but investigates the wider context of such occurrences, examining the

---

3   Joseph Glanville, *Saducismus Triumphatus: or, Full and Plain Evidence Concerning Witches and Apparitions* (London: S. Lownds, 1689); also compare Richard Olson, 'Spirits, Witches and Science', *Skeptic* 1.4 (1992): 34–43.

4   Daniel Defoe, *The History of the Devil* (London: for. T. Warner, 1727), pp. 16–17.

states of mind of those who claimed to have confronted the devil and questioning the truthfulness of their reports. His scientific approach to the subject embraces many serious moments but it also contains countless witty observations. Defoe's work wavers between representing scientific discourse and offering parodic subversions of science's grand aspirations to truth. In one place, Defoe rejects the idea that madness can be interpreted as evidence that 'the devil has taken possession of a particular person: ... pretending to Possession, and to have the Devil in them, when really it is not so; certainly the Devil must take it very ill, to have all their demented, lunatic Tricks charg'd upon him; some of which, nay, most of which are so gross, so simple, so empty, and so little to the Purpose, that the Devil must be asham'd to see such Things pass in his Name, or that the World should think he was concern'd in them.'[5]

Defoe next scrutinizes oral traditions about the devil's alleged motives and powers. He is particularly opposed to the petty trickery ascribed to the devil. As is emphasized by the frontispiece of Defoe's book (Figure 6), the devil is considered to be a grand personage, who presides over a magnificent court, second neither to that of the Pope nor to any worldly ruler of the period. The one distinguishing feature that makes it clear that this is the court of the devil consists of a cloven foot owned by all members of his court. While this subtle marker of the devil's inalienable characteristic ridicules trite superstitions, it draws attention to the similarities between a worldly court and imaginary notions about the devil's place of habitation. But Defoe's analysis sketches a whole range of different devils – or views of the devil. On the literal level, Defoe insists that the devil is not simply a figment of the imagination and therefore describes supposedly genuine cases of Possession – instanced by the 'deserv'd' death by fire of the Witch of Ipswich, executed in 1646,[6] but he places them alongside 'some merry Popes, who, *if Fame lies not*, were Sorcerers ... and became what we call *Devils Incarnate*.'[7]

Defoe's devil is a complex blend of different characters which cannot be reduced to a façade for a mechanistic attitude along the lines of La Mettrie's description of man as a machine.[8] Such an interpretation would go against the grain of the concluding statement of the book:

It is enough to us that this Torment of the *Devil* is represented to us by Fire, it being impossible for our confin'd Thoughts to conceive of Torment by any Thing in the world more exquisite; whence I conclude, that *Devils* shall at last receive a Punishment suitable to their spirituous Nature, and as exquisitely Tormenting as a burning Fire would be to our Bodies.[9]

---

5   Defoe, *History*, p. 375.
6   Defoe, *History*, pp. 355–7.
7   Ibid., p. 203.
8   Julien Offray La Mettrie, *L'homme machine: A Study in the Origins of an Idea*, ed. A. Vartanian (Princeton: Princeton University Press, 1960).
9   Defoe, *History*, p. 407.

Fig. 6   Frontispiece from Defoe's *History of the Devil*, London: for T. Warner, 1727.

Emphasis on the non-objective nature of representation and experience becomes absolutely central in the concluding passage. While the courtly scene of the frontispiece primarily satirizes polite culture, the final passage concentrates on the figure of the devil. But rather than concluding with an assertion of the horrible powers of incarnated evil, the treatise leaves us with an ambiguous devil who may either have material existence or simply be a representation of imaginary views.

Regardless of whether the devil is physically real or a force of the imagination, his ability to instigate emotional turmoil gives him a certain kind of reality. This is how Defoe's tongue-in-cheek approach draws attention to his period's wide-ranging and mutually incompatible beliefs about the devil. His comic techniques may be neither consistent nor obvious but they are by no means atypical for a period that sought to pull together disparate arguments and grasp the full complexity of topics ridden with contradictions and conflicting opinions.

Seven years before *The History of the Devil*, Defoe had written *Robinson Crusoe* (1719), an immensely popular novel about the formation of European identity in the isolation of an exotic wilderness. Its hero's sense of self is threatened by his encounter with primitive society but it is consolidated once again when Crusoe rallies his wits to persuade his indigenous companion-servant Friday of the existence of the devil:

> I found it was not so easie to imprint right Notions in his Mind about the Devil, as it was about the Being of a God. Nature assisted all my Arguments to Evidence to him, even the Necessity of a great first Cause and over-ruling governing Power, a secret directing Providence, and of the Equity, and Justice, of paying Homage to him that made us, and the like. But there appeared nothing of all this in the Notion of an evil Spirit, of his Original, his Being, his Nature, and above all, of his Inclination to do Evil, and to draw us in to do so too.[10]

Crusoe famously rescued Friday from cannibalism in a dual sense: he saved him from being slaughtered by an enemy tribe and convinced him that it was morally objectionable to eat human flesh. In spite of having grown up in a cannibalistic society, Friday is nevertheless a noble savage with a sharp sense of reason and justice, which enables him to refute Crusoe's most persuasive arguments with the simple question: '*if God much strong, much Might as the Devil, why God no kill the Devil, so make him no more do wicked?*'[11] The confrontation between a member of a primitive society and the shipwrecked westerner sparks off an exciting drama about the contradictory nature of Christian beliefs. By expressing himself in the broken English of the indigenous Friday, Defoe could give voice to sentiments which he would have found difficult to voice openly, for although the expression

---

10 Daniel Defoe, *The Life and Strange Surprizing Adventures of Robinson Crusoe* (London: Oxford University Press, 1972), p. 217.

11 Defoe, *Crusoe*, p. 218, emphasis in original.

of materialist atheism had ceased to be a crime, and was no longer a cause for capital punishment, social pressure continued to be severe.

As a journalist, or hack writer, who depended on the good will of the public, Defoe had to shun the epithet of an atheist, or freethinker, which, in his time, amounted to pretty much the same thing.[12] However, he was not afraid to dramatize a farcical dialogue on religious belief, in which a moderately intelligent, stranded sailor and a reformed cannibal defend their respective positions and thus demonstrate how incapable ordinary people are of grasping theological arguments. More than that, Crusoe's watered-down version of Christian belief fails most miserably when he explains its premises in commonsensical terms, so much so that he is really forced to give Friday the last word. Crusoe is finally forced to admit that he has 'more Sincerity than Knowledge' to save 'the Soul of a poor Savage, and bring him to the true Knowledge of Religion, and of the Christian Doctrine'.[13] His difficulties in persuading Friday suggest that Christian beliefs are founded on counterintuitive or even flawed assumptions.

A quarter of a century later, Andrew Ramsay gave vent to his outrage that 'the fatalistic doctors have disfigured and dishonoured the sublime mysteries of our holy faith'.[14] Defoe refrains from indicting anybody; at least he does not do so explicitly, but instead resorts to satirical techniques to draw attention to the inconsistencies and absurdities of Christian dogma. Furthermore, unlike David Hume, whose recognition that '[t]he whole is a riddle, an aenigma, an inexplicable mystery' induced him to 'make [his] escape, into the calm, though obscure, regions of philosophy,'[15] Defoe did not suggest that religion necessarily amounts to superstition. Even though his *History* casts a satirical light on most reported appearances of the devil, it treats them as culturally defined projections for the expression of abstract and ultimately ungraspable metaphysical concepts. The decision to refrain from articulating a more adequate interpretation can smack of befuddled ignorance. But it also enables a playful approach to the mysteries of existence. A work like Defoe's *History of the Devil* is not overtly funny but it is written in a playfully independent spirit. By treating as a history what orthodox believers would define as a perennial and timeless conflict between good and evil, Defoe's work belongs to a category of fiction that radically questions human beliefs about life and death, while retaining the capacity to marvel at the mysteries of being.

---

12 Cf. Paula R. Backscheider, *Daniel Defoe: His Life* (Baltimore: Johns Hopkins University Press, 1989).

13 Defoe, *Crusoe*, p. 220.

14 Andrew Ramsay, *Philosophical Principles of Natural and Revealed Religion* (1748–49), quoted in David Hume, *The Natural History of Religion*, ed. A. Wayne Colver, and *Dialogues Concerning Natural Religion*, ed. John Valdimir Price (Oxford: Clarendon Press, 1976), footnote 91.

15 Hume, *Natural History of Religion*, p. 299.

Defoe's comic treatment of God, death and the devil draws on a long tradition of literary humour. While presenting themselves as studies of evil, that is to say, historical overviews of different manifestations of evil, such treatments elucidate the impact of an individual's evil deeds on the stability of an entire society. At issue are the values and mentalities that safeguard the intellectual and moral integrity of a society. This means that the attempt to subject the complex diversity of issues associated with the devil to scrutiny has the tendency to result in a work that both frightens and amuses its readers.

While choosing the devil as a subject for a comprehensive history was not in itself an innovation, the light-heartedness of Defoe's approach to the topic was new. One of the earliest serious studies of the nature, origin and objectives of the devil is Johann Weyer's work *De praestigiis daemonum* (1583). This discussion of good and bad spirits, psychological disturbances, mental delusions, witchcraft and medicine also devotes much effort to the analysis of transgressions.[16] There is a certain comic ring to his self-presentation as someone who possesses unlimited insight into all issues pertaining to the borderlines between legitimate natural magic (or scientific approaches to nature) and vicious abuses of the gullible masses, but the book offers no genuine reasons for laughter. Weyer's aim of offering a rational approach to metaphysical questions is demonstrated by chapter titles, such as 'The body can be carried through suitable spaces only and cannot be in different places at the same time,' (XIII) or 'Uneducated physicians and surgeons attribute what is really their own ignorance and error to witchcraft and to the saints' (XVIII). His treatise may be an excessively confident attempt to set right all misconceptions about the devil but its seriousness certainly allows for no intentional humour. When Defoe embarked on the same task of drawing a comprehensive picture of all manifestations of uncanny forces some 150 years later, Weyer's sober self-confidence is no longer available. The humorous dimensions of Defoe's work, therefore, give expression to the contradictory perceptions of good and evil.

Writing closer to Weyer's era, Ben Jonson's satirical comedy *The Alchemist* (1610) describes alchemists as exploitative scoundrels. The play interrogates the nature of knowledge but more important are its dissections of the nature of human wishes and desires. Jonson's dramatic programme goes beyond the ambit of the Faustus theme, but it is a key influence on Thomas Shadwell's portrait of the science of the Restoration.

It is worth remembering at this point that late medieval traditions about a comic devil continued to influence dramatic renditions of transgressive behaviour into the seventeenth century and beyond. Mystery play cycles, as well as other popular drama of the medieval period, tended to dramatize the devil's defeat by Christ as a comic spectacle. For example, the Harrowing of Hell, a dramatic transformation of the Gospel of Nicodemus, illustrates Christ's descent into the underworld to

---

16 John Shea, trans., *Witches, Devils and Doctors in the Renaissance: Johann Weyer, De praestigiis daemonum* (1583) (Binghampton, NY: Medieval and Renaissance Texts and Studies, 1991).

liberate the penitent sinners from the clutches of Satan. Already the Latin versions of this theme, performed in the context of liturgical ceremonies inside the church, contained some humorous components.[17] When they were translated into the vernacular, and came to be an integral part of the mystery play cycles performed, for example, in fifteenth-century York, Chester or Wakefield, the devil became a famous butt of low comedy. Luther Link comments on the consequences of reducing the personification of evil to the human scale:

> In the Harrowing of Hell, Hell considers Satan to be a source of trouble. It is a Hell that Satan cannot control, and this fact is emphasized when Christ forces Hell Mouth to give up its entrapped souls. … Hell speaks, argues with Satan, blaming him for the arrival of Christ: 'Just look what you've done, you bloody fool!'[18]

Although popular drama liked to portray the devil as a fool, who might be chased howling from the stage, the fascination with dramatic personifications of evil goes beyond the simple pleasure of laughing at a disempowered devil. The devil, and other representatives of his realm, are complex figures with at least a certain appeal as challengers of established order. David Bevington hence explains the popularity of the Vice figure in morality plays and its continuing influence on Renaissance theatre. He describes Tityvillus, the Vice in *Mankind* (1471?), as the 'chief attraction' of the play but also explains that the Vice had the longest and most highly developed speaking parts of contemporary morality plays.[19]

Many of Shakespeare's villains, such as Richard III and Iago, are heavily indebted to the tradition of the Vice figure. On the surface, these figures are held up as embodiments of evil that are meant to elicit horror and aversion, but they also have an irresistible appeal. The representations of evil are always ambivalently pitched between illustrating the horrible consequences of transgressions and exemplifying the attractions of an immoral life. The enduring fascination with ambivalent devils and attractive transgressors will be treated in my discussion of various farcical versions of the Faustus drama. Before turning to these transformations of the legend, I want to comment on a dramatic treatment of a scientific scholar that leaves no scope for the hero's final escape from ruin and public scorn.

The Virtuoso (1776), Thomas Shadwell's disillusioned analysis of scientific innovation and intellectual daring, draws a strong link between science and morality, concluding that the period's preoccupations with the new science caused

---

17 For a detailed discussion of Latin versions of *The Harrowing of Hell*, see Karl Young, *The Drama of the Medieval Church* (Oxford: Clarendon Press, 1933), vol 1, pp. 149–77.

18 Luther Link, *The Devil: A Mask without a Face* (London: Reaktion Books, 1995), p. 76. Also compare Frederic T. Wood, 'The Comic Elements in the English Mystery Plays', *Neophilologus* 25.1 (1940): 39–48.

19 David Bevington, *From 'Mankind' to Marlowe: Growth of Structure in the Popular Drama of Tudor England* (Cambridge, MA: Harvard University Press, 1962), p. 15 and pp. 79–83.

the moral decay of a weak-headed society. However, the situation is not quite as simple as this. By linking scientific concerns to a general scrutiny of knowledge, the play enters into a complex study of the morality of a society whose belief in perennial values was fundamentally challenged during the Interregnum.

Science on the Restoration Stage: Shadwell's *Virtuoso*

Although the title of Shadwell's *Virtuoso* explicitly targets amateur scientists as social nuisances, scientific experimentation is scrutinized along with philosophical and moral forms of knowledge. This detail strikes us most forcefully when we remind ourselves that the insipid orator Sir Formal Trifle, who appears in the role of attendant and flatterer to Sir Nicholas Gimcrack, is equally the target of Shadwell's satire. The empirical scientist and the orator complement each other in so far as one of them specializes in discovering new knowledge about the material world and the other takes on the role of communicating such information to a lay audience. Both treat knowledge as a means of self aggrandizement: there is no rational purpose behind the Virtuoso's time-consuming and expensive habits of observing the secrets of nature and there is no meaning in the orator's empty phrases.

Sir Formal's dismal address to the weavers who feel threatened by the inventions of the new science graphically illustrates his inability to understand and calm an enraged crowd. His florid description of their 'unheard-of torrent of tempestuous rage' (5.3.40) is powerless to cool the anger of a crowd, much as Sir Gimcrack is incapable of running his own household.[20] For these reasons the play treats the misguided application of intellectual faculties as a major offence. That the play considers Sir Gimcrack to be an evil character is demonstrated by the fact that he ends up losing everything. Since the public taste of the Restoration period demanded comedies, Shadwell structures his study of society around the ultimately successful union between Sir Gimcrack's nieces and their sprightly young suitors. In spite of the happy ending required by the comic mode, *The Virtuoso* leaves its audience with a disheartening portrait of its society.

At first glance Sir Gimcrack has little in common with Faustus. The main parallel is that Sir Gimcrack also aspires to knowledge and is eventually punished for his excessive curiosity. The secular context of the play, however, forbids an ending whereby Sir Gimcrack's body will be mangled and his soul sent to hell. In spite of being a comedy, the play nevertheless finishes on a note of unmitigated disaster. Gimcrack is bankrupt, loses his prospects of inheriting the fortune of his uncle, and is abandoned both by his adulterous wife and his mistress, and hence suffers the punishments of a secular Faustus.

---

20 All references are to Thomas Shadwell, *The Virtuoso*, eds. Marjorie Hope Nicolson and David Stuart Rodes (Lincoln: University of Nebraska Press, 1966), p. 3.

Although he lacks wit and willpower, there are further parallels between the befuddled scientist and the Faustian quest for knowledge. For example, Faustus' hubristic craving for insight into the secrets of nature similarly fires Sir Gimcrack's studies. In the laboratory of a Restoration scientist, however, the sinful attempt to spy into the secrets of the creator has been downsized into a wasteful and useless endeavour, so that Sir Gimcrack turns into an impotent shadow of Faustus. However, it is important to keep in mind that it is Sir Gimcrack's supposedly useless pieces of information which have proved indispensable for science's desire to imitate nature. The twentieth-century philosopher of science Hans Georg Gadamer reminds us that microscopic study of minute organisms yielded not only crucial information in the fight against diseases but that the analysis of phenomena like the blue in cheese provided scientific support for a pantheistic attitude towards the material world. He argues that the microscope opened up a vital perspective on 'microscopic creatures and infusoria – which provided the first great confirmation of the "animation" present in all beings, that is, the soul within them.'[21] The purpose of grasping the essence – or quintessence – of the creator, however, has no place in Shadwell's portrait of Sir Gimcrack. Intellectual obtuseness may be a reason for this character's failure to recognize why seventeenth-century scientists engaged in microscopic studies.

A side glance at the work of Henry Power and Robert Hooke, key figures in seventeenth-century science, who were recognizably satirized by the play, reminds us that especially Power's work shows him to have been entranced by the beauties of minute organisms. He was one of many scientists of the period who were not just interested in gathering factual information about the world but who studied phenomena like the growth of mould in cheese so as to grasp underlying principles about all organisms. He rationalizes the objectives of microscopic studies as follows: 'modern Industry ... hath discover'd this advantageous Artifice of Glasses, and furnish'd our necessities with such artificial Eys, that now neither the fineness of the Body, nor the smallness of the parts, nor the subtility of its motion, can secure them from our discovery.'[22]

Sir Gimcrack, by contrast, has been formed as a dull and insensitive character who is incapable of drawing any inferences from his observations. But why is he punished so severely for his seemingly harmless bumbling? It may be possible to answer this question if we ask what would happen if the play's scientist was a focused and gifted investigator, rather than a disorganized and gullible fool. If he were an ingenious scholar, he might have excelled the rather brilliant Robert Hooke and reached the level of Mary Shelley's Victor Frankenstein. Rather than collecting an array of trivial bits of information, he might have been able to bypass the ordinary course of nature and given life to an artificially produced human being.

---

21 Hans-Georg Gadamer, *The Enigma of Health*, trans. Jason Gaiger and Nicholas Walker (Stanford: Stanford University Press, 1996), p. 148.

22 Henry Power, *Experimental Philosophy, in Three Books: Containing New Experiments Microscopical, Mercurial, Magnetical* (London: T. Roycraft, 1664), c3r.

For the most part Shadwell's insistence on the Virtuoso's feeble intellect and judgement neutralizes the evil that might result from his research. Snarl's vitriolic comment: 'in sadness, nephew … you will never leave lying and quacking with your transfusions and fool's tricks' (2.2.195) is just one passage in the play that draws attention to the Virtuoso's limited knowledge and skills. Whatever comic effects may have resulted from the presumptive transformation of madmen into sheep, Snarl also points out that his scientific nephew 'kill'd four of five that I know with your transfusion' (2.2.214). In spite of his minimal knowledge and skills, Sir Gimcrack causes some serious problems. The protests of the ribbon weavers, who lost their subsistence because of the invention of a mechanic loom, further illustrates that every scientific or technological innovation, regardless of whether it is a small step or a gigantic leap, unbalances an established order of things. Since the impact of new inventions, and the social interventions caused by them, is extremely difficult to fathom, argues Shadwell, society must keep a careful eye on scientific advancements.

Shadwell styled himself after the example of Ben Jonson, a similarly severe critic of the presumptive possession of special knowledge. Of course, Jonson's quick-witted scoundrels have no interest in expanding the period's knowledge about the natural world; they only dabble in alchemical pseudo-science in order to impose themselves on gullible victims. In order to be successful in their impostures they needed a special kind of knowledge that allowed them to discover the weaknesses of others. At the end of the play, their pretence of possessing magical skills is finally exposed. The play also reveals the remarkable skills of impostors to fathom what people hope to gain by the use of irrational and supernatural means. Face and Subtle can practice fraud precisely because they are intimately familiar with the workings of human desires. But Jonson treats this fact with proto-Darwinist equanimity, implying that in an environment directed by self-interest, cleverness and wit determine the competition for wealth and resources. A similar contest over who possesses the most suitable skills to survive and succeed in a competitive environment is staged in Shadwell's *Virtuoso*.

In spite of his dismissive attitude towards the empirical science practiced by the early Royal Society, Shadwell's *Virtuoso* offers a more comprehensive scrutiny of his period's scientific and intellectual endeavours. The satirical thrust of the play is directed at contemporary developments in the history of science. *The Virtuoso* contains explicit references to Gresham College, and there are historical reports that contemporaries almost pointed at Robert Boyle and Robert Hooke as the targets of Shadwell's satire. Marjorie Nicolson has identified a whole list of activities of the Royal Society satirized in the play.[23] The main dramatic object of the satire was to indict the Virtuoso for wasting his time and money on useless investigations, inviting us to laugh at the fact that Sir Gimcrack has 'spent two thousand pound in

---

23 Cf. Nicolson's introduction to *The Virtuoso*; also compare her *Science and Imagination* (Ithaca, NY: Great Seal Books, 1956), pp. 172–4.

microscopes to find out the nature of eels in vinegar, mites in a cheese, and the blue of plums which he has found out to be living creatures' (1.2.11ff).

Responses to Shadwell (from Pope to twentieth-century interpretations) have ascribed his wholesale attack on science to his inability to understand that theoretical (or speculative) science necessarily complements applied science. A good deal of the play's anti-intellectualism attaches to moments that show Sir Gimcrack in a state of advanced imbecility when he, for example, learns to swim in his laboratory because he 'hates water', explaining that 'I content myself with the speculative part of swimming; I care not for the practice. I seldom bring anything to use; 'tis not my way. Knowledge is my ultimate end' (2.2.84–6). This is to say that such passages jibe at a type of science that fails to examine the meanings and consequences of its discoveries.

Responsibility is a key issue for the play. While it purports to scrutinize both the scurrilities and the potentially dangerous consequences of scientific investigations, the main focus of the play is on social responsibility. Sir Gimcrack is ridiculed not only for his natural historical tomfoolery but also for his failure to comprehend human nature. He may be gathering factual knowledge but he is shown to be incapable of assessing how it may affect the society that will put it to further use. Worst of all, he lacks discernment; this is to say he is unable to see through the flattery of his sycophantic adulators and is incapable of ruling his household, particularly its women.

The play opens with a dialogue between the two young male characters Bruce and Longvil which follows on from Bruce reading aloud a Latin quotation from Lucretius. Both young men are libertines about to have their excessive sexual cravings restrained by marriage. Modelled on historical characters like John Wilmot, second Earl of Rochester (1647–1680), the libertine was a stock character of Restoration comedy: a dashing cavalier who had to show his bravado during the upheavals of the Interregnum but whose energies and instincts needed to be curtailed after the Restoration of Charles II. In Rochester's case, the riotous existence of a young man without proper purpose was only curbed by his early death. The question of how to transform aggressive and licentious young men into useful members of society after the political tempests have blown over remained urgent in the 1670s. Shadwell's answer to the problem agrees with the general mentality of Restoration comedy, proposing that the sexuality of the young libertines should not be constrained too rigidly but that the objects of their intellectual interests should be considered carefully.

The two young libertines raise the spectre of atheism when they quote Lucretius's description of the Epicurean gods. An interesting coincidence is that it was in 1676, the same year as *The Virtuoso* was first performed that Rochester translated the extended context of the passage quoted by Bruce. Rochester's translation of Lucretius reads as follows:

> The Gods, by right of Nature, must possess
> An everlasting Age of perfect Peace:

Far off removed from us and our Affairs;
Neither approached by Dangers, or by Cares;
Rich in themselves, to whom we cannot add:
Not pleased by Good Deeds; nor provoked by Bad.[24]

As I have argued in my analysis of the chapbooks, Faustus' wish to encounter the being who created nature fires his desire to spy into Paradise, the place where the purpose of the material creation was believed to exist in a state of perfection. The indifference of Lucretius's gods, by contrast, renders such endeavours pointless. A materialistically organized cosmos offers no incentives for a spiritual quest, but nor does it hold up a code of morality that regulates the behaviour of passionate young men in a world without moral restraint.

To return to the opening of *The Virtuoso:* for those who could understand the Latin, the quotation from Lucretius is a simple echo of the language of learning for the less erudite members of the audience but for those who understand Latin it introduces the topic of atheism. Tellingly enough, the dialogue of the play begins with Longvil's comment: 'what an unfashionable fellow art thou, that in this age art given to understand Latin'. Mastery of Latin, the lingua franca of science and learning, becomes a factor in the play's assessment of knowledge. For those who understood Latin and recognized the context of the quotation, the scandal of atheism is associated with natural philosophers, regardless of whether they adopted a theoretical or empirical approach to the study of nature. Their attitude towards nature as the origin and cause of all 'natural laws' challenged the traditional understanding of God as the unique and sole source of order. As the example of Robert Burton has demonstrated, natural philosophers did not necessarily embrace atheism, but a scientific approach to nature nevertheless encouraged a differentiation between a creator, who maintains a never-ending relationship with his creatures, and a creative principle which disregards all concerns for good and evil.

The chief point of reference in the quotation from Lucretius is 'Nature'. When Rochester's translation talks about the idea that things are done 'by right of nature', he suggests that nature has not only become vastly more important than God but that both nature and (the) god(s) are indifferent to human concerns. As Lorraine Daston argues, the shift from identifying a divine instance that guarantees the stability of norms and values to accepting the anonymous and indifferent authority of nature goes along with the establishment of the self-interested values of a materialist society.[25]

In *The Virtuoso*, Shadwell describes a society from which religion has disappeared. The Gods evoked in the opening scenes are those of Epicurean philosophy who remain indifferent to the events of earth. It portrays a society that

---

24   Reproduced as a footnote to Act 1.1.7–12 in Nicolson's edition of *The Virtuoso*, p. 9.
25   Daston, Lorraine, 'The Nature of Nature in Early Modern Europe', *Configurations* 6.2 (1998): 149–72.

is morally corrupt, sexually unfaithful, cruel, vindictive and ungenerous. Miranda underlines the ruthless principles of her society when she exclaims: 'O unjust custom that has made women but passive in love as if nature had intended us for ciphers only, to make up the number of the creation' (3.4.127ff). On the other hand, the play's open acceptance of the idea that the sympathetically depicted male characters have sexual intercourse with Lady Gimcrack for the mere sake of the drive confirms a hypocritical convention that insists on female chastity while being much more accepting of male promiscuity. But all characters of the play display a ruthless selfishness and unembarrassed hypocrisy. As a matter of fact, the play rejects the very idea that any of its characters might be innocent: even Clarinda and Miranda ruthlessly use their admirers as tools to promote their own plans.

The play's comic plot portrays the decay of moral standards as a consequence of the weak powers of reasoning that have become the rule of the day. But the sexual intrigue of Shadwell's plot is also very much part of the play's satirical statement on science: desire for intellectual knowledge is contrasted to desire for sexual knowledge. While the play appears to argue that reason will win out against the offensive figure of the Virtuoso, there is no real alternative to his weak-minded science and morality. The play certainly gives the upper hand to Bruce and Longvil, not just because they show themselves to be in possession of common sense but also because at heart they acknowledge religion as an integral part of their lives. The young people may tease each other about having gone to church in order to look at the opposite sex, rather than to worship God (2.1.44ff), but the church nevertheless features as an important moral backdrop to their encounter. In spite of their intellectual flirtation with Epicurean philosophy, the young men continue to acknowledge the moral authority of the Christian God.

Sir Gimcrack's household and mind, by contrast, is characterized by confusion and chaos. Catherine Wilson argues that, however different their methodologies, historians of science agree that 'truth may emerge out of error but cannot emerge out of confusion'.[26] One of Sir Gimcrack's serious faults consists of rejecting the idea of observing 'men and their manners' (3.3.89); another is that he is given to doctoring the results of his empirical observations. For example, when he describes the tarantula's sympathy for music (cf. 3.3.93ff), he blurs the boundaries between speculation and invention and thus overturns the laws of nature. Longvil gives vent to his outrage when he says: 'As there is no lie too great for their telling, so there's none too great for their believing' (3.3.48ff). The Virtuoso's science is blamed for promoting a state of intellectual confusion and thus is far removed from its role as a harbinger of Enlightenment. In so far as scientific error is equated with a wilful expression of untruths (or lies), moreover, Shadwell severely indicts a science that is indifferent towards false conclusions. Describing the scientist's motives as a simple wish to celebrate his intellect, Shadwell denies the probity of

---

26 Catherine Wilson, *The Invisible World: Early Modern Philosophy and the Invention of the Microscope* (Princeton: Princeton University Press, 1995).

the experimental witness that Steven Shapin has shown to be so significant for the validity of observed facts.[27]

But although the play ends with the victory of two young men who hate the science of a befuddled experimental scientist, it does not offer conclusive evidence that they are right and good. Bruce and Longvil are selfish, licentious (both engage in casual sex with Lady Gimcrack) and indulge in excessive cruelty towards the would-be wits. They win the competition with Sir Gimcrack not because they have proved him wrong but simply because they are physically and intellectually stronger. In some sense, of course, they win because they have the better science. Overtly they say that their science amounts to recognising the necessity of studying mankind; implicitly, though, theirs is not an alternative science but a science that legitimates self-interest. Bruce's parody of theoretical science is a simple excuse for the gratification of his desire. The scientific witticism 'I shall forget the speculative part of love with Clarinda and fall to the practice with her [Lady Gimcrack]' (3.1.140) detracts from the fact he simply asserts his right to do as he wishes.

The play therefore not only points to the necessity of studying human nature (instead of the nature of mites and the blue of plums) but reveals that morality is no more than a disguise behind which to hide passion and self-interests. Shadwell may be discrediting the methods of his period's science and questioning the appropriateness of its objects of study, but on a deeper level he is producing an analysis of the influence of passion on the social conception of knowledge.

To some extent the savagery of Shadwell's satire is owing to the fact that he challenges the objective validity of knowledge. The early Royal Society and its amateur dabblings were the overt object of his satire but he also examines the practical context of rationality. The conflict between the terrified Sir Gimcrack and the ribbon weavers, resolved by Bruce and Longvil, presents a telling study of rationality. The two young men master the situation because they realize that only brute force can disperse an enraged crowd. As regards moral standards, both young men audaciously breach the ideal of matrimonial faithfulness, but when they expect chastity from their wives, they enforce a hypocritical double standard. This means that they do not apply the principles of rationality but enforce their view of rationality on others.

When Shadwell has his female characters complain against the curtailment of the liberty of 'free-born women' (1.1.23), he offers examples of why it is so important to study the motivations of those in possession of power. The science advocated by him needs to investigate the reasons for social practices in order to ensure that rationality cannot be bent and twisted beyond recognition. He may be rather too dogmatic in his views, but he also invites his audience to judge for themselves whether the standards presented to them are acceptable. They are invited to laugh

---

27 Cf. Steven Shapin, *A Social History of Truth: Civility and Science in Seventeenth-century England* (Chicago: University of Chicago Press, 1994).

openly, as a statement of their own assessment of the values examined by the play and as an indication that they object to gross abuses of common sense.

William Mountfort's Farcical Faustus

Although Shadwell's *Virtuoso* does not really take issue with the Faustus theme, it highlights contemporary views about knowledge and experimentation and as such adds an additional perspective to William Mounfort's *The Life and Death of Doctor Faustus Made into a Farce* (written and first performed between 1684 and 1688).[28] This adaptation of Christopher Marlowe's *Doctor Faustus* expands the burlesque scenes of Marlowe's play and embeds Faustus' dealings with the devil in improvized squabbles between Harlequin and Scaramouche. The farcical version retains the dramatic contest between the God and Bad Angel and is also structured as a cautionary tale. However, Faustus' great dread of the termination of the twenty-four years stipulated by the pact is only lightly sketched. The comically condensed version of the tragedy suggests that the audience was familiar with the key features of the Faustus drama. The same tacit awareness of the arguments discussed by the Faustus legend is implied by the farce's portrayal of some of its concerns in the comic interludes between Harlequin and Scaramouche.

Owing to the elaborate stage machinery of the Dorset Garden Theatre, the farce can satisfy one of the seminal wishes of the mythical Faustus. The desire to see heaven falls by the wayside but Faustus' request to 'see Hell once, and return safe' (12) is granted not only to the hero of the play but to the entire audience. Rather than simply narrating an account of Faustus' damnation, the play invites its audience to witness the event by offering a spectacular reproduction of hell on stage. By contrast with Marlowe's final focus on the mangled body of Faustus,[29] Mountfort shows the entry of his transgressive hero into hell. As I have argued in Chapter 3, Marlowe's period tended to interpret the spectacle of the violated body as evidence for the irredeemable sinfulness of Faustus, because a violent death still counted as an indication that the dead person was damned and sent to hell.[30] While Marlowe invited his audience to question the inevitability of Faustus' damnation,

---

28 Cf. Anthony Kaufman's introduction to the facsimile edition that was first published in 1697, *The Life and Death of Doctor Faustus Made into a Farce* (Los Angeles: William Andrews Clark Memorial Library, 1973), p. viii.

29 The A-text concludes with the mangled body of Faustus as a stage metaphor for his damnation, which only the most undaunted among Marlowe's audience would have challenged. By contrast, the B-text finishes with an additional scene where a group of scholars come together to enumerate mitigating circumstances for Faustus' behaviour. Even if their qualified homage is not interpreted as downright acquittal, the simple fact that the play does not conclude on the note of a violently distorted body gives Faustus the benefit of the doubt.

30 Heiko Obermann, *Luther: Man between God and the Devil*, trans. Eileen Walliser-Schwarzbart (New Haven: Yale University Press, 1989), pp. 3–4.

Mountfort resolves all ambiguity. There is no doubt that his Faustus goes to hell. But it is the hell of farce.

It is tempting to conclude that the spectacle afforded by Mountfort's farcical hell amounts to a wholesale rejection of the Faustus legend's customary warnings against intellectual curiosity and magic. The increased significance of the comic subplot, which already plays a vital role in Marlowe's version, shrugs off Scaramouche's dabbling in magic as a by no means unusual way to secure a livelihood. The sympathies of the audience are with the petty criminal's struggles for survival, regardless of whether the inexhaustible resourcefulness of Mountfort's play involves the devil or describes a rogue who pockets the handouts he is supposed to distribute among the poor (22–3). Standing at the bottom of the social hierarchy, Harlequin and Scaramouche have nothing to lose. They endear themselves to the popular taste because of their capacity to survive without wealth and education. The gravity of Faustus' offence is relativized by comparison. However, he does not practice magic as a last resort in his struggle for survival; nor can he plead the simple naivety of Harlequin.

Although the intellectual outlook of the late seventeenth century had legitimated curiosity, it continued to oppose everything that resembled witchcraft. Hostility frequently targeted carnivalesque public spectacles along with overt practices of magic. Discussing the experience of devil costumes in French streets, Stuart Clark comments that for an observer like Pierre Le Loyer, 'public play and licence were satanic in principle; just as the devil who led the masqueraders in Hogarth's engraving of 1724, *Masquerades and Operas*, referred to a specific vocabulary of costume and, at the same time, signified the supposedly demonic origins and values of the entertainment'.[31] Frequently it was merely a matter of formulating a trite dismissal of public festivities. While the devil was of course not the direct instigator of such spectacles, at one level or another, they embraced an attempt to come to terms with the nature of demons and their influence on the daily lives of early modern people. It does not matter that they were personifications, or metaphors for abstract forces, rather than 'real', transcendental agents. What matters is that it is in the nature of bacchanalian revels to try to come to terms with that which connects temporal human existence with higher and supposedly perennial forces.

The colourful and noisy spectacle of the farcical hell harks back to several popular traditions, chief among them displays of hell in morality plays and other rituals designed to break the power of evil. But the theatrical feat of staging hell also interrogates popular assumptions about the nature of hell. Historical accounts

---

31 Stuart Clark's study of witchcraft shows that the preoccupation with demons and black magic dominated European culture between the fifteenth and the eighteenth century: *Thinking with Demons: The Idea of Witchcraft in Early Modern Europe* (Oxford: Oxford University Press, 1997), p. 21. Also compare Terry Castle, *Masquerade and Civilization: The Carnivalesque in Eighteenth-century English Culture and Fiction* (London, 1986), pp. 1–51.

of the stage machinery used to dramatize Mountfort's hell do not survive. It is likely, though, that it would have involved pyrotechnic marvels as well as a spectacle of devils swishing through the air, utilising similar dramatic effects as are depicted on the frontispiece of Evaristo Gherardi's *Arlequin empereur dans la lune* (1684).[32]

When Mountfort brought *The Life and Death of Doctor Faustus Made into a Farce* onto the London stage in the 1680s, he pandered to his audience's taste for farce.[33] In his introduction to the facsimile edition of Mountfort's play, Anthony Kaufman points out that several Italian *commedia dell'arte* actors had visited London since the Restoration and had inspired English imitations, the first of them being Edward Ravenscroft's *Scaramouch a Philosopher, Harlequin a School-Boy, Bravo, Merchant, and Magician* (1677).[34] It is striking that the first task given to an English Harlequin is to come to terms with philosophy and magic. The choice of this dramatic subject indeed illustrates how important were abstract knowledge and practical skills for a period that struggled to reinvent itself after the traumas of regicide and civil war. Ravenscroft's analysis of magic, similarly as Aphra Behn's extremely popular play *The Emperor of the Moon* (1687), revolves around Harlequin's surprising transformational abilities. These farcical plays celebrate the protean hero whose elusive appearance guarantees his success in an upwardly mobile society, which is to say he illustrates the aspirations of his period's increasingly powerful middle classes, rather than performing more typical acts of conjuration.

The magic of Mountfort's Faustus play revolves around stereotypical ideas of magic. It boasts the paraphernalia of a magical wand and a book of formulae. While Marlowe contrasts the magic of Doctor Faustus with the fraudulent tricks of Dick and Robin (especially Act 3.3), there is nothing to indicate that the magic of Mountfort's Scaramouche might not be as effective as that of his master. But if magic depends on the ability to pronounce the right formulae, anyone in possession of a conjuring book should be able to create the desired effects. The idea that the insolent servant's intrusion into his master's study allows him to perform magical tricks likewise belongs to the core components of Marlowe's Faustus but once again, Mountfort further emphasizes this dramatic element. When Scaramouche is willing to satisfy Harlequin's wish to have a devil punish his former master for turning him out of doors, he tells him that 'for a Crown a Week I'll lett thee out a Devil, as they do Horses at Livery' (9). This episode underlines the business

---

32 Evaristo Gherardi, *Les intrigues d'Arlequin*, in: *Le Théâtre Italien de Gherardi, ou le receuil générale de toutes les Comedies & sçenes Françoises jouées par les Comediens Italiens du Roy, pendant tout les temps qu'ils one été au Service de la Majesté* (Marchand Libraire prés le Dam: chez Adrian Braakman, 1701).

33 Kaufman, *Doctor Faustus Made into a Farce*, p. ix.

34 Kaufman, *Doctor Faustus Made into a Farce*, p. ix. For Edward Ravenscroft's play see: *Scaramouche a Philosopher, Harlequin a School Boy, Bravo, Merchant and Magician, a comedy after the Italian manner* (London: for Robert Sollers, 1677).

deal behind Faustus' pact with the devil but it also ridicules popular ideas that supernatural assistance can be purchased similarly as a horse can be rented for a particular occasion.

So as to impress the ignorant Harlequin, Scaramouche leads him to believe that he has command over a whole stable of devils. Although he is only bragging about his magical skills, the fleshed-out metaphor of the devil in livery, performing the whims of those who pay for his services, reminds us that it is only human to imagine that it is possible to enter into a business deal with supernatural powers: much as it was believed that five dozen 'Hail Marys' might 'buy' the favour of the heavenly virgin. Scaramouche's behaviour further parodies the idea that a devil can be bespoken in order to carry out every whim of his temporary master. Once he has sized up his customer as an ignorant sinner, Scaramouche behaves like a horse dealer rather than a magician. Although his transgressions are as serious as those of Faustus, he comes across as both too ludicrous and too insignificant to warrant the wrath of God.

Marlowe's tragic history of Faustus had already contrasted the grand breach of the divine Law with the more venal sins of his low characters. Mountfort's adaptation likewise focuses on mundane human concerns. Harlequin formulates a burlesque request when he asks for a devil or two 'of a strong Constitution, that may swallow up his [former master's] Turpentine Pills as fast as he makes 'em, that he may never cure poor Whore more of a Clap; and then he'll be undone, for they are his chief patients' (8). His account of how he had himself 'devour'd Three Yards of *Diaculum* Plaister instead of Pancake' describes a poor apprentice close to starvation but it also conjures up a grotesque type of physicality.

Exaggeration and farcical behaviour detract from the tragic seriousness of the plot, but these features also open the gates to a whole range of typically human emotions and responses. According to the plot of the play, Harlequin is an unemployed servant who is angry but also guilt-ridden and therefore frightened at the possible consequences of his unlawful revenge. When Harlequin arrives in front of the Doctor's house, the stage directions say that he 'opens the Door, peeps about, and shuts it'. His hesitancy dramatizes his inner conflicts between the desire to have his request granted and fear of the devil. He illustrates a deeply human trait when he peeps timidly. Rather than balancing the pros and cons, however, he is simply proceeding slowly and cautiously, guarding himself against the physical aggression he might have to face when encountering the devil. He is not really worrying about the loss of his soul. If he had a choice, he would much prefer not to have anything to do with any metaphysical agent but he believes himself to be compelled to this step as a last resort. Being weak and powerless himself, he demands the help of a strong figure to punish his opponent. The play does not therefore dramatize the devil's successful seduction of good people but instead shows the dabbling in magic of characters who have already been written off as low character and sinners. Faustus accordingly persuades Scaramouche that it is a great privilege to work in his household because his special relationship with the devil offers protection to all its inmates. He exclaims: 'the Devil loves Sinners at his Heart', which persuades Scaramouche to swap his 'Chimney-sweeping Trade' for a more metaphorical 'black Art' (3).

Mountfort's shortened version of Marlowe's play changes some crucial episodes. A telling instance occurs during the first dialogue between Faustus and Mephostopholis: when Faustus provocatively exclaims 'I think Hell's a meer Fable', and drops the qualifying subclause, his spirit simply agrees to his statement: 'Ay, think so still' (6), instead of warning him that he will find out differently in due course, as Marlowe's spirit does: 'Ay, think so still, till experience change thy mind' (A and B: 2.1.128). Although the main characters of the farce have shed their individual characteristics, the play also takes many liberties with religious taboos. However, it would be mistaken to interpret the farce as an atheistic manifesto. Its portrayal of a banquet conjured up by magic, for instance, challenges theatrical make-believe: the most sophisticated ropes and pulleys and wheels of the playhouse are used to render visible the banquet's elusive qualities. This episode illustrates the popular belief that the devil's handiwork disappears when the name of the Lord is mentioned. Harlequin's persistence in thanking heaven for the bountiful meal logically removes it from his grasp (14–16). In spite of his transgression in soliciting the help from the devil, he demonstrates himself to be a simple human being who is humbly grateful for his daily bread. While the visual spectacle of the 'running Banquet', as Harlequin calls it, is clearly amusing, a contemporary audience might have laughed at the logical absurdity of showing Christian thankfulness for the devil's food, but it would not have laughed at the Christian sentiments themselves.

A characteristic of farce and other more ephemeral theatrical techniques is to display spectacles at the same time as drawing attention to their illusory qualities. While hell is at first only visible in the background, the final scene takes place inside hell itself, the location where the limbs of Faustus come together again, after they have been '[a]ll torn asunder by the Hand of Hell'. The final stage directions read 'A Dance, and Song', reminding us of the impossibility of pinning down and explaining the true nature of what we have just witnessed. It is also important to be aware that the play offers no sympathy for the damnation of Faustus. The farcical framework operates at a remove from the legend's customary engagement with damnation and salvation, allowing the reassembled limbs of Faustus to join into the final dance. This might be a Dance of Death, another symbolic ritual of the late Middle Ages.[35] But although the farce dramatizes the necessity of Faustus' damnation, it leaves us with a sense of utter bafflement about the meanings of the theatrical spectacle of hell.

Another interesting feature is that although Harlequin and Scaramouche imitate the behaviour of Faustus, they do not necessarily have to go to hell with him. The simple reason for this is that they are indestructible. Embodying the weaknesses of

---

35 Hans Holbein the Younger made a famous illustrated series of images about the different experiences of death and dying; cf. *The Dance of Death* (1538), facsimile edition, ed. Werner L. Gundesheimer (New York: Dover Publications, 1971).

humanity and suffering the difficulties associated with servitude and poverty, their native wit always saves them. In spite of their grossly frivolous dealings in black art, the play does not even consider destroying them along with their master Faustus. As stock characters, they are defeated only temporarily and always reappear in the next play. It is impossible for them to leave behind their working class identities as servants, chimneysweeps, artisans and knaves but this context also renders their transgressions more forgivable. The physical and psychological resilience of these low-life characters also reflects a deeply rooted sense of tolerance towards human foibles. Whereas a Calvinist or Puritan work would have taken all sinners to task, Mountfort's farce tolerates a certain amount of transgression.

Laughter enables a moment of recognition for its audience, so that it can accept that, yes, this is what we are like. *Commedia dell'arte*, as well as other comic art forms which borrowed certain components from popular drama, cultivated a spirit of solidarity among the poor which was eagerly applauded by an urban audience that no longer subscribed to Puritan austerity. Farces and comedies that endorsed a certain licence, therefore, showed more accepting views of human weaknesses which, for example, informed Bernard Mandeville's argument about the economic benefits of vice and selfishness in *The Fable of the Bees; or, Private Vices, Publick Benefits* (1714). The tolerant attitudes of popular art forms hence reflect the perspective of an upwardly mobile society that thrived best in the peripheries of legality.

Scaramouche's obituary on the recently deceased husband of the employer, for whom he is working after leaving Doctor Faustus' household, accordingly contains a whole list of offences: he squandered his property, swore, raped his maids and, finally, forswore his oath. After dismissing all of these acts as minor issues, Scaramouche comments on the breach of his oath: 'Words are but wind, and he meant no more harm than a sucking Pig does by squeaking' (23). The argument in defence of the deceased husband draws attention to the fact that meaning is itself a kind of magic. Scaramouche's skewed dissection of a very serious offence reveals that everything is possible for those who have control over meaning. In this sense the *commedia dell'arte* figures abandon Faustus because he is only one among many who possess illicit but effectual means of enriching themselves. Since Mountfort's farcical heroes are only interested in wealth, they leave Faustus for other masters who will afford easier profits for their underlings.

Harlequin in Hell: Evaristo Gherardi and the Conventions of *Commedia dell'Arte*

Joking references to the black art of Scaramouche ridicule the magical aspirations of a character whose main occupation is that of a chimneysweep. But of course, the fact that Scaramouche performs a messy task in an urban household also reinforces his resemblances to popular representations of the devil. The parallels between a chimneysweep and a devil are symbolically underlined because the passage through the chimney connects higher and lower spheres of life at the same time as the chimneysweep's dealings with ashes and soot suggest first-hand knowledge of the transformation happening to the body after physical death.[36] It is likely that in popular belief, the chimneysweep is frequently thought to be a harbinger of good luck because his occupation demands that he should cross the symbolic boundaries between high and low, life and death.

Carnivalesque comedies, or *commedia dell'arte*, emerged in sixteenth-century Italy as a way of challenging the hierarchies of bourgeois urban society. However, it also retained close links with the festivities of the medieval church. The original emphasis was on challenging order, which is why *commedia dell'arte* was well suited for the representation of a rapidly changing world. While the harlequinade that established itself during the seventeenth century is focused on bawdy parodies of courtship rituals and grotesque duels between rivals, Harlequin and Scaramouche also retain traces of their earlier participation in popular festivals to dispel the devil.[37] Their ambiguous nature reflects an inalienable confusion between the devil, his victims and anybody trying to expel him.

While it was still impossible to gain knowledge about the true nature of hell, the invention of Galileo's telescope (1610) suggested that technology finally enabled knowledge about a cosmic space that played an important role in western mythology.[38] The moon has always been an object of special interest. Associated with the night, madness and the world of fantasies, this celestial body was peculiarly suited as a dramatic setting to discuss new knowledge about material and metaphysical matters. Its proverbial elusiveness, together with the uncertainty as to the nature of this location, were a fertile ground for exploring the resemblances

---

36 Ulrike Reiss argues that Harlequin has his origin in the medieval understanding of the devil; see, *Harlequin: eine Ausstellung im Oesterreichischen Theatermuseum* (Wien: Hermann Böhlaus, 1984). Other speculations concerning his black face can be found in Pierre Louis Duchartre, *The Italian Comedy:The Improvisations, Scenarios, Lives, Attributes, Portraits, and Masks of the Illustrious Characters of the Commedia dell'Arte*, trans Randolph T. Weaver (London: George G. Harrap, 1929), pp. 123ff. See also Thelma Niklaus, *Harlequin Phoenix or The Rise and Fall of a Bergamask Rogue* (London: The Bodley Head, 1956).

37 For a discussion of the origins and history of *commedia dell'arte*, see Winifred Smith, *The Commedia dell'Arte* (New York: Benjamin Blom, 1964). See also Kenneth Richards and Laura Richards, *The Commedia dell'Arte: A Documentary History* (Oxford: Basil Blackwell for The Shakespeare Head Press, 1990).

38 Galileo Galilei, *The Sidereal Messenger of Galileo Galilei and a part of the preface to Kepler's Dioptrics Containing the Original Account of Galileo's Astronomical Discoveries* (London: Dawsons, 1960). Also compare *Kepler's Dream, with the Full Text and Notes of 'Somnium sive astronomicum lunaris Johannis Kepleri'* (Berkley: University of California Press, 1965).

between the moon's imagined inhabitants and traditional notions about spirits, devils and angels.[39]

An exploration of the spaces brought closer and made accessible by the new science furnished a wonderful task for Harlequin. Regardless of whether Harlequin took his origin in ritual expulsions of the devil or whether he is simply a saucy entertainer, he is an ideal figure for the exploration of unfamiliar, remote and mythical locations. The exploration by pantomime of real and imaginary places, indeed, brings about an odd blend between realism and fantasy. Living in an intellectual and geographic landscape that is rapidly changing, Harlequin can adjust to all situations. While his adaptability can be decried as offensive elusiveness it also represents an ingenious resourcefulness that will prevent him from being defeated.

A writer of harlequinades that heavily influenced English Restoration comedy was Evaristo Gherardi, the director of the Italian comedy in Paris. My brief glimpse at some of his plays will not be able to pay tribute to the richness of his art but it hopes to shed light on the significance of the harlequinade as a vehicle for the examination of the borderlines between magic and scientific knowledge. At this point I want to highlight a few aspects of Gherardi's harlequinade in order to explain some important influences on the farcical and pantomimical portrayals of the Faustus theme.

The formulation of Gherardi's title *Arlequin Protée* (1683)[40] draws attention to Harlequin's need to adjust and transform himself in order to succeed in an unpredictable world. Increasingly sophisticated techniques of theatrical deceptions and *trompe l'oeil* presented the pantomime as a spectacle that challenged social hierarchies and questioned existing notions of reality. This is why Gherardi's Harlequin is sent on a voyage to the underworld and to the moon, two similarly imaginary and liminal locations. A fascinating example that brings together fact and fiction is *Arlequin empereur dans la lune* (1684) which, among others, inspired Aphra Behn's immensely popular farcical play *The Emperor of the Moon* (1687).[41] In Gherardi's play, Harlequin lives in the household of a besotted adherent to the idea that the moon is a world in its own right. He therefore uses his transformational skills in order to pass himself off as an ambassador of the emperor of the moon. The play concludes with the appearance of three eminently

---

39 Samuel Butler was another contemporary figure to write a satire about the period's enthusiastic speculations about the world of the moon; see 'The Elephant in the Moon', *Satires and Miscellaneous Poetry and Prose*, ed. René Lamar (Cambridge: Cambridge University Press, 1928).

40 Evaristo Gherardi, *Arlequin Prothée*, in: *Le Théâtre Italien, ou le receuil générale de toutes les Comedies et Scènes françaises jouées par les Comediens Italiens du Roi* (Geneva: Slakine Reprints, 1969), vol. 1, pp. 74–120. Harlequin's transformational powers are also emphasized in Gherardi's *Arlequin, empereur de la lune*, p. 167.

41 For the influence of the Italian comedy on Aphra Behn, see Leo Hughes and A.H. Scouton, *Ten English Farces* (Austin, TX: The University of Texas Press, 1948).

ridiculous *'Chevaliers du Soleil'* – or Knights of the Sun (King) – who come to punish Harlequin for his imperial aspirations. Although Harlequin is punished for his presumption, the play does not conclude with the re-instatement of a rational perspective according to which inhabitants of the moon are derided as figments of the imagination. On the contrary, the impersonator of a fantasy is simply defeated by competing impersonators, as a result of which Harlequin gets away with tampering with reality, even if he cannot escape a good beating.

In another more elaborate pantomime entitled *Les intrigues d'Arlequin*, Harlequin resorts to magic in order to force his master to agree that the two young women under his guardianship can marry the husbands of their choice. With the help of a magical wand, he transforms himself into a scientist who knows everything about the sun, the moon and the planets.[42] *Les intrigues d'Arlequin* was published four years after *commedia dell'arte* had been banished from the French stage and one year after Gherardi's death. Entitled 'Letter from Cardan, written on the Meadows of Eternal Bliss to Monsieur xxx [sic]',[43] the preface plunges the reader into speculations about the possibility of gaining knowledge about life after death.

The setting of the preface is an ambiguous blend between hell and the Greek underworld. Pluto, the generous lord over this world, treats his distinguished vassals to a comedy. To this end he calls for Harlequin, as he describes him 'a little man who had come to him from the other world some time ago'.[44] The frontispiece is divided into a number of different scenes. Harlequin, about whom the preface says that he 'on his own amounts to a comedy', is set apart from Pluto and his illustrious company (Figure 7). The royal company resembles that of Louis XIV (1638–1715), in whose service Gherardi had once been employed, who is featured as the implied point of reference for the lord of the underworld. The background offers us a good view of many activities associated with the act of running a world (or underworld): wheels are pointing us into astrological theories and/or theatrical displays of such theories. But the wheel is also the wheel of fortune from which we see a hapless figure tumbling into the abyss. In the background, Sisyphus and Tantalus endure their eternal tortures while devils and other hellish fowl are fluttering to and fro. All signs agree that this is hell, but of course we are only observing an imaginary hell that insidiously resembles an absolutist state. The scope of the harlequinade for drawing attention to the workings of the earthly wheels of power explain why such plays came to be banished from the French stage.

Harlequin, the masked comedian, is the ruler over the spectacle through which he guides us. The mask sets him off as an archetypal stranger who can take his audience through the most unreal environments. That the attempt to play

---

42 Gherardi, *Les intrigues d'Arlequin*, pp. 434–539.

43 French 'Lettre de Cardan, écrite des Champs Elisée a Monsieur xxx [sic.]', *Les intrigues d'Arlequin*, p. 434.

44 Evaristo Gherardi, *Les intrigues d'Arlequin*, p. 444.

Fig. 7   'Harlequin in Hell', frontispiece for Evaristo Gherardi, *Les intrigues d'Arlequin*, in *Le Théâtre Italien de Gherardi*, Marchand Libraire prés le Dam: chez Adrian Braakman, 1701, p. 444.

Harlequin without a mask turned out to be a complete failure demonstrates how strongly his power depended on his mask.[45] Because of his masked face he stands at a remove from the events around him, which also allows him to take on the role of an absolutist ruler. In particular, it puts him in the position of the lord over the dramatic spectacle, so that he can reveal the cheap quality of the stage properties used to legitimate the forces of wealth and power.[46]

Harlequin Faustus

The Italian comedy reached a peak of popularity during the 1720s. The unprecedented enthusiasm of its reception was, however, matched with some savage criticism. When Alexander Pope published the first version of his *Dunciad* in 1728, his swan song on the cultural sanity of the period, he argued that the existence of such works must be a sure indication that the end was nigh. After his contemptuous reference to the 'sable sorcerer' (3.233) portrayed by John Thurmond's *Harlequin Doctor Faustus* (1723) and John Rich's rivalling play *The Necromancer* (1723), Pope expresses his censorious outrage about the disgraceful scenes on the popular stage:

> Thence a new world to Nature's laws unknown,
> Breaks out refulgent, with a heav'n its own:
> Another Cynthia her new journey runs,
> And other planets circle other suns.
> The forests dance, the rivers upward rise,
> Whales sport in woods, and dolphins in the skies;
> And last, to give the whole creation grace,
> Lo! one vast egg produces human race. (3.241–48)[47]

Pope's indignant observation illustrates that the stage machinery of contemporary theatres tampered with the basic laws of nature. As was instanced by the devil's banquet in Mountfort's farcial Faustus play, Pope's description reminds us that harlequinades entertained their audiences by suspending the law of gravity and even confronting them with surreal alternatives to the creation of a human being. What offends Pope most is not lack of piety in acknowledging the Christian God

---

45 Leo Hughes, *Ten English Farces*, p. 42. gives Cibber as a source for this argument. See also *An Apology for the Life of Colley Cibber, with an Historical View of the Stage during his own Time Written by Himself* (1740), ed. B.R.S. Fone (Ann Arbor: University of Michigan Press, 1968), I, 150ff.

46 John O'Brien, 'Magic and Mimesis: Harlequin Doctor Faustus and the Modernity of English Pantomime,' *Harlequin Britain: Pantomime and Entertainment, 1690–1760* (Baltimore: Johns Hopkins University Press, 2004), pp. 93–116.

47 Alexander Pope, *Poems*, ed. John Butt (London: Methuen, 1963).

as the sole creator of all living beings, but the idea that the unrestrained exertion of imaginative powers has challenged the natural order of things.

There is something prudish about Pope's judgements but he is of course right that the harlequinades of the 1720s were provocative to the point of challenging the order of nature. This is demonstrated, for example, by the stage directions for the final scene of John Thurmond's *Harlequin Doctor Faustus*:

> When the Songs are ended, it Thunders and Lightens; two Fiends enter and seize the Doctor, and are sinking with him headlong thro' Flames; other Devils run in, and tear him piece-meal, some fly away with the Limbs, and others sink. Time and Death [two characters] go out.

> The musick changes, and the Scene draws, and discovers a Poetical Heaven with the Gods and Goddesses rang'd in order, on both sides the Stage, expressing their Joy in Dances for the Enchanter's Death (who was suppos'd to have Power over the Sun, the Moon, and the Seasons of the Year).[48]

What is in practical terms a rapid stage transformation from one pantomime to another also opens up a perspective on human and metaphysical agents.

As I have already mentioned, David Bevington and Eric Rasmussen prefer as the basis of their edition the previously less highly esteemed A-text of Marlowe's *Doctor Faustus*, because the B-text is more conscious of theatrical tricks; this is to say that the concrete visualization of hell, '*discovered*' at the back of the playing area, undercuts the horror with which Faustus is expected to stare '[i]nto that vast perpetual torture-house' (B: 5.2.121–2).[49] Showing the eternal tortures of hell on the stage subverts their psychological terror because, however sophisticated the stage machinery of the theatre might be, the audience was aware that hell was merely a spectacle; a fantasy rendered visible by theatrical technology. By showing a ludicrous group of gods who rejoice at the destruction of Faustus, Thurmond's pantomimical spectacle draws attention to the petty-minded human characteristics attributed to metaphysical agents. Who would damn Doctor Faustus after observing the behaviour of such gods?

It does not surprise, therefore, that the introduction to John Rich's *The Necromancer, or, Harlequin Doctor Faustus* makes an effort to demystify the infernal reputation of Doctor Faustus:

> He was born in *Germany*, about the Beginning of the 14th *Century*, a Period of Dullness and Barbarism. *Monkery* and *Imposition* prevail'd much stronger than, perhaps, they ever

---

48 John Thurmond, *Harlequin Doctor Faustus: With the Masque of the Deities* (London: for T. Corbett, 1724), p. 10.

49 David Bevington and Eric Rasmusseen, 'Introduction', *Doctor Faustus* (Manchester: Manchester University Press, 1993), p. 46

will again: And Knowledge was in so few Hands, that an *uncommon* Share of *Learning*, or *uncommon Qualifications*, were sufficient to make a Man thought a *Conjurer*.[50]

This passage argues that Faustus was only described as a magician because his contemporaries wanted to slander him. Samuel Palmer, another historical commentator, argued that Faustus had discovered the art of printing and was accused of practicing magic because he carried a larger number of books 'than it was possible for several men to transcribe in their whole life, and the pages of each copy so exactly alike, ... he was seiz'd, try'd and condemn'd for *Magick* and *Sorcery*, and was accordingly dragg'd to the stake to be burnt; but upon discovering his Art, the parliament at *Paris* made an act to discharge him from all prosecution, in consideration of his admirable invention'.[51]

By explaining that the Faustus legend emerged in response to a particularly gifted technological innovator, Rich's introduction suggests that the harlequinade indirectly laughs at those who condemned Faustus. But what does it mean when Harlequin Faustus is sent to hell? As we hear in a satirical description of its dramatic performance, Faustus was carried to hell in an elaborately designed machine that looked like a dragon:

> The Dragon roaring, opens wide
> His Sparro-Mouth, from side to side,
> And down he gulps him at one swallow
> …
> Now peals of Thunder rowl aloud,
> To terrify the gazing Croud,
> And render the tremendous Scene,
> More frightful than it need have been;
> The Dragon roaring mounts up higher,
> And gapes, to show his Mouth's on fire,
> Which like a flaming Oven looks
> When heating at the Pastry-Cooks.
> The Devils, to conclude the Jest,
> Cling close to the departing Beast,
> Among the rest the Doctor's Zany,

50　[John Rich,] *The Vocal Parts of an Entertainment, Call'd the Necromancer: Or, Harlequin Doctor Faustus*, As Perform'd at the Theatre Royal in Lincoln's Inn Fields (London: A. Dodd, 1723), pp. v–vi.

51　Samuel Palmer (with additions by George Psalmanazar), *The General History of Printing* (London: printed by the author, 1732), pp. 87–8 and 31–2. A similar argument is presented in Daniel Defoe's *The History of the Principal Discoveries and Improvements in the Several Arts and Sciences* (London: for W. Mears, 1727), pp. 223–4. Also compare Adrian Johns, *The Nature of the Book: Print and Knowledge in the Making* (Chicago: University of Chicago Press, 1998), pp. 324–79.

Who made the Croud more sport than any,
Catch'd hold o' th' Dragons Duggs and there
He held and hung 'twixt Earth and Air ...[52]

The absurdity of the scene suppresses all other responses to the event. The dragon presents itself as a grotesque hybrid between a fire-spouting flying machine and an apocalyptical beast.[53] While such spectacles were enormously popular, a whole range of the period's critics were infuriated by the popular plays' breaches of both established beliefs and natural laws.

The final apotheosis of Harlequin Faustus happens in a pantomime by Lewis Theobald performed after the two initial Faustus Harlequinades. In Theobald's *A Dramatick Entertainment, call'd Harlequin a Sorcerer* (1725), the hero is introduced as the 'contracted Son' of the Lord of the Underworld.[54] Since Harlequin has changed his role of Faustus to that of the devil, the themes of temptation and damnation have dropped out altogether. The plot now revolves around the legend of Pluto's forceful abduction of Proserpine. In this version of the tale she complains about the boredom of the underworld until Harlequin is fetched to entertain her. When Pluto hears of Harlequin's arrival, he moreover gives orders that the traditional tortures of hell should now be terminated:

Most welcome are thy Tidings – Hence,
To Hell's far Bounds the Sound dispence
Let not a Fiend presume to wear
The Face of Sorrow or Despair;
But all, in merriest Mood, unite,
To give their mighty Prince Delight.
Let rack'd *Ixion* now advance;
Prometheus too prepare to dance;
Let *Sysiphus* and *Tiphon* play;
The Fatal Sisters too be gay:
E'en watchful *Cerberus* shall rest,

---

52 *The Dancing Devils: Or, the Roaring Dragon. A Dumb Farce. As It was lately Acted at Both Houses, but Particularly at One, with Unaccountable Success* (London: printed by A. Bettesworth, 1724), pp. 69–70.

53 Cf. the most prominent biblical reference to the physical translation of Elijah into heaven: 'And it came to pass, as they still went on, and talked, that, behold, there appeared a chariot of fire, and horses of fire, and parted them both asunder; and Elijah went up by a whirlwind into heaven.' (*Authorized King James Version of the Bible* [1611], 2 *Kings* 2.9). As Eugen Wolff points out, there had been a long tradition of celebrating Luther as the last Elijah, which in turn provoked a parodic tradition by his opponents; cf. Eugen Wolff, *Faust und Luther: ein Beitrag zur Entstehung der Faust-Dichtung* (Halle a.S.: Max Niemeyer, 1912), p. 78.

54 Theobald, Lewis, *A Dramatick Entertainment, Call'd Harlequin a Sorcerer: with the Loves of Pluto and Proserpine*, London: T. Wood, 1725.

And *Tantalus* shall freely feast:
This is my Will – – – proclaim it round,
And in loud Triumphs spread the Sound. (p. 11)

It is not new that Harlequin is emphatically eulogized as somebody who can make his audience happy. In his role as entertainer of the court of the underworld, however, Harlequin Faustus suggests the conclusion that even in hell suffering comes into being when a ruler is unhappy, rather than being a punishment for acts of transgression.

The story of the pantomime, then, explains that the now happy monarch Pluto, who has replaced torments with courtly entertainments, cannot fail but be successful in his courtship of Proserpine. As a result of his improved mood, the general atmosphere of his underworld changes. Because Proserpine is a lot happier with her new environment, she responds favourably to Pluto's courtship:

With utmost Pleasure, now I see
The Monarch of my Heart and Me.
No more great *Pluto* sues in vain,
No more my Anger I retain;
I view thy Empire, richly wide,
Partner of all thy Pow'r and Pride.
Where Vassal Peers thy Nod obey,
And scepter'd Slaves their Homage pay. (p. 12)

While the Harlequin Faustus plays of 1723 trivialized the transgressions of Faustus, Theobald's extension of the Faustus typology sketches a world where transgressive acts are pardonable as long as they provide entertainment.

Conclusion

The portrayals of hell as a spectacle for the entertainment of popular audiences reflected a secular disregard for the metaphysical significance of this symbolic space. But the popularity of the Faustus theme also gave rise to a renewed demand for the printed formulae that were supposed to have been used by the historical Doctor Faustus. But as Frank Möbus explains, the main purpose of such publications concerned the mysterious art of locating treasure and discovering hidden riches.[55] The main purpose of eighteenth-century harlequinades and popular plays about jester-devils, however, was to entertain gaping crowds. Of course it is impossible to know what exactly the enthusiastic audiences saw in the comically

55   Frank Möbus, 'Kein Meister über die Geister', *Faust, Annäherung an einen Mythos*, eds. Frank Möbus, Friederike Schmidt- Möbus and Gerd Unverfehrt (Göttingen: Wallstein Verlag, 1995), p. 38.

distorted versions of hell and the underworld. It would be inaccurate to conclude that the majority of these audiences consisted of atheists, but a key factor in the popularity of Harlequin Faustus must have consisted of its irreverent treatment of the cautionary tale. By this time, traditional warnings about the exploration of new knowledge had become ridiculous.

Eighteenth-century harlequinades thrived particularly well in a materialist environment, where magic was reduced to a portrayal of stereotypical views about heaven and hell. Popular treatments of the Faustus theme also offered an unprecedented empowerment to those at the bottom of the social hierarchy: the crowds of an urban society. Of course urban audiences possessed some commercial clout, and they were willing to pay for performances that portrayed characters who were struggling to get on in the world. For such audiences, the magic of Harlequin Faustus was located not in the magical formulae but in the fact that a socially disadvantaged hero could prosper by his own resources. The unquestioned survival of the indigent Harlequin and Scaramouche pays tribute to the invincibility of those born without any privileges: the apprentices, artisans, shop-keepers and common labourers who had to thrive by their wit and occasional disregard for rules and prohibitions.

This chapter simply offers a brief overview of comic forms that were used in the late seventeenth and early eighteenth century. Sketching a broad-picture view of the arguments and counterarguments that circled around the Faustus theme, however, reveals the overarching significance of literary perspectives that diminished the weight of topics of unwieldy metaphysical proportions and hence transformed them into a human scale. This chapter embraced Defoe's half-serious account of the devil's involvement in human affairs, Shadwell's satire, Mountfort's farcical Faustus play, and the exuberantly sensual harlequinades about Faustian magician. All of these works were immersed in a culture of savage controversies related to whether the popular culture of the eighteenth century systematically undermined the established values of the period, or alternatively, gave vent to the imagination of a highly controlled society.

Conclusion

This study has traced the development of the Faustus legend from the late sixteenth to the early eighteenth century, starting from the moment when semi-oral versions of the typology were transformed into literary format, and concluding with the decade of the 1720s, when the popular hero was re-invented as Harlequin Faustus. In spite of having been recorded in writing and performed as a popular tragedy, an already well-known theme became even more popular when Marlowe's *Doctor Faustus* was first performed. Throughout the eighteenth century, it continued to belong to the repertoire of traveling companies and puppet players.

Johann Wolfgang Goethe's treatment of the material was the first to acquire the status of canonical literature. Even though it is outside the scope of this book to analyse Romantic and subsequent versions of the tale, it is worth mentioning how strongly Goethe's transformation changed the public perception of the Faustus theme. In *Faust I*, the first and generally best known part of his *Faust*, he considers the moral implications of his hero's quest to gratify his desires, rather than studying his acts of intellectual daring.[1] A wider range of ideas about the magic qualities of nature are explored in *Faust II*. In the first part, which imagines a contemporary context for the traditional elements of the story, however, magic is primarily a means to an end, rather than a path towards understanding and experiencing the principles that hold the cosmos together. These ideas resonate in the background of the first part but it is only in the second part that Goethe concentrated on the traditional concerns of the tale. The thematic complexity of *Faust II*, coupled with the extreme difficulty of staging this play, dampened its potential influence, while *Faust I* became probably the most widely read play in the German language.

The different versions of the Faustus legend, written in the hundred and fifty years after the German and English Faust Books first appeared, concentrate on exploring the place of humans in the natural order. While examining different meanings and uses of magic, these works draw close parallels between the desire to employ magic and an archetypal yearning to be at one with nature. Since such a desire is sometimes touted as an act of naivety and sometimes praised as a vital aspiration, the narrative typology wavers between comic, tragic and burlesque modes. Its uneasy generic identification, then, reflects the psychological uncertainties of an age that still had to figure out the differences between wanting to obtain command over the natural world and wanting to enter into a harmonious relationship with nature.

That the early versions of the Faustus legend found expression in many generic forms – ballads, broadsheets, plays, poetry, literary prose and pantomime – reflects

---

1   Johann Wolfgang Goethe, *Faust* (München, Hanser, 1999).

its popularity, showing that the typology expressed essential concerns for a period that, among other things, had to come to terms with the rise of the new science. The Faustus legend offered itself as a welcome instrument for exploring the consequences of an increasingly secularized understanding of nature. There is a subversive message to the story in defiance of its ostensible purpose as a cautionary tale, which legitimated the intellectual ventures of the enquiring mind. But its complex tapestry of ambiguities is also the result of an attempt to re-connect to the secret, or magical, energies of nature that were being discredited as a result of materialist descriptions of nature becoming generally accepted. The twin objectives of gleaning factual information about nature and instilling a sense of awe had long been closely enmeshed. Ironically enough, the scientific endeavours growing out of early investigations of nature – also known as natural magic – threatened to destroy the sense that nature harboured its own enchantment.[2] The idea that there was a magical quality to nature was embraced both by popular superstitions about personified figures of good and evil and in an abstract reverence for nature's patterns of growth and decay. Such a response to nature was suspect both for proponents of Christianity and Enlightened materialists: what the former indicted as a mark of superstition, the latter decried as a deplorable absence of reason.

While many members of the early Enlightenment intelligentsia no longer believed in a devil, this figure retained his presence in popular imagination. But of course, the physically concrete devil of folk mythology differed strongly from the abstract principle of evil that informed theological controversies. Equally divergent were contemporary views about the legitimacy of curiosity and ideas concerning the rights and duties of the scientific experimenter. It was precisely because there were widely diverging attitudes about the meanings and uses of scientific knowledge that the Faustus legend became such a popular vehicle for exploring these issues. But those who sought to restrain the liberties of the explorer and those who demanded a liberation of the mind argued their case with similar eloquence, which is why the subversive messages of the Faust Books came to co-exist with the cautionary tale's vociferous condemnation of the hubristic aspirations of an unrestrained mind.

A feature that provides a shared dimension for all versions of the Faustus legend, therefore, is that they reflect the age-old idea that humankind's bond to the metaphysical world is determined by some primordial battle between good and evil. The Faustus legend builds on the notion that a human being is always somehow at the mercy of an endless battle between opposing forces. The cautionary tale accordingly argues that Faustus is damned, not only because he voluntarily sides with the forces of evil, but also because the battle fought over him (for instance symbolized by the Good and Bad Angels of Marlowe's play) has been determined in favour of the evil combatant. In spite of complex attempts to explain the causal

---

2 Cf. Giambattista della Porta, *Natural Magic*, facsimile edition of an anonymous English translation printed in London in 1658 (New York: Basic Books, 1958); the original Latin edition was first published in 1558.

relations between the damnation and the behaviour of Faustus, on one level, at least, it is a matter of chance which of the two forces gains the upper hand.[3] This explains why, for example, Marlowe's dramatic arrangement of his characters can be seen to dismiss the conflict between the two personifications of good and evil as a petty squabble.

Not all versions of the legend (whether explicit imitations or works with similar thematic emphases) equally condone the behaviour of Faustus and rather than salvaging Faustus from hell and damnation, the versions of the Faustus legend discussed here make us think about the injustice of such a view of human destiny. From a drama about obedience and insubordination, the Faustus narrative hence turns into a study of human attempts to deal with responsibility and moral self-determination.

In many early versions of the tale, the chief goal of Faustus is to gain control over natural forces. The gratification of this desire, of course, gives him a pleasurable awareness of his own powers, but it also forces him to recognize that having all his wishes granted does not necessarily give rise to a feeling of fulfillment. The inner emptiness of Faustus is the result of his experience that however great his skills may be they are nevertheless limited. What is more, no amount of knowledge, or command over nature, could satisfy his desires unless he learns to be at one with himself and the world.

In the chapbooks the drama relates to the separation between humankind and nature, while Marlowe's and later transformations of the myth concentrate on the power-pleasure nexus. At their best, especially in the early versions, the legend reminds us that Faustus' disobedience is primarily motivated by his desire to re-connect with the natural and social environments from which he has been separated and alienated. It is his painful awareness of his isolation that motivates his intellectual and metaphysical quests. Being not just a deep thinker but also a man of action, Faustus sets out to explore every corner of the three-partite cosmology of his age: heaven, hell and earth. The condition of the pact according to which he can become a spirit himself sketches a method of re-connecting, which is why I have argued that this feature is as vital to the Faust Books as their innovative treatment of the three journeys through physical and symbolic space. Although Faustus' quest for a union with the cosmos may be enmeshed in many ambiguities, it remains a vital element of the early versions of the tale.

In many ways the farcical transformations of the Faustus legend are far removed from the topic of emotional fulfillment. However, it is only as Harlequin Faustus that he can be seen to have achieved his long-standing wish of becoming a spirit. When Harlequin Faustus is sent to hell, in compliance with the severe verdict of the cautionary tale, he is in one version revealed to be an honoured

---

3   For a discussion of the idea, emerging in the seventeenth century, that chance and probability played a major role in human existence, see Lorraine Daston, *Classical Probability in the Enlightenment* (Princeton: Princeton University Press, 1988).

vassal of the king of the underworld,[4] and in another version responds by showing a childish fascination for the fire-spouting machinery of hell.[5] While seemingly complying with the condemnation of the challenger of convention and tradition, popular comedy exposes established beliefs about heaven and hell as pure fantasy. Even though Harlequin Faustus could not care less about the metaphysical interests of earlier Faustus figures, he at least gets his fair share of fun. Neither a severe Christian judge of human pleasures nor even a devil can squash his spark of life. It diverges strongly from the belief in an inner light, which inspired the mystic undercurrents of Milton's *Paradise Lost*. But Harlequin Faustus' confident resistance to all enemies of worldly pleasure nevertheless asserts an ineradicable belief in a human nature that deserves to unfold its potentials without constraint.

My study has argued that the versions of the Faustus legend written between approximately 1580 and 1730 share some important concerns. Next to the process of legitimating curiosity and gesturing towards a sense of unity between humankind and the natural world, the simple portrayal of a character endowed with enormous intellectual and imaginative powers is important. Of course, the hypothetical question of what might happen if the almost boundless energies of the Renaissance man Faustus were released posed an enormous threat to social order. This is why the voice of the cautionary tale condemned not just the sinful dealings of Faustus with the devil but also indicted him for the possession of a strong character and a penchant for adventure. In the early modern period, however, initiative and individual effort were also turning into highly cherished qualities. But for a long time the opposing attitudes towards the value of an adventurous mind were at loggerheads. It does not surprise, therefore, that they are equally present in the Faustus typology and indeed generate an eloquent controversy between the voice of the cautionary tale and a thinly disguised admiration for intellectual daring. The final fact of Faustus' death leaves us unable to decide which of the two voices is right. But the creative energy that radiates from the depiction of Faustus' adventures suggests that all versions discussed here were on the side of Faustus, even if the arguments in his favour are expressed in parallel with those of the prophet of doom.

4　Cf. [John Rich,] *The Vocal Parts of an Entertainment, Call'd the Necromancer: Or, Harlequin Doctor Faustus, As Perform'd at the Theatre Royal in Lincoln's Inn Fields* (London: A. Dodd, 1723). See also Theobald, Lewis, *A Dramatick Entertainment, call'd Harlequin a Sorcerer: With the Loves of Pluto and Proserpine* (London: T. Wood, 1725).

5　Cf. John Thurmond, *Harlequin Doctor Faustus: With the Masque of the Deities* (London: for T. Corbett, 1724).

Bibliography

Editions of Key Works Discussed in Text

Browne, Thomas, *The Prose of Sir Thomas Browne*, Garden City, NY: Anchor Books, 1967.

EFB (English Faust Book): John Henry Jones, ed., *The English Faust Book: A Critical Edition Based on the Text of 1592*, Cambridge: Cambridge University Press, 1994.

Fontenelle, Bernard le Bovier de, 'A Discovery of New Worlds' (1686), trans. Aphra Behn (1688), in *The Works of Aphra Behn*, vol. 4, ed. Janet Todd, London: William Pickering, 1993.

GFB (German Faust Book, published by Johann Spies, 1587): Helmut Wiemken, ed., *Doctor Fausti Weheklag: die Volksbücher von D. Johann Faust und Christoph Wagner*, Bremen: Carl Schünemann, 1961.

Marlowe, Christopher, *Doctor Faustus: A- and B-texts*, eds. David Bevington and Eric Rasmussen, Manchester: Manchester University Press, 1993.

Milton, John, *Paradise Lost*, in *Complete English Poems, Of Education, Areopagitica*, ed. Gordon Campbell, London: Everyman, 1993.

Farcical Versions of Doctor Faustus

Merrivale, Thomas, *The Necromancer: or, Harlequin Doctor Faustus: A Poem*, London: J. Roberts, 1724.

Mountfort, William, *The Life and Death of Doctor Faustus Made into a Farce* (1697), intro. Anthony Kaufman, The Augustan Reprint Society, no. 157, Los Angeles: William Andrews Clark Memorial Library, 1973.

[Rich, John and Thomas Merrivale] *The Vocal Parts of an Entertainment, call'd the Necromancer: Or, Harlequin Doctor Faustus*, As performe'd at the Theatre Royal in Lincoln's Inn-Fields. To which is Prefix'd, a Short Account of Doctor Faustus; and how he came to be reputed a Magician, London: printed at the Book-seller's Shop, 1723.

Shadwell, Thomas, *The Virtuoso* (1676), eds. Marjorie Hope Nicolson and David Stuart Rodes, Lincoln: University of Nebraska Press, 1966.

The British Stage; Or, the Exploits of Harlequin: a Farce, Design'd as an After-Entertainment for the Audiences of Harlequin Doctor Faustus, and the Necromancer, London: printed for T. Warner, 1724.

The Dancing Devils: or, The Roaring Dragon: A Dumb Farce, As it was lately Acted at both Houses, but particularly at one, with unaccountable Success, London: printed by A. Bettesworth et al., 1724.

The Surprising Life and Death of Doctor John Faustus. To which is now added, *The Necromancer: Or, Harlequin Doctor Faustus*, As performed at the Theatre Royal, in Lincoln's Inn Fields. Likewise the whole *Life of Fryer Bacon, the Famous Magician of England: And the merry Waggeries of his Man Miles*, London: printed and sold by the Booksellers, 1727.

Theobald, Lewis, *A Dramatick Entertainment, call'd Harlequin a Sorcerer: With the Loves of Pluto and Proserpine*, London: T. Wood, 1725.

Thurmond, John, *Harlequin Doctor Faustus* [first performed in 1723]*: With the Masque of the Deities*, London: T. Corbett, 1724.

Other References

Abraham, Lyndy, *Marvell and Alchemy*, Aldershot: Scolar Press, 1990.

———, *A Dictionary of Alchemical Imagery*, Cambridge: Cambridge University Press, 1998.

Agrippa of Nettesheim, Henry Cornelius, *The Philosophy of Natural Magic* (1533), Seacaucus, N.J.: University Books, 1974.

Albertus Magnus, *Book of Minerals*, trans. Dorothy Wyckoff, Oxford, 1967.

Allen, Don Cameron, *Doubt's Boundless Sea: Skepticism and Faith in the Renaissance*, Baltimore: Johns Hopkins University Press, 1964.

Altman, Joel, *The Tudor Play of Mind*, Berkeley: University of California Press, 1978.

Anderson, Benedict, *Imagined Communities: Reflections on the Origin and Spread of Nationalism*, London: Verso, 1983.

Anon., *Der Schlüssel von dem Zwange der Höllen oder die Beschwörungen und Prozesse des Doctor Johannis Faustae, von der öfters practicirten göttlichen Zauber-Kunst ex Originalibus*, Hamburg: L.M. Glogan Sohn, 1609.

Anon., *Histoire prodigieuse et lamentable de Jean Fauste, grand et horrible enchanteur, avec sa mort espouventable*, Rouen: chez Clement Malassis, 1667.

Anon., *Historisch-kritische Untersuchung über das Leben und die Thaten des als Schwarzkünstler verschrieenen Landfahrers Doctor Johannes Fausts, des Cagliostro seiner Zeiten*, Leipzig: Dykische Buchhandlung, 1791.

Aristotle [pseud.], *Secretum Secretorum: Nine English Versions*, ed. M.A. Manzalaoui, Oxford, 1977.

Armstrong, Megan C., *The Politics of Piety*, Rochester: University of Rochester Press, 2004.

Ashmole, Elias, ed. *Theatrum Chemicum Britannicum*, ed. Allen G. Debus, New York, 1967.

Auerbach, Erich, *Mimesis: The Representation of Reality in Western Literature* (1945), trans. Willard R. Strask, Princeton: Princeton University Press, 1974.

Augustine, Aurelius, *The City of God*, trans. Marcus Dods, New York: Modern Library, 1950.

———, *The Anti-Manichaean Writings*, ed. Philip Schaff, vol. 4 of *The Early Church Fathers: Nicene and Post-Nicene Fathers*, New York: The Christian Literature Publishing, 1890; available electronically under Christian Classics

Ethereal Library, accessed 23 August 2006, http://www.ccel.org/ccel/schaff/
npnf104.html.

———, *Four Anti-Pelagian Writings*, trans. John A. Mourant and William J.
Collinge, Washington: Catholic University of America Press, 1992.

Bacon, Francis, *The Advancement of Learning and New Atlantis*, ed. Arthur
Johnston, Oxford: Clarendon Press, 1974.

———, *Novum Organum, with Other Parts of the Great Instauration* (1620), trans.
and eds. Peter Urbach and John Gibson, Chicago: Open Court, 1994.

Bailey, Margaret Lewis, *Milton and Jacob Boehme: A Study of German Mysticism
in Seventeenth-century England*, New York: Haskell House, 1964.

Bann, Stephen, *Romanticism and the Rise of History*, New York: Twayne
Publishers, 1995.

Bartels, Emily Carroll, ed., *Critical Essays on Christopher Marlowe*, London:
Prentice Hall International, 1997.

Barthelemy, Anthony Gerard, *Black Face Maligned Race: The Representation
of Blacks in English Drama from Shakespeare to Southerne*, Baton Rouge:
Louisiana State University Press, 1987.

Bates, Paul A., *Faust, Sources, Works, Criticism*, New York: Harcourt, Brace and
World, 1969.

Bateson, Gregory and Mary Catherine Bateson, *Angels Fear: An Investigation
into the Nature and Meaning of the Sacred*, London: Rider, 1987.

Bath, Michael, *Speaking Pictures: English Emblem Books and Renaissance
Culture*, London: Longman, 1994.

Behn, Aphra, *The Works of Aphra Behn* (1688), 5 vols., ed. Janet Todd, London:
William Pickering, 1993.

Belsey, Catherine, *The Subject of Tragedy: Identity and Difference in Renaissance
Drama*, London: Methuen, 1985.

Benjamin, Walter, *Illuminations*, ed. Hannah Arendt, trans. Harry Zohn, New
York: Schocken, 1969.

Benz, Richard E., ed., *Deutsche Volksbücher*, Heidelberg: Schneider, 1956.

———, *Historia von D. Johann Fausten, dem weitbeschreyten Zauberer und
Schwarzkünstler*, Stuttgart: Reclam, 1968.

Bergerac, Cyrano de, *Histoire comique des États et Empire de la Lune*,
ed. C. Nodier, Paris: Club des Editeurs, 1961.

Bernouilli, Christoph, ed., *Romantische Naturphilosophie*, Jena: Eugen Diedrichs,
1926.

Best, Michael R. and Frank H. Brightman, eds., *The Book of Secrets of Albertus
Magnus of the Virtues of Herbs, Stones and Certain Beasts, also A Book of the
Marvels of the World*, Oxford: Clarendon Press, 1973.

Bevington, David, *From 'Mankind' to Marlowe: Growth of Structure in the Popular
Drama of Tudor England*, Cambridge, MA: Harvard University Press, 1962.

———, ed. *Mediaeval Drama*, Boston: Houghton Mifflin, 1975.

The Bible, Authorized King James Version (1611).

Blackburn, William, 'Heavenly Words: Marlowe's Faustus as a Renaissance
Magician,' *English Studies in Canada* 4.1 (1978).

Boas, Marie, *The Scientific Renaissance 1450–1630*, New York: Harper Torchbooks, 1962.

Boerner, Peter and Sidney Johnson, *Faust through Four Centuries: Retrospect and Analysis*, Tübingen: Max Niemeyer, 1989.

Brown, Peter, *Augustine of Hippo: A Biography*, London: Faber, 1967.

Browne, Thomas, *Pseudodoxia Epidemica*, 2 vols., ed. Robin Robbins, Oxford, 1981.

———, *The Works of the Learned Thomas Brown* [sic], London: for Tho. Barnet, Ric. Chiswell, Tho. Sawbridge, Charles Mearn and Charles Brome, 1686.

Brückner, Albert, *Faustus von Mileve*, Basel: Friedrich Reinhardt, 1901.

Bruno, Giordano, *On the Infinite Universe and Worlds*, in *Giordano Bruno: His Life and Thought*, ed. and trans. Dorothea Waley Singer, New York: Abelard-Schulman, 1950.

Bunyan, John, *Pilgrim's Progress* (1678), ed. R. Sharrock, Harmondsworth: Penguin, 1968.

Burckhardt, Jacob, *The Civilisation of the Renaissance in Italy* (1860), trans. S.G.C. Middlemore, London: Allen & Unwin, 1944.

Burnet, Thomas, *Sacred Theory of the Earth: containing an account of the original of the earth, and of all the general changes which it hath already undergone, or is to undergo, till the consummation of all things* (1684), London: printed for John Hooke, 1719.

Butler, E.M., *The Fortunes of Faust*, Cambridge: Cambridge University Press, 1979.

———, *The Myth of the Magus*, Cambridge: Cambridge University Press, 1948.

Butler, Samuel, *Satires and Miscellaneous Poetry and Prose*, ed. René Lamar, Cambridge: Cambridge University Press, 1928.

Byrd, Max, *Visits to Bedlam: Madness and Literature in the Eighteenth Century*, Columbia: University of South Carolina Press, 1974.

Calvin, Jean, *Calvin: Institutes of the Christian Religion*, 2 vols., ed. John T. McNeill, trans. Ford Lewis Battles, Philadelphia: Westminster, 1960;

———, *Institutes of the Christian Religion*, trans. Henry Beveridge, London for Bonham Norton, 1599; accessed 15 August 2006, http://www.reformed.org/master/index.html?mainframe=/books/institutes/.

Cantor, Paul A., *Creature and Creator: Myth-making and English Romanticism*, Cambridge: Cambridge University Press, 1984.

Castle, Terry, *Masquerade and Civilization: The Carnivalesque in Eighteenth-century English Culture and Fiction*, London, 1986.

Cavendish, Margaret, *Poems and Fancies: written by the right honourable, the Lady Newcastle* (1653), Menston: Scolar Press, 1972.

Chambers, E.K., *The Medieval Stage*, 2 vols., Oxford: Oxford University Press, 1978.

Chamisso, Adalbert, *Peter Schlemihls wundersame Geschichte* (1814), ed. J. Boyd, Oxford: Basil Blackwell, 1962.

Chance, Jane and R.O. Wells, eds., *Mapping the Cosmos*, Houston: Rice University Press, 1985.

Clark, Stuart, *Thinking with Demons: The Idea of Witchcraft in Early Modern Europe*, Oxford: Clarendon Press, 1997.

Cole, Douglas, *Suffering and Evil in the Plays of Christopher Marlowe*, Princeton: Princeton University Press, 1962.

Coleridge, Samuel Taylor, *Biographia Literaria or Biographical Sketches of My Literary Life and Opinions* (1817), eds. James Engell and W. Jackson Bate, in *The Collected Works of Samuel Taylor Coleridge*, Princeton: Princeton University Press, 1983.

———, *Seven Lectures on Shakespeare and Milton*, introd. J.P. Collier, New York: B. Franklin, 1968.

Coudert, Allison, *Alchemy: the Philosopher's Stone*, Boulder, 1980.

Cox, John D., *The Devil and the Sacred in English Drama, 1350–1642*, Cambridge: Cambridge University Press, 2000.

Craik, T.W., 'Faustus' Damnation Reconsidered,' *Renaissance Drama*, NS 2 (1969): 189–96.

Creeds of Christendom, accessed 14 February 2006, http://www.creeds.net.

Danielson, Dennis Richard, ed, *The Cambridge Companion to Milton*, Cambridge: Cambridge University Press, 1989.

Danson, Lawrence, 'The Questioner,' *Christopher Marlowe: Modern Critical Views*, ed. Harold Bloom, New York: Chelsea House Publishers, 1986, pp. 183–206.

Darnton, Robert, *The Kiss of Lamourette: Reflections in Cultural History*, New York: Norton, 1990.

Darwin, Erasmus, *The Botanic Garden* (1791), Menston: The Scolar Press, 1973.

Daston, Lorraine, *Classical Probability in the Enlightenment*, Princeton: Princeton University Press, 1988.

———, 'The Nature of Nature in Early Modern Europe', *Configurations* 6.2 (1998): 149–72.

Daston, Lorraine and Catherine Park, *Wonders and the Order of Nature, 1150–1750*, New York: Zone Books, 1998.

De Huszar Allen, Marguerite, *The Faust Legend: Popular Formula and Modern Novel*, New York: Peter Lang, 1985.

Dear, Peter, *Discipline and Experience: The Mathematical Way in the Scientific Revolution*, Chicago: University of Chicago Press, 1995.

Deats, Sara Munson, 'Doctor Faustus: From Chapbook to Tragedy', *Christopher Marlowe: Doctor Faustus*, Columbia University Press, 2004.

———, *Sex, Gender and Desire in the Plays of Christopher Marlowe*, Newark: University of Delaware Press, 1993.

Debus, Allen, *The English Paracelsians*, London, 1965.

Defoe, Daniel, *The History of the Principal Discoveries and Improvements in the Several Arts and Sciences*, London: for W. Mears, 1727.

———, *The History of the Devil*, London: for. T. Warner, 1727.

Dobbs, Betty Jo Teeter, *The Foundations of Newton's Alchemy: Of, 'The Hunting of the Greene Lyon'*, Cambridge: Cambridge University Press, 1975.

Dollimore, Jonathan, *Radical Tragedy: Religion, Ideology and Power in the Drama of Shakespeare and His Contemporaries*, Brighton: Harvester, 1984.

Donne, John, 'Holy Sonnet V', *Poems* (1635), Literature Online, accessed 12 July 2006, http://gateway.proquest.com/openurl?ctx_ver=Z39.88-2003&xri:pqil: res_ver=0.2&res_id=xri:lion-us&rft_id=xri:lion:ft:po:Z400340775:4.

Douglas, Aileen, 'Popular Science and the Representation of Women: Fontenelle and After', *Eighteenth-Century Life* 18.2 (1994): 1–14.

Dryden, John, *The Works of John Dryden*, ed. H.T. Swedenberg Jr. et al., 19 vols, Los Angeles: University of California Press, 1956.

Duffy, Eamon, *The Stripping of the Altars: Traditional Religion in England, 1400–1580*, New Haven: Yale University Press, 1994.

Eamon, William, *Science and the Secrets of Nature: Books of Secrets in Medieval and Early Modern Culture*, Princeton: Princeton University Press, 1994.

Ellis, Frank H., ed., *Poems on Affairs of State: Augustan Satirical Verse, 1669–1714*, New Haven, 1970.

Empson, William, *Essays on Renaissance Literature*, vol. 1: *Donne and the New Philosophy*, ed. John Haffenden, Cambridge: Cambridge University Press, 1993.

———, *Faustus and the Censor: The English Faust-Book and Marlowe's 'Doctor Faust'*, ed. John Henry Jones, Oxford: Basil Blackwell, 1987.

———, *Milton's God*, London: Chatto and Windus, 1961.

Engels, Friedrich, 'Die deutschen Volksbücher', in Karl Marx and Friedrich Engels, *Über Kunst und Literatur*, Frankfurt: Europäische Verlagsanstalt, 1968.

Feinaug, Johannes, *Der Tübinger Reim-Faust von 1587/88, aus dem Prosa-Volksbuch 'Historia von D. Johann Fausten' (1587) in Reime gebracht*, facsimile, s.l.: Jürgen Schweier Verlag, 1977.

Ficinio, Marsilio, *Three Books on Life*, eds. and trans. Carol V. Kaske and John R. Clark, Binghampton, NY, 1989.

Figulus, Bendictus, *A Golden and Blessed Casket of Nature's Marvels* [*Pandora Magnalium Naturalium Aurea et Benedicta*, 1608] (1893), trans. Arthur Edward Waite, London, 1963.

Filoramo, Giovanni, *A History of Gnosticism*, trans. Anthony Alcock, Oxford: B. Blackwell, 1990.

Findlen, Paula, 'Between Carnival and Lent: The Scientific Revolution at the Margins of Culture', *Configurations* 6.2 (1998): 243–67.

Fitzpatrick, Martin, Peter Jones, Christa Knellwolf and Iain McCalman, eds., *The Enlightenment World*, London: Routledge, 2004.

Fletcher, Angus, '*Doctor Faustus* and the Lutheran Aesthetic', *English Literary Renaissance* 35 (2005): 187–209.

Fontenelle, Bernard le Bovier de, *Dialogues of the Dead* (1683), trans. John Hughes, London: printed for Jacob Tonson, 1708.

———, *Entretiens de la pluralité des mondes*, Paris, 1686.

Force, James E. and Richard H. Popkin, *The Books of Nature and Scripture: Recent Essays on Natural Philosophy, Theology, and Biblical Criticism in the Netherlands of Spinoza's Time and the British Isles of Newton's Time*, Dordrecht: Kluwer Academic, 1994.

Forsyth, Neil, *The Old Enemy: Satan and the Combat Myth*, Princeton: Princeton University Press, 1987.

———, *The Satanic Epic*, Princeton: Princeton University Press, 2003.

Foucault, Michel, *The History of Sexuality*, vol. 1, New York: Random House, 1978.

Frazer, James, *The Golden Bough: A Study in Magic and Religion*, Ware: Wordsworth Editions, 1993.

Friedenreich, Kenneth, Roma Gill and Constance B. Kuriyama, eds., 'A Poet and a Filthy Play-Maker', *New Essays on Christopher Marlowe*, New York: AMS, 1988.

Galileo Galilei, *Dialogue Concerning the Two Chief World Systems*, trans. Stillman Drake, Berkley, 1967.

———, *The Sidereal Messenger of Galileo Galilei* (1610), London: Dawsons, 1960.

Gardner, Iain and Samuel N.C. Lieu, eds., *Manichean Texts from the Roman Empire*, Cambridge: Cambridge University Press, 2004.

Gatti, Hilary, *The Renaissance Drama of Knowledge: Giordano Bruno in England*, New York: Routledge, 1989.

Geissler, H.W., ed., *Gestaltungen des Faust*, 3 vols., München: Verlag Parcus, 1974.

Geneva, Ann, *Astrology and the Seventeenth Century Mind: William Lilly and the Language of the Stars*, Manchester: Manchester University Press, 1995.

Gherardi, Evaristo, *Arlequin Prothée*, in *Le Théâtre Italien, ou le receuil générale de toutes les Comedies et Scènes françaises jouées par les Comediens Italiens du* Roi, Geneva: Slakine Reprints, 1969.

———, *Les intrigues d'Arlequin*, in *Le Théâtre Italien de Gherardi, ou le receuil générale de toutes les Comedies & sçenes Françoises jouées par les Comediens Italiens du Roy, pendant tout les temps qu'ils one été au Service de la Majesté*, Marchand Libraire prés le Dam: chez Adrian Braakman, 1701.

Gibbons, Brian J., *Spirituality and the Occult from the Renaissance to the Modern Age*, London: Routledge, 2001.

Ginzberg, Carlo, 'High and Low: The Theme of Forbidden Knowledge in the Sixteenth and Seventeenth Centuries', *Past and Present* 73 (1976): 28–41.

Goldberg, Jonathan, 'Sodomy and Society: The Case of Christopher Marlowe', *Southwest Review* 69 (1984): 371–8.

Golowin, Sergius, Mircea Eliade and Joseph Campbell, *Die grossen Mythen der Menschheit*, Verlag Hohe, Erststadt, 2007.

Goodich, Michael, 'Miracles and Disbelief in the Late Middle Ages', *Mediaevistik* 1 (1988): 23–38.

Goodman, Dena, *The Republic of Letters: A Cultural History of the French Enlightenment*, Ithaca: Cornell University Press, 1994.

Grant, Robert M., ed., *Gnosticism: A Source Book of Heretical Writings from the Early Christian Period*, New York: Harper and Brothers, 1961.

Grantley, Daryll and Peter Roberts, eds., *Christopher Marlowe and English Renaissance Culture*, Aldershot: Scolar Press, 1996.

Greenblatt, Stephen, 'Marlowe and the Will to Absolute Play', *Renaissance Self-Fashioning: From More to Shakespeare*, Chicago: University of Chicago Press, 1980, pp. 193–221.

Greene, Robert, *Friar Bacon and Friar Bungay*, ed. Daniel Seltzer, Lincoln: University of Nebraska Press, 1963.

Greg, W.W., 'The Damnation of Faustus,' *Modern Language Review* 41.2 (1946): 97–107.

Grell, Ole Peter and Andrew Cunningham, eds., *Religio Medici: Medicine and Religion in Seventeenth-Century England*, Aldershot: Scolar Press, 1996.

Grell, Ole Peter, Jonathan I. Israel and Nicholas Tyacke, eds., *From Persecution to Toleration*, Oxford: Oxford University Press, 1991.

Guthke, Karl, *Die Mythologie der entgötterten Welt: ein literarisches Thema von der Aufklärung bis zur Gegenwart*, Göttingen: Vandenhoeck & Ruprecht, 1971.

Habermas, Jürgen, *The Structural Transformation of the Public Sphere: An Inquiry into a Category of Bourgeois Society*, trans. Thomas Burger with Frederick Lawrence, Cambridge, MA: Harvard University Press, 1989.

Haile, H.G., *Das Faustbuch nach der Wolfenbüttler Handschrift*, Berlin: E. Schmidt, 1963.

———, *The History of Doctor Johann Faustus*, Urbana: University of Illinois Press, 1965.

Hannaway, Owen, *The Chemists and the Word: The Didactic Origins of Chemistry*, Baltimore: Johns Hopkins University Press, 1975.

Hardison, O.B., *Christian Rite and Christian Drama in the Middle Ages*, Baltimore: Johns Hopkins University Press, 1965.

Hariot, Thomas, *A Brief and True Report of the New Found Land of Virginia*, Frankfurt a. M.: Theodor de Bry, 1590.

Harth, Erica, *Cartesian Women: Versions and Subversions of Rational Discourse in the Old Regime*, Ithaca: Cornell University Press, 1992.

Harvey, John, *An Astrological Addition* to: *The Learned Worke of Hermes Trismegistus, intitulet, Iatromathematica, that is, his Physical Mathematiques, or Mathematical Phisickes*, London: by Richard Watkins, 1583.

Harvey, William, *The Circulation of the Blood* (1628), trans. Kenneth J. Franklin and Andrew Wear, London: Everyman, 1990.

Haynes, Jonathan, 'Representing the Underworld: *The Alchemist*', *Studies in Philology* 86.1 (1989): 18–41.

Heninger, S.K., Jr., *Touches of Sweet Harmony: Pythagorean Cosmology and Renaissance Poetics*, San Marino, 1974.

————, *The Cosmographical Glass: Renaissance Diagrams of the Universe*, San Marino, 1977.

Hermes Trismegistus, His Divine Pymander, trans. John Everard, London, 1650.

Hill, Christopher, *Intellectual Origins of the English Revolution*, Oxford: Clarendon Press, 1965.

————, *The World Turned Upside Down: Radical Ideas during the English Revolution*, London, 1974.

————, *Milton and the English Revolution*, London: Faber, 1977.

Hobbes, Thomas, *Leviathan*, ed. J.C.A. Gaskin, Oxford: Oxford University Press, 1996.

Hoelzel, Alfred, *The Paradoxical Quest: A Study of the Faustian Vicissitudes*, New York: Peter Lang, 1988.

Holmyard, E.J., *Alchemy*, Harmondsworth: Penguin, 1957.

Honan, Park, *Christopher Marlowe: Poet and Spy*, Oxford: Oxford University Press, 2005.

Honderich, Pauline, 'John Calvin and Doctor Faustus', *Modern Language Review* 68 (1973): 1–13.

Hopkins, Arthur John, *Alchemy: Child of Greek Philosophy* (1933), New York, 1967.

Houlbrooke, Ralph, *Death, Religion, and the Family in England 1480–1750*, Oxford: Oxford University Press, 1998.

Hughes, Leo, *A Century of English Farce*, Princeton: Princeton University Press, 1956.

Hume, David, *An Enquiry Concerning the Principles of Morals*, ed. P.H. Nidditch, Oxford: Clarendon Press, 1975.

Hunter, Ian, *Rival Enlightenments: Civil and Metaphysical Philosophy in Early Modern Germany*, Cambridge: Cambridge University Press, 2001.

Hunter, Michael, *Science and Society in Restoration England*, Cambridge, 1981.

Israel, Jonathan I., *Radical Enlightenment: Philosophy and the Making of Modernity 1650–1750*, Oxford: Oxford University Press, 2001.

Jacob, Margaret C., *The Cultural Meaning of the Scientific Revolution*, New York: McGraw Hill, 1988.

————, *Living the Enlightenment: Freemasonry and Politics in Eighteenth-Century Europe*, New York: Oxford University Press, 1991.

————, *The Radical Enlightenment: Pantheists, Freemasons, and Republicans*, London: Allen & Unwin, 1981.

Jaffe, Bernard, *Crucibles: The Story of Chemistry from Ancient Alchemy to Nuclear Fission*, New York: Dover, 1976.

James, E.D., 'Fontenelle's *Entretiens sur la pluralité des mondes* and their Intellectual Context', in *Actes de Columbus: Racine, Fontenelle: Entretiens sur la pluralité des mondes, Histoire et littérature*, Paris: *Papers on French Seventeenth-Century Literature*, 1990, pp. 133–48.

Johns, Adrian, *The Nature of the Book: Print and Knowledge in the Making*, Chicago: University of Chicago Press, 1998.

Johnson, Francis A., 'Marlowe's Astronomy and Renaissance Skepticism', *English Literary History* 13 (1946): 241–54.

Jonas, Hans, *The Gnostic Religion: The Message of the Alien God and the Beginnings of Christianity*, Boston: Beacon Press, 1958.

Jones, Chris, *Radical Sensibility: Literature and Ideas in the 1790s*, London: Routledge, 1993.

Jonson, Ben, *The Alchemist*, ed. Alvin B. Kernan, New Haven: Yale University Press, 1974.

————, *The Devil is an Ass*, ed. Peter Happé, Manchester: Manchester University Press, 1994.

Kaempfer, Engelbert, *The History of Japan*, London: for Thomas Woodward, 1728.

Kastan, Scott, ed., *Christopher Marlowe: Doctor Faustus*, New York: W.W. Norton, 2005.

Keefer, Michael, 'History and the Canon: the Case of *Dr. Faustus*', *University of Toronto Quarterly* 56 (1987): 498–522.

————, 'Verbal Magic and the Problem of the A and B Texts of *Doctor Faustus*', *Journal of English and Germanic Philology* 82 (1983): 324–46.

Kepler, Johannes, *Kepler's Dream, with the Full Text and Notes of 'Somnium sive astronomicum lunaris Johannis Kepleri'* (1634), ed. Patricia F. Kirkwood, Berkley: University of California Press, 1965.

Kiessling, Nicholas, 'Doctor Faustus and the Sin of Demoniality,' *Studies in English Literature, 1500–1900*, 15.2 (1975): 205–11.

King-Hele, Desmond, *The Essential Writings of Erasmus Darwin*, London: MacGibbon & Kee, 1968.

Kircher, Athanasius, *Ars magna sciendi*, Amsterdam, 1669.

Klimkeit, Hans-Joachim, ed., *Hymnen und Gebete der Religion des Lichts: iranische und türkische liturgische Texte der Manichäer Zentralasiens*, Opladen: Westdeutscher Verlag, 1989.

Klinger, Friedrich Maximilian, *Fausts Leben, Taten und Höllenfahrt* (1791), Frankfurt a. M.: Insel, 1964.

Klossowski de Rolla, Stanislas, *Alchemy: The Secret Art*, London, 1973.

Knellwolf, Christa, 'The Mechanic Powers of the Spirit: Medicine and Mock-Heroic in Samuel Garth's *The Dispensary*', *Signatures* 1 (2000): 88–106. (http://www.signatures.ucc.ac.uk/)

————, 'Robert Hooke's *Micrographia* and the Aesthetics of Empiricism', *The Seventeenth Century* 16.1 (2001): 177–200.

————, 'The Science of Man', *The Enlightenment World*, eds. Martin Fitzpatrick, Peter Jones, Christa Knellwolf and Iain McCalman London: Routledge, 2004, pp. 194–206.

————, 'Women Translators, Gender and the Cultural Context of the Scientific Revolution', *Translation and Nation: Towards a Cultural Politics of Englishness*, eds. Roger Ellis and Liz Oakley Brown, Clevedon: Multilingual Matters, 2001), pp. 48–85.

Knellwolf, Christa and Jane Goodall, *Frankenstein's Science: Experimentation and Discovery in Romantic Culture, 1780–1830*, Aldershot: Ashgate, 2008.

Kocher, Paul H., *Science and Religion in Elizabethan England*, San Marino, 1953.

Kretzenbacher, Leopold, *Teufelsbündner und Faustgestalten im Abendlande*, Klagenfurt: Verlag des Geschichtvereines für Kärnten, 1968.

Kuhn, Thomas, *The Structure of Scientific Revolutions*, Chicago: University of Chicago Press, 1962.

Kuriyama, Constance, *Hammer or Anvil: Psychological Patterns in Christopher Marlowe's Plays*, New Brunswick: Rutgers University Press, 1980.

Latour, Bruno, *We Have Never Been Modern*, trans. Catherine Porter, Cambridge, MA: Harvard University Press, 1993.

Layton, Bentley, *The Gnostic Scriptures: A New Translation with Annotations and Introductions*, Garden City, NY: Doubleday, 1987.

Lennep, Jacques van, *Art et alchimie: Étude de l'iconographie hermetique et ses influences*, Brussels: Meddens, 1971.

Levin, Harry, *The Overreacher: A study of Christopher Marlowe*, Cambridge: Cambridge University Press, 1952.

Levine, Joseph M., *The Battle of the Books: History and Literature in the Augustan Age*, Ithaca: Cornell University Press, 1991.

Lindberg, David C., ed., *Science in the Middle Ages*, Chicago: University of Chicago Press, 1978.

Linden, Stanton J., ed., *Darke Hierogliphicks: Alchemy in English Literature from Chaucer to the Restoration*, Lexington: University Press of Kentucky, 1996.

——, *The Mirror of Alchimy: composed by the thrice-famous and learned fryer, Roger Bachon*, New York: Garland, 1992.

Link, Luther, *The Devil: A Mask without a Face*, London: Reaktion Books, 1995.

Lobet, Marcel, *Le feu du ciel: Introduction à la littérature prométhéennne*, Bruxelles: la renaissance du livre, 1969.

Locke, John, *An Essay Concerning Human Understanding*, in *Works*, Aalen: Scientia Verlag, 1963.

Logan, Donald F., *A History of the Church in the Middle Ages*, London: Routledge, 2002.

Logeman, H., ed., *The Historie of the Damnable Life and Deserved Death of Doctor John Faustus* [The English Faust Book] (1592), Gand: H. Engelcke, 1900.

Lukács, Georg, *Goethe and his Age* (1947), trans. Robert Anchor, New York: H. Fertig, 1978.

Luther, Martin, *Werke: Kritische Gesamtausgabe*, 10 vols., Weimar: H. Böhlaus, 1964.

Lyotard, Jean François, *Le différend*, Paris: Minuit, 1983.

McAdam, Ian, *The Irony of Identity: Self and Imagination in the Drama of Christopher Marlowe*, Newark: University of Delaware Press, 1999.

McAlindon, T., 'The Ironic Vision: Diction and Theme in Marlowe's *Doctor Faustus*', *Review of English Studies* 32 (1981): 9–41.

Macfarlane, Alan, *The Origins of English Individualism*, Oxford: Basil Blackwell, 1976.

McGinn, Bernard, *Antichrist: Two Thousand Years of the Human Fascination with Evil*, San Francisco: HarperCollins, 1994.

Mâle, Emile, *Religious Art in France, the Late Middle Ages*, Princeton: Princeton University Press, 1986.

Mann, Thomas, *Doktor Faustus: das Leben des deutschen Tonsetzers Adrian Leverkühn, erzählt von einem Freunde* (1947), Berlin: S. Fischer, 1949.

Marcus, Leah, 'Textual Indeterminacy and Ideological Difference: the Case of *Dr. Faustus*', *Renaissance Drama* 20 (1989): 1–29.

———, *Unediting the Renaissance: Shakespeare, Marlowe, Milton*, London: Routledge, 1996.

Marlowe, Christopher, *Christopher Marlowe's 'Doctor Faustus': the A-Text*, eds. David Ormerod and Christopher Wortham, Nedlands: University of Western Australia Press, 1985

———, *Doctor Faustus: A- and B-texts* (1604, 1616), eds. David Bevington and Eric Rasmussen, Manchester: Manchester University Press, 1993

———, *Doctor Faustus and Other Plays*, eds. David Bevington and Eric Rasmussen, Oxford: Oxford University Press, 1995.

Martz, Louis Lohr, *The Paradise Within: Studies in Vaughan, Traherne and Milton*, New Haven: Yale University Press, 1964.

Mebane, John S., *Renaissance Magic and the Return of the Golden Age: The Occult Tradition and Marlowe, Jonson, and Shakespeare*, Lincoln: University of Nebraska Press, 1989.

Mee, Jon, *Romanticism, Enthusiasm, and Regulation: Poetics and the Policing of Culture*, Oxford: Oxford University Press, 2003.

Mendelsohn, J. Andrew, 'Alchemy and Politics in England, 1649–1665', *Past and Present* 135 (1992): 30–78.

Milton, John, *Treatise on Christian Doctrine*, 2 vols., London, 1904.

Möbus, Frank, Friederike Schmidt-Möbus and Gerd Unverfehrt, eds., *Faust, Annäherung an einen Mythos*, Göttingen: Wallstein Verlag, 1995."

Montgomery, John Warwick, *Cross and Crucible: Johann Valentin Andreae (1586–1654), Phoenix of Theologians*, 2 vols., The Hague, 1973.

Morgan, Gerald, 'Harlequin Faustus: Marlowe's Comedy of Hell', *Humanities Association Bulletin* 18.1 (1967): 22–34.

Mulligan, Lotte, '"Reason", "Right Reason", and "Revelation" in Mid-Seventeenth-Century England', in *Occult and Scientific Mentalities in the Renaissance*, ed. Brian Vickers, Cambridge: Cambridge University Press, 1984.

Munson, Sara Deats, '*Doctor Faustus*: From Chapbook to Tragedy', *Essays in Literature* 3 (1976): 3–16.

Nauert, Charles G., Jr., *Agrippa and the Crisis of Renaissance Thought*, Urbana: University of Illinois Press, 1965.

Neubert, Franz, *Vom Doctor Faustus zu Goethes Faust*, Leipzip, 1932.

Newton, Isaac, *The Correspondence of Isaac Newton*, 7 vols., ed. H.W. Turnbull et al., Cambridge, 1959–1977.

Nicolson, Marjorie Hope, *Newton Demands the Muse: Newton's Opticks and the Eighteenth-Century Poets*, Princeton: Princeton University Press, 1946.

————, *Science and Imagination*, Ithaca, N.Y.: Great Seal Books, 1956.

Nimmegen, Mariken van, *Mary of Nimmegen* (1518–19), facsimile edition, introd. Harry Morgan Ayres and Adriaan Jacob Barnouw, Cambridge, MA: Harvard University Press, 1932.

Nokes, David, *Raillery and Rage: A Study of Eighteenth-Century Satire*, New York: St. Martin's Press, 1987.

Nowell, A. and T. Norton, *A Catechism, or First Instruction and Learning of Christian Religion*, London: printed by Iohn Daye, 1570.

Nuttall, A.D., *The Alternative Trinity: Gnostic Heresy in Marlowe, Milton, and Blake*, Oxford: Clarendon Press, 1998.

Oberman, Heiko A., *Luther: Man Between God and the Devil*, trans. Eileen Walliser-Schwarzbart, New Haven: Yale University Press, 1989.

O'Brien, John, *Harlequin Britain: Pantomime and Entertainment, 1690–1760*, Baltimore: Johns Hopkins University Press, 2004.

O'Donnell, Joseph, *Augustine, Sinner and Saint: A New Biography*, London: Profile, 2005.

O'Keeffe, John, *The Plays of John O'Keeffe*, ed. Frederick M. Link, New York: Garland, 1981.

Oort, Johannes, Otto Wermelinger and Gregor Wurst, eds., *Augustine and Manichaeism in the Latin West: Proceedings of the Fribourg-Utrecht Symposium*, Leiden: Brill, 2001.

Orr, Bridget, *Empire on the English Stage, 1660–1714*, Cambridge: Cambridge University Press, 2001.

Pagel, Walter, *Paracelsus: An Introduction to Philosophical Medicine in the Era of the Renaissance*, New York, 1958.

Pagels, Elaine, *The Origin of Satan*, New York: Random House, 1995.

Palmer, Philip Mason and Robert Pattison More, *The Sources of the Faust Tradition: from Simon Magus to Lessing*, New York: Octagon Books, 1966.

Palmer, Samuel, *The General History of Printing*, London: printed by the author, 1732.

Paracelsus, *The Hermetic and Alchemical Writings of Aureolus Philippus Theophrastus Bombast, of Hohenheim, Called Paracelsus the Great*, ed. Arthur Edward Waite, New Hyde Park, NY: University Books, 1967.

Parkin, David, ed., *The Anthropology of Evil*, Oxford: Blackwell, 1985.

Parry, Graham, 'A Troubled Arcadia', in *Literature and the English Civil War*, eds. Thomas Healy and Jonathan Sawday, Cambridge: Cambridge University Press, 1990, pp. 38–55.

Peltonen, Markku, ed., *The Cambridge Companion to Bacon*, Cambridge: Cambridge University Press, 1996.

Pico della Mirandola, *On the Dignity of Man*, trans. Charles Wallis, New York: Bobbs-Merrill, 1965.

Pope, Alexander, *A Critical Edition of the Major Works*, ed. Pat Rogers, Oxford: Oxford University Press, 1993.

Porta, Giambattista della, *Natural Magic* (1658), facsimile edition, New York: Basic Books, 1958.

Porter, Roy, *The Creation of the Modern World: The Untold Story of the British Enlightenment*, New York: Norton, 2000.

Praz, Mario, *Studies in Seventeenth-Century Imagery*, 2nd ed., 2 vols., Roma: Edizioni di storia et letteratura, 1964–1974.

Purver, Marjorie, *The Royal Society: Concept and Creation*, Cambridge, MA, 1967.

Quarles, Francis, *Emblems*, London, 1634.

Ravenscroft, Edward, *Scaramouch a Philosopher, Harlequin a School-Boy, Bravo, Merchant, and Magician. A Comedy after the Italian Manner*, London: for Robert Sollers, 1677.

Read, John, *Prelude to Chemistry: An Outline of Alchemy*, Cambridge, MA: Harvard University Press, 1966.

Redwood, John, *Reason, Ridicule and Religion: The Age of Enlightenment in England 1660–1750*, London: Thames and Hudson, 1996.

Ricks, Christopher, '*Doctor Faustus* and Hell on Earth', *Essays in Criticism* 35.2. (1985).

Ricoeur, Paul, *The Symbolism of Evil*, trans. Emerson Buchanan, New York: Harper & Row, 1967.

Riggs, David, 'Marlowe's Quarrell with God', in *Critical Essays on Christopher Marlowe*, ed. Emily Carroll Bartels, London: Prentice Hall International, 1997.

———, *The World of Christopher Marlowe*, London: Faber and Faber, 2004.

Rivers, Isabel, *Reason, Grace and Sentiment: A Study of the Language of Religion and Ethics in England, 1660–1780*, 2 vols., Cambridge: Cambridge University Press, 1991.

Roberts, Gareth, 'Necromantic Books: Christopher Marlowe, Dr. Faustus, and Agrippa of Nettesheim', in Darryll Grantley and Peter Roberts, eds., *Christopher Marlowe and English Renaissance Culture*, Aldershot, Hants.: Scolar Press, 1996, pp. 148–71.

Rogers, John, *The Matter of Revolution: Science, Poetry, and Politics in the Age of Milton*, Ithaca, NY: Cornell University Press, 1996.

Rose, William, ed., *The History of the Damnable Life and Deserved Death of Doctor Faustus*, s.l.: George Routledge and Sons, 1925.

Rossi, Paolo, *Francis Bacon: From Magic to Science*, London, 1968.

Rulandus, Martinus, the elder, *A Lexicon of Alchemy* [*Lexicon Alchemiae*, 1612], trans. Arthur Edward Waite, London, 1964.

Schneider, G. and E. Arndt, eds., *Fortunatus* (1509), Müller & Kiepenheuer, 1964.

Schoonhovius, Florentius, *Emblemata*, Leyden: Elzeviriana, 1626.

Schuler, Robert M., *Alchemical Poetry 1575–1700: From Previously Unpublished Manuscripts*, New York: Garland, 1995.

———, 'Some Spiritual Alchemies of Seventeenth-Century England', *Journal of the History of Ideas* 41 (1980): 293–318.

Schultz, Howard, *Milton and Forbidden Knowledge*, New York: Modern Language Association of America, 1955.

Shadwell, Thomas, *The Lancashire Witches and Tegue o Divelly the Irish Priest, a comedy acted at the Duke's Theatre*, London: for John Starkey, 1682.

Shapin, Steven, *A Social History of Truth: Civility and Science in Seventeenth-Century England*, Chicago: University of Chicago Press, 1994.

Shapin, Steven and Simon Schaffer, *Leviathan and the Air-Pump: Hobbes, Boyle and the Experimental Life*, Princeton: Princeton University Press, 1985.

Shelley, Mary, *Frankenstein or the Modern Prometheus (The 1818 Text)*, ed. Marilyn Butler, Oxford: Oxford University Press, 1998.

Shelley, Percy Bysshe, *The Complete Works of Percy Bysshe Shelley*, 10 vols., New York: Gordian, 1965.

Shepherd, Simon, *Marlowe and the Politics of Elizabethan Theatre*, Brighton: Harvester, 1986.

Shumaker, Wayne, *Natural Magic and Modern Science: Four Treatises 1590–1657*, Binghampton, N. Y., 1989.

Simpson, James, ed., *The Oxford English Literary History*, vol. 2: *Reform and Cultural Revolution 1350–1547*, Oxford: Oxford University Press, 2002.

Sinfield, Alan, *Faultlines: Cultural Materialism and the Politics of Dissident Readings*, Berkeley: University of California Press, 1980.

———, *Literature in Protestant England, 1560–1660*, London: Croom Helm, 1983.

Smith, Jeffrey Chipps, *Sensuous Worship: Jesuits and the Art of the Early Catholic Reformation in Germany*, Princeton: Princeton University Press, 2002.

Stafford, Barbara Maria, *Body Criticism: Imaging the Unseen in Enlightenment Art and Medicine*, Cambridge, MA: MIT Press, 1991.

Stevenson, David, *The Origins of Freemasonry: Scotland's Century, 1590–1710*, Cambridge, 1988.

Stewart, Larry, *The Rise of Public Science: Rhetoric, Technology, and Natural Philosophy in Newtonian Britain, 1660–1750*, Cambridge: Cambridge University Press, 1992.

Suchten, Alexander von, *An Explanation of the Natural Philosopher's Tincture, of Theophrastus Paracelsus*, in Bendictus Figulus, *A Golden and Blessed Casket*, London: Elliot, 1893, pp. 192–258.

Svendsen, Kester, *Milton and Science*, Cambridge, MA: Harvard University Press, 1956.

Tagart, Edward, 'Socinus', *Sketches of the Lives and Characters of the Leading Reformers of the Sixteenth Century: Luther, Calvin, Zwingle, Socinus, Crammer, Knox*, London: John Green, 1943.

Taylor, F. Sherwood, *The Alchemists*, St. Albans, 1976.

Thomas, Keith, *Man and the Natural World*, London: Allen Lane, 1983.

———, *Religion and the Decline of Magic: Studies in Popular Beliefs in Sixteenth and Seventeenth Century England*, London: Weidenfeld and Nicolson, 1971.

Thoms, William J., ed., *Friar Bacon*, in *A Collection of Early Prose Romances*, vol. 1, London: William Pickering, 1828.

Thorndike, Lynn, *A History of Magic and Experimental Science during the First Thirteen Centuries of Our Era*, 8 vols., New York: Columbia University Press, 1923–58.

Thurmond, John, *The Miser: Wagner and Abericock, A Grotesque Entertainment*, London: for W. Trott, 1727.

Tilley, Morris P.A., *A Dictionary of the Proverbs in England in the Sixteenth and Seventeenth Centuries*, Ann Arbor, 1950.

Toon, Peter, ed., *The Millenium and the Future of Israel: Puritan Eschatology 1600–1660*, London, 1970.

Traister, Barbara Howard, *Heavenly Necromancers: The Magician in English Renaissance Drama*, Columbia: University of Missouri Press, 1984.

Tydeman, William, *'Doctor Faustus': Text and Performance*, Basingstoke: Macmillan, 1984.

———, *English Medieval Theatre 1400–1500*, London: Routledge & Kegan Paul, 1986.

Vaughan, Thomas, *The Works of Thomas Vaughan*, ed. Alan Rudrum, Oxford, 1984.

Völker, Klaus, *Faust, ein deutscher Mann: die Geburt einer Legende und ihr Fortleben in den Köpfen*, Belin: Wagenbach, 1975.

Walker, Daniel P., *The Decline of Hell: Seventeenth-Century Discussions of Eternal Torment*, London: Routledge, 1964.

———, *Spiritual and Demonic Magic, from Ficino to Campanella*, Studies of the Warburg Institute, vol. 22, Nendeln: Kraus Reprint, 1969.

Webster, Charles, *The Great Instauration: Science, Medicine and Reform 1626–1660*, London, 1975.

Weinberger, Jerry, *Science, Faith, and Politics: Francis Bacon and the Utopian Roots of the Modern Age*, Ithaca: Cornell University Press, 1985.

Weyer (aka Wier), Johann, *Witches, Devils, and Doctors in the Renaissance: Johann Weyer, De praestigiis daemonum* (1583), trans. John Shea, Binghamton, N.Y.: Medieval & Renaissance Texts & Studies, 1991.

White, Hayden V., *Tropics of Discourse: Essays in Cultural Criticism*, Baltimore: The Johns Hopkins University Press, 1978.

Whitney, Geoffrey, *Choice of Emblemes, and Other Devises, For the most part gathered out of sundrie writers*, Leyden: Francis Raphelengius, 1586.

Widmann, Georg Rudolf, *Fausts Leben* (1599), ed. Adelbert von Keller, Hildesheim: Georg Olms, 1976 (1880).

Williams, Raymond, *Keywords: A Vocabulary of Culture and Society*, London: Flamingo, 1983.

Wilson, Catherine, *The Invisible World: Early Modern Philosophy and the Invention of the Microscope*, Princeton: Princeton University Press, 1995.

Wolff, Eugen, *Faust und Luther: Ein Beitrag zur Entstehung der Faust-Dichtung*, Halle a. S.: Max Niemeyer, 1912.

Wood, Frederik T., 'The Comic Elements in the English Mystery Plays', *Neophilologus* 25.1 (1940): 39–48.

Woodman, David, *White Magic and Renaissance Magic*, Rutherford: Fairleigh Dickinson University Press, 1973.

Wright, Thomas D.D., *The Passions of the Minde* (1601), facsimile reprint, Hildesheim: Georg Olms, 1973.

Wymer, Rowland, '"When I Behold the Heavens": a Reading of *Doctor Faustus*', *English Studies* 67 (1986): 505–10.

Yarbro-Collins, Adela, *The Combat Myth in the Book of Revelation*, Missoula, MT: Scholars Press, 1976.

Yates, Frances A., *Giordano Bruno and the Hermetic Tradition*, London: Routledge, 1964.

——, *The Rosicrucian Enlightenment*, London: Routledge, 1972.

Yeo, Richard, *Encyclopaedic Visions: Scientific Dictionaries and Enlightenment Culture*, Cambridge: Cambridge University Press, 2001.

Young, Karl, *The Drama of the Medieval Church*, 2 vols., Oxford: Clarendon Press, 1933.

Zacher, Christian K., *Curiosity and Pilgrimage: The Literature of Discovery in Fourteenth-Century England*, Baltimore: Johns Hopkins University Press, 1976.

Index